TAKING ON GENERAL MOTORS

A Case Study Of
The Campaign To Keep GM Van Nuys Open

TAKING ON GENERAL MOTORS

A Case Study Of
The Campaign To Keep GM Van Nuys Open

ERIC MANN

Center for Labor Research and Education

Institute of Industrial Relations

University of California, Los Angeles

Institute of Industrial Relations
Publications
University of California, Los Angeles 90024-1478

ISBN 0-89215-141-2

For my grandmother, Sarah Mandell
and my wonderful daughters
Lisa
Celia
and
Melinda.

ABOUT THE AUTHOR

Eric Mann has spent more than twenty years as a civil rights, anti-war, and labor organizer, beginning with his involvement with the Congress of Racial Equality and Students for a Democratic Society. He has worked as an assembly line worker and UAW member since 1978; has worked at the GM Van Nuys plant since 1982; and has been an active member of UAW Local 645, where he served as Coordinator of the Campaign to Keep GM Van Nuys Open. He has written many articles on the auto industry and the labor movement for the *New York Times*, the *Los Angeles Times* and *The Nation*.

CONTENTS

PART THREE THE CAMPAIGN TO KEEP GM VAN NUYS OPEN

PART FOUR DRAWING LESSONS FROM THE VAN NUYS CAMPAIGN

FOREWORD

In the Fall of 1985, the Center for Labor Research and Education, UCLA Institute of Industrial Relations, became the "home" for the author of this book. Eric Mann was one of two trade unionists selected by a committee to receive a three-month stipend offered by the Lucy and Harry Lang Memorial Internship fund. Established in 1965, the Lang endowment provides for a periodic monetary award to trade unionists in the Southern California area. The objective of the internship is to provide a union member with the opportunity to undertake a union-related research project which provides for personal growth and whose final product offers information to the labor movement or generates timely discussion within the movement.

When Eric appeared before the interviewing committee, comprised of three Labor Center coordinators, the late Paul Bullock, who at the time was the Institute's research economist, and Naomi Lang, the daughter of the Langs, he was working at the General Motors (GM) plant in Van Nuys. A night shift employee and an active five-year member of UAW Local 645, Eric was deeply involved in the campaign to keep GM Van Nuys open in the face of a possible permanent shutdown. He sought time away from his night shift work at the plant. He wanted to study the history of General Motors by focusing on the men who headed up the corporation over the years. His objective was to bring to himself and others a better understanding of GM in relation to GM's threat to close the Van Nuys operation and how best to respond to that threat. He also wanted to relate the story of the genesis and development of the labor-community campaign which was geared to boycott GM products in the event the company closed the plant employing 5,000 bargaining unit workers.

About the time this book was ready for publication, a certain event occurred: the inauguration of the "team concept" at the Van Nuys facility. The training of UAW members in the new method of production was followed by a lively union election between pro- and anti-team concept advocates. As a result, Eric asked for and received an extension of time to incorporate these developments into his book.

Eric Mann presents a viewpoint which is controversial. If nothing else, the book should serve as a dialogue within the labor movement, since a myriad of issues flow from the lines of this publication. Anyone who believes that the trade union movement is monolithic in temper and thought will be disabused of that view upon reading of the internal conflict in this one UAW local. In some ways, the story that unfolds in these pages is a microcosm of both labor and public policy issues that are being addressed by the national AFL-CIO in its self-analysis of the changing situation of workers, though clearly less polemical and dramatically different in tone and style. Discussion and debate are part and parcel of the labor movement's present-day mood and objective as it grapples with a changing work environment.

Professor Rosen of Columbia University praises the book because of its detailed insight into a local union. It is more than that. For it is a story not only of a local union with divergent views within its halls, but it is a story of a union that is feeling the pinch and pain of a major happening in this country--plant closings. Closings and threats of closings pose the threshold policy question of why our industrial base is eroding. And whether the "team concept" is the threshold answer to the erosion of our industrial base, or even a partial response to worldwide competition, awaits the pragmatic test of time.

This book provides the reader with a basis for timely and lively discussion within and outside of the trade union movement. If this occurs, the time and effort of all concerned in offering the publication for readership will have been well spent.

Geraldine Leshin
Assistant Director for
Labor Research and Education
UCLA Institute of Industrial Relations

PREFACE

This is a book about organizing. Since graduating from Cornell University in 1964 and beginning work as a field organizer for the Congress of Racial Equality (CORE), I've spent more than twenty years as a part of three mass movements: the civil rights movement, the movement to end the war in Vietnam, and the labor movement. Each of those social movements did not come into being spontaneously, although spontaneous rebellion and protest were critical components. They were the product of the planning, consciousness, and dedication of thousands of people--the organizers.

As America has moved rightward in the 1980s, the achievements of those movements are being reversed while their history is being rewritten to serve the objectives of a conservative political agenda. The "history" of the civil rights movement is reduced to brief TV shots of Martin Luther King giving a speech about having a dream, while the 200,000 demonstrators at the Washington monument are portrayed as silent extras from central casting. The history of a decade of anti-war organizing has been systematically censored so that a new generation may have to fight and die before the lessons are relearned. The history of the labor movement is reduced to images of "labor bosses" or, at best, nostalgic reminiscences of past events that appear to have little relevance to the present.

My historical optimism and my decision to become involved in the labor movement are products of the great accomplishments of the civil rights and anti-war movements. One of the objectives of *Taking on General Motors* is to encourage those with political roots in the sixties to appreciate the critical strategic importance of today's labor movement; while another is to encourage those in the labor movement to see that many of the approaches of the civil rights and anti-war movements are essential to labor's resurgence. Another goal is to popularize the idea of labor organizing, both as a social science and a subject of greater mass appreciation; while still another is to use the significant achievements of the Campaign to Keep GM Van Nuys Open as a vehicle to help generate a broader debate about union strategy, economic policy and, ultimately, what structural changes in the system will be necessary to serve working people and their unions.

With those objectives in mind, I made several conscious decisions. I chose to tell more about the subject than less. For me, after five years of working at the Van Nuys plant I feel I am sharing a wealth of information and analysis, and have carefully edited out what seemed to be extraneous or redundant. But when faced with the choice between serving the interests of the dedicated organizer or scholar, for whom the factual foundations of the analysis are essential and hopefully fascinating, and the reader who might want me to move through the story at a little faster pace, I opted in favor of an in-depth treatment.

Similarly, I want to emphasize that the historical work on both General Motors and the UAW is not "interesting background" but an essential part of the story. The successes at Van Nuys in both keeping a doomed plant open far beyond the doctor's prognosis and successfully resisting company efforts to impose an oppressive labor relations system were at least partially the product of union organizers who had an historical view of both the company and the union--and who used that analysis as a building-block of their strategy. I attempted to develop all the major players, both past and present, as complex, comprehensible figures carrying out strategies based on their class interests, their political perspectives and, at times, their personal idiosyncrasies. Fairness, objectivity, and a certain historical appreciation of one's political opponents is essential to good scholarship--and effective organizing work.

Finally, I think the case study methodology is an excellent format with which to raise broader issues. The rich history of the Van Nuys movement has provided a workshop of immense value, one that social scientists, labor organizers, and those concerned about the future of America's working people and their unions should study carefully. In the context of the late 1980s, in which anti-labor and pro-business ideology is dominant, it is difficult to know how to push the pendulum back to the left. It is shocking to me to witness the degree to which many liberal, progressive, and generally open-minded people have adopted, often without realizing it, a world view based on pro-company and anti-labor assumptions.

By rooting this story in the detailed description of five years in the life of one UAW local, it is hoped that many readers will realize that they have a lot to learn about today's labor movement and the real-life workers who comprise it. In a small way, it is hoped that *Taking On General Motors* and the successful movement it describes can demand a fair hearing for views about the labor movement and the society at large that have been systematically excluded from our nation's "free marketplace of ideas."

I was able to begin this project through the generous help provided by the Lucy and Harry Lang Family Fellowship, administered by UCLA's Center for Labor Research and Education at the UCLA Institute of Industrial Relations. I am very grateful to Naomi Lang, daughter of Harry and Lucy Lang, for continuing the Lang Family Fellowship. The initial months of concentrated time away from the assembly line and the day-to-day pressures of union politics allowed me to begin the process of research and writing which I have continued for a year and a half.

I enjoyed my association with the Institute and the Center for Labor Research and Education. I thank the

Institute's director, Daniel J.B. Mitchell, and associate director, Archie Kleingartner, for their thoughtful and critical analyses of my initial research. Geraldine Leshin, the Labor Center's director, has been very supportive of my work. While sharing my interest in the historical background, she always reminded me to "bring it back to the present," and took particular care in responding to my manuscript.

A number of people have helped transform the manuscript into book form. Ron Stringer, copy editor at the *LA Weekly*, was an invaluable editor of many of my early drafts. At the Institute's Publications Center, Jane Wildhorn supervised production and, with Judith Richlin-Klonsky, edited later drafts. Margaret Zamorano was invaluable in entering numerous editorial changes with skill and good nature. She was ably joined in this and other production tasks by Brikti Abraha.

This book was read in manuscript form by several labor activists and writers, all of whom have contributed significantly to its development: Peter Olney, an organizer for the ILGWU and Coalition activist; Mark Masaoka, one of the primary organizers of the Van Nuys Campaign; Jack Metzgar, editor of the *Midwest Center for Labor Research Review*; Mike Davis, author of *Prisoners of the American Dream*; and Marianne Brown of UCLA's Center for Labor Research and Education. They all provided a supportive and critical matrix for the development of the book, while of course I take full responsibility for its final outcome.

Pete Beltran, my local's past president and present shop chairman, has given me an invaluable five-year course in labor leadership and the politics of the UAW. I am appreciative of the help of West Coast Regional Director Bruce Lee, who has kept his commitment to "an open region" in which debate over the direction of the UAW is understood as a necessary condition for a stronger union.

My mother-in-law, Melinda Hurst, was indispensable in providing friendship and family support throughout the long process of this book. My mother, Libby Mann, helped me to cross the finish line--as she has all my life. My wife, Lian Hurst Mann, who began this journey with me on an assembly line at the Ford Milpitas plant, has provided encouragement and insight throughout my work in the UAW, and has been essential in the editing, formatting, and design of the final product.

Finally, *Taking On General Motors* is only possible if there is a movement based on dedicated organizers and committed allies. I would like to especially thank Mark Masaoka, Mike Gomez, Nate Brodsky, Kelley Jenco, Manuel Hurtado, Jose Silva, Jake Flukers, Willie Guadiana, Dorothy Travis, Santos Murguia, Rudy Acuña, Jack Koszdin, Eloy Salazar, Father Luis Olivares, Bishop Juan Arzube, Rev. Frank Higgins, Bill Coleman, Nadine Kerner, Bob Flamer, Rev. Dick Gillett, Ed Asner, Howard Berman, Christina Perez, Jim Blatt, Michal Goldman, and our friends at the Wellspring Fund, the Liberty Hill Foundation, the Shalan Foundation, and the Youth Project. I hope that those whose contributions have not been acknowledged because of space limitations will accept my apologies.

Part One

SETTING THE STAGE

Chapter One

THE CAMPAIGN IN CONTEXT

> When this plant was opened after the war there was nothing around it. But now a whole community has grown up around General Motors. So the question we have to ask, as it concerns plant closings and capital flight, is: What gives General Motors the right to come into a community and use our people's energies for twenty, thirty, and forty years, pollute our water and poison our air, and then when they're finished with us, to throw us away as casually as we would throw away an orange peel? They have a social responsibility to keep this plant open! We know they do. But the job of the Campaign is to force General Motors to live up to that responsibility.[1]

These are the words of Pete Beltran, president of United Auto Workers Local 645 in Van Nuys, California, just north of Los Angeles. The "Campaign" he refers to is the Campaign to Keep GM Van Nuys Open, a grass roots movement of the local and its community supporters to stop a plant closing before it happens.

Beltran's words, spoken in 1983 at a Campaign rally of over 1,000 supporters, would have seemed quite tame to the workers who occupied GM's Fisher Body plants in the 1937 Flint sit-downs and forced the corporation to recognize the UAW. Those workers debated about "changing the system," and while disagreeing about the relative merits of socialism versus a highly regulated capitalism, virtually all of the early UAW leaders saw the union as part of a broader movement for increased worker control over the factories and expanded working class power in the nation's political life. In contrast, Beltran's analysis was expressed in the framework of "corporate social responsibility" more than workers' insurgency. Still, the concept popularized by the Campaign--that workers and communities were not going to allow GM to close a plant that it legally "owned," and, if necessary, would resort to a boycott against the corporation to keep the plant open--was a radical departure from the prevailing ideology and strategy of today's labor movement.

At the time the Campaign was initiated in 1982 few believed that a single UAW local could take on General Motors, and certainly not on an issue as central to the corporation's self-conception as its "right" to open and close plants as it saw fit. Yet, after five of California's six auto plants had been closed between 1980 and 1982--and GM openly threatened to close Van Nuys as well--there was a growing sentiment within the local that something had to be tried.

Five years later, the Campaign to Keep GM Van Nuys Open had lived up to its name. Five years of organizing--demonstrations, marches, thousands of consumer letters to GM Chairman Roger Smith, a face-to-face meeting with GM president F. James McDonald, and a seemingly endless string of tactics to keep the pressure on the corporation--had produced a rare victory. On November 6, 1986, GM announced the closing of eleven plants in the GM system. GM Van Nuys, which had been commonly acknowledged to be one of the first plants scheduled for closing, was kept open.

There are certainly instances when organizers have made extravagant claims and taken credit for events over which, in actuality, they had little or no influence. This case study, however, will argue that the Campaign was the decisive factor in GM's decision to keep the plant open.

While the Campaign's victory took place in the context of personal tragedy for the workers at the eleven closed plants, it was not because the Van Nuys movement tried to go it alone. Just the opposite. It was only after years of unsuccessful efforts to build a movement *within* the UAW for a more unified strategy to prevent plant closings in the industry that UAW Local 645 had to focus its limited resources on the difficult enough job of trying to save one plant. It is hoped that, through this victory, organizers in other UAW locals, locals of other labor unions throughout the country, and community groups threatened with plant closings will learn from and apply the many lessons of the Campaign to their own situation. It is with that objective, and the concomitant goal of contributing to a broader public debate on economic and industrial policy, that this book was written.

The Van Nuys Campaign came into being as workers in basic industry, beginning in the mid-1970s, tried to respond to the massive hemorrhaging of the nation's manufacturing plants: "the deindustrialization of America."[2] Cities that had once raised a generation of hard-working, proud industrial workers--Cleveland, Buffalo, Pittsburgh, Youngstown, Gary, Detroit, Birmingham--had become symbols of economic and psychological depression. TV news crews learned to package plant closings into a neat and predictable format: opening shots of boarded-up stores and abandoned factories, then a close-up of a depressed and perplexed autoworker (or steelworker or rubberworker) sitting in his living room with his family, saying, "I don't know what we're going to do. I worked twenty years at the plant, and now I have nothing."

Study after study provided statistical validation for what millions of workers had come to understand through direct experience. "Between January 1979 and January 1984, 11.5 million workers over the age of twenty lost jobs because of plant closings or cutbacks." One study of displaced autoworkers found that two years after the plant closing, their income had dropped on the average of 43 percent.[3]

While the workers' suffering was enormous, they directed very little anger and even less organized protest against management. Despite more than a decade of poor management planning, inferior quality and design, and stratospheric executive salaries and bonuses in America's basic industries, an angry public responded to each announcement of massive layoffs or plant closings with a slap on the wrist for management and a slap in the face for the discarded workers and their unions. Corporate management had transformed its own failure into a political victory. A sympathetic media repeated management's simple, easy-to-memorize analysis of America's economic decline and prescription for its revitalization, which in turn was adopted as gospel by leaders of both major political parties, by the professional classes, by many "neoliberal" intellectuals and, most frighteningly, even by many workers. The typical management argument went as follows:

> American industry, threatened with competition from low-wage countries, is fighting for its life. While management admits that our complacency led to many of the problems, America cannot rebuild its basic industries unless management is protected from a meddling government and greedy unions and given a free hand to get industry back on track. In Japan, big business has a government that gives tax relief instead of imposing hostile regulation and labor unions that realize that cooperation and corporate profits are the key to the workers' welfare.
>
> Management agrees that American product quality and productivity have declined, but that cannot be corrected without a revolutionary change in labor's attitude. Featherbedding, laziness and sloppy workmanship--all protected by union contracts--have become the rule, and a bloated paycheck is pricing the American worker out of a job. Management hates layoffs and plant closings and understands the pain they cause, but if companies cannot

> dramatically cut labor costs and become "lean and mean" there will be no American comeback and no jobs for anyone.[4]

The corporate public relations departments had done their job so effectively that layoffs and plant closings were barely challenged. Few questioned whether a plant really had to be closed, what the social costs of the closing were, or what other alternatives existed. Almost no one asked whether a plant had been closed because there was no market for its products, or because management had milked it for profits and reinvested them in more profitable enterprises, or because it was still profitable, but not quite as profitable as other sources of capital investment--investments in speculative and paper transactions that produce little social wealth. Worse, many members of the middle class who had long resented the wage levels of unionized workers in basic industry, swallowed the management catechism whole and began to repeat mechanically that plant closings were actually a blessing in disguise--weeding out the deadwood and preparing the way for a state-of-the-art, high-tech America.

While some believe that government's unrestrained support for capital's reorganization began under Ronald Reagan, it was, in fact, the Carter administration, as evidenced by the harsh terms imposed on the UAW in the Chrysler reorganization, that led the way both practically and ideologically. Carter's Commission for a National Agenda for the '80s, addressing the problem of declining industrial productivity, argued that "It may be in the best interest of the nation to commit itself to locationally neutral economic and social policies rather than spatially sensitive urban policies that either explicitly or inadvertently seek to preserve cities in their historic roles."[5]

The Carter report used evasive and abstract language to cloak a brutal social policy--that in order to allow capital the maximum flexibility to restore previous levels of profitability the government would allow, if not encourage, corporations to abandon communities and workers. Corporations should not be compelled to stay in communities that had served them for decades, where they could rebuild older plants or build new ones while helping to reconstruct declining urban infrastructures. That would be uncompetitive utopianism. If communities and cities were destroyed in the process, according to the report, this was an inevitable part of the creative destruction necessary for economic growth.

When Ronald Reagan assumed the presidency in 1981, he was able to construct his edifice of social Darwinism on the foundation laid by Carter. Attacked by the corporations and abandoned by the Democrats as well as the Republicans, many in the labor movement latched onto the "three opiates": *protectionism, realism, and concessionism.*

"Protectionism" railed against foreign competition, mainly the Japanese, and searched for a return to the "good old days" when America ruled the world and problems of wage competition with other manufacturing nations did not have to be addressed. While there are certainly inequities in Japan's trade policies, the UAW seemed unwilling to confront the inequities of *American* trade policies, most specifically vis-a-vis third world countries. The union's almost obsessive focus on Japanese imports--despite the fact that American corporations still controlled 70 percent of the domestic auto market while planning to bring in imports of their own--led to a scapegoating of the Japanese and an avoidance of confrontations with the Big Three automakers.

"Realism" was the repetition of company arguments by union officials with an air of fatalism: "It hurts me to admit it, but the company is right. Costs have to be cut, and if we don't give up some of our benefits and wages the responsibility for plant closings will fall on the union."

"Concessionism," was retreat raised to the level of strategy. It argued that by financing the reorganization of ailing corporations through contract concessions, the workers could contribute to the rebuilding of American industry and the preservation of their own jobs. Worse, instead of explaining concessions as a tactical retreat imposed on the workers and their union by company coercion, it portrayed the concessions as a clever trade off of financial give-backs in return for greater union "control" over corporate decision making--a claim, as will be argued later, that proved to be spurious.

In practice, protectionism led to autoworkers smashing Toyotas in parking lots and placing anti-Japanese placards ("Unemployment, made in Japan") on the walls of their union halls. Realism led to a passive response to layoffs and plant closings since, in some way, the workers believed that their demise was inevitable--perhaps even historically necessary. Concessionism led to Chrysler workers voting to accept massive wage cuts to save the corporation, only to have ten plants closed, and 57,000 workers permanently laid off while Lee Iacocca gained fame and fortune based on the Chrysler "miracle." The combined effect of the three opiates was that, in the early 1980s, there was little if any resistance by auto workers to plant closings.

In this historical context, the Campaign to Keep GM Van Nuys Open (hereafter referred to as the Campaign) provides a valuable laboratory for labor strategy. Several critical components of the Campaign explain why it warrants an in-depth study.

1) *The high level of conscious planning.* When labor unions announce strikes or boycotts, the media often portray them as spontaneous or poorly thought out responses to company strategies. And all too often this is accurate. In recent years, the labor movement has been chronically deficient in plotting out its own strategies. By contrast, the Campaign, from its inception, has been the product of strategic planning by a core of UAW organizers, and for five years has undergone a continuous process of reassessment. If for no other reason than its high degree of conscious organization, both the accomplishments and weaknesses of the Campaign can provide a valuable analytical model.

2) *The boldness of the plan.* Confronted with the declining position of many American corporations in the world economy, some unions have pursued a defensive strategy of cutting their losses--bargaining over *how many* layoffs are necessary, trying to limit *the number* of plant closings, negotiating over *how many* dollars in concessions per hour are appropriate. The Campaign has

been able to advance the movement against plant closings by:

– anticipating a plant closing before it happened and taking preemptive action to stop it;

– rejecting the nonadversarial, concession-oriented path and, instead, threatening GM with a boycott of its products in Los Angeles County if it should close the Van Nuys plant;

– demanding that GM keep the plant open for at least ten years. The Campaign was able to build a popular consciousness among many constituencies in Los Angeles that such a demand was both morally justifiable and economically feasible. Perhaps most importantly, it advanced a demand that both restricted the mobility of capital and advanced the power of labor at a time when, overall, capital's power was dramatically expanding and labor's declining.

3) *The expansion of the scope of labor's influence.* When the Campaign first began, the vast majority of the local's own members didn't even know it existed. Five years later, it had become the subject of heated debate within the Los Angeles labor movement and a highly popular cause among many political and community leaders throughout the city. The Campaign organized rallies of more than one thousand supporters; involved highly visible allies such as actor Ed Asner, singer Jackson Browne, and the Reverend Jesse Jackson; and became the subject of more than one hundred newspaper stories, as well as receiving national attention in both *Business Week* and the *New York Times.* One of the Campaign's objectives has been to generate broad policy debate over the issues of plant closings and labor's response, which it has accomplished through its many organizing successes and its high degree of public visibility.

4) *The achievement of the Campaign's main objective.* Too often in these discouraging times for labor, case studies of labor's activities end with: "While the plant was closed, (or the strike was lost), valuable lessons were learned." But so far, the Campaign has contributed both lessons and victory to the broader labor movement.

The Campaign began in 1982. After several years of organizing, some of the Campaign's most enthusiastic supporters claimed: "If it weren't for the Campaign, the plant would be closed down today." But that wasn't accurate; for in fact, between late 1982 and late 1986, GM did not close down *any* plants, and those UAW locals that did nothing appeared to be doing just as well as the Van Nuys local which had been organizing nonstop for four years.

As 1986 began, however, predictions by industry analysts of imminent plant closings within the GM system became widespread, and in virtually every news account, GM Van Nuys was at the top of the list of those to be closed. Finally, in November 1986, when GM announced the closing of eleven plants, the Van Nuys workers were able to echo Mark Twain's observation that "the reports of our death have been greatly exaggerated."

The "saving" of the Van Nuys plant is quite possibly a temporary development. In the wake of GM's announced plans to close several more plants in the late 1980s, the future success of the Campaign is by no means assured. Still, at a time of so many defeats for labor, when a local union begins organizing four years in anticipation of a plant closing and manages to hold off what first appeared to be an inevitable management decision, an analysis of the inner workings of the Campaign becomes all the more critical.

5) *The Campaign's ability to combine a movement against plant closings with a movement to reestablish workers' influence on the shop floor.* At the time the movement began, the main issue at controversy was GM's threat to close the plant. After the Campaign's first round of success, however, GM shifted its strategy to impose a so-called "Japanese-style" "cooperative" management system on the union local. The analysis of how the movement to save the plant contributed to and joined with a movement to resist the company's "team concept" plan adds a critical dimension to the Van Nuys story.

6) *The willingness of the Campaign's leadership to subject their work to analytical scrutiny.* For those who believe that such processes as labor union and community organizing can be approached analytically, and to some degree scientifically, it is as important to

examine the weaknesses and setbacks of a movement as it is to examine its accomplishments. An American labor movement that has declined from representing 35 percent of the workforce in 1954 to less than 19 percent in 1987 needs to reexamine many of its assumptions and take a more self-critical approach to its work.[6] In this context, the strategic disagreements within the local, the disagreements between some local officers and the International leadership, and the setbacks and breakthroughs of the Campaign are presented to encourage broader discussion and debate about labor and community strategies.

Studying the history of General Motors--the entrepreneurial machinations of Billy Durant that constructed the early GM empire; the ruthless, profit-driven catechism of Alfred P. Sloan that made GM the unchallenged leader of the American auto industry for six decades; the high-tech wheeling and dealing of Roger Smith--is fascinating in itself, and a prerequisite for effective organizing. In recent years, labor organizers have come to realize that developing a "corporate profile" of the company you plan to confront is essential to generating creative strategy and tactics. Through digging into that history and rigorously unraveling a complex tapestry, and through the scientific application of analysis, strategy, and organizing, workers and their unions can transform themselves from students of history to historical actors.

Taking On General Motors continues with an historical essay on the development of GM and the UAW, moves to a case study covering five years in the life of a UAW local, and ends with a discussion of some of the broader issues raised by the Van Nuys movement.

NOTES

1. Speech by UAW Local 645 President Pete Beltran, May 14, 1983, from the film *Tiger By the Tail*, directed by Michal Goldman and produced by the Labor Community Coalition, Van Nuys, California, 1983.
2. Barry Bluestone and Bennett Harrison, *The Deindustrialization of America* (New York: Basic Books, 1982). This book was the first systematic effort to place the problems of plant closings at the doorstep of the large corporations and to encourage labor's counterstrategies. It remains the essential foundation for any discussion of the subject.
3. Leonie Sandercock and John Friedmann, "Economic Restructuring and Community Dislocation: The Challenge to Planners," Graduate School of Architecture and Urban Planning, University of California, Los Angeles, December 1985, p. 7.
4. There are literally hundreds of articles reflecting the same, "recovery at the workers' expense" analysis. Two bookends for the summary I have presented are: "The Reindustrialization of America," *Business Week* (Special Issue), June 30, 1980, and "Can America Compete?" *Business Week*, April 20, 1987.
5. *U.S. President's Commission on an Agenda for the 80's*, quoted in Sandercock and Friedmann, pp. 11, 12.
6. "Labor Leaders Foresee a Turning Point," *Los Angeles Times*, February 22, 1987, p. 28.

Part Two

THE GENERAL MOTORS STORY: MANAGEMENT'S HISTORY AS A PRELUDE TO LABOR'S STRATEGY

Chapter Two

BILLY DURANT AND THE FORMATION OF GENERAL MOTORS

The Entrepreneurial Period of the Early Auto Industry (1908-1920)

The stereotyped view of General Motors is that of a cold, faceless institution whose managerial cast of characters is cut from dies that produce identical and interchangeable parts. But the early years of GM were shaped by the flamboyant, idiosyncratic, and brilliant personality of William Crapo Durant. Those were the days when entrepreneurs, far more than managers, were needed to usher in an industry that didn't even exist. The Ford Motor Company was founded by Henry Ford, Buick by David Dunbar Buick, Oldsmobile by Randsom Olds, and Cadillac by the more modest Henry Leland. When Durant later experienced personality conflicts with some of his top staff, Charles Nash resigned and subsequently formed the Nash Motor Company, and Walter Chrysler founded what would become the second largest auto company in the United States. This was the age of pioneers, the age of industrial innovators and risk-takers; and no greater genius and riverboat gambler existed than Billy Durant, who would lay the groundwork for the vast General Motors empire.

While GM's formal incorporation took place in 1908, the histories of Durant and GM are so inextricably intertwined that we must begin the story in 1890. Durant, son of an alcoholic father who eventually deserted his family; devoted son to a mother who raised both Durant boys; grandson to one of Michigan's first governors; and former laborer, insurance salesman, and cigar vendor, stumbled onto a near-bankrupt manufacturer of horse-drawn "road carts." Short on capital but long on ambition, Durant enlisted his friend, J. Dallas Dort, borrowed $1,000 from a bank, and for $2,000 bought the product, the patent, and the equipment to set up the Flint Road Cart Company in his hometown of Flint, Michigan.[1]

Having no factory, Durant took the plans to W.A. Patterson, Flint's leading carriage manufacturer, who agreed to make the road carts for $12.50 each. Durant then sold them to dealers for $17.00. The light, sturdy road car was an instant success, and sales reached 100,000 within a few years.

Durant first began subcontracting his carriages to other manufacturers, but he quickly saw that they would copy his ideas and start to build competing models. Durant began to build factories, hire workers, and manufacture his own road cars and carriages. He soon realized, however, that as long as other companies manufactured his parts and his factories merely carried out the assembly process, he would have no substantial advantage over his competitors. In response, he began a practice he was later to refine with General Motors, that is, seeking out the best parts manufacturers and integrating them directly into his own operation. This allowed him to cut costs, control quality, and increase profits.

In 1895, Durant took the profits from his road-cart venture and formed the Durant-Dort Carriage Company to manufacture full-sized carriages. By the early 1900s the company had become the leading carriage manufacturer in the country, selling 50,000 carriages a year. Durant, forty years old, had become a millionaire.[2]

Durant was very fond of the city of Flint and eventually became known as the "father of Flint" for transforming the city into one of the nation's largest auto manufacturing centers. But Durant was also known as "the father of General Motors" and began the tradition of threatening communities with the lever of the runaway shop to gain profitable concessions. Faced with the need for investment capital (and vacillation on the part of the city's fathers to provide it) Durant threatened to take his business elsewhere. *The Gennessee Democrat* on June 30, 1891, ran the following story:

Flint Road Cars Works Go To Saginaw

> We regret to leave Flint [said Durant], but the inducements offered to us in the way of improved facilities were such that, from a business standpoint we couldn't afford to disregard them.[3]

Confronted with Durant's threat of a runaway, the Flint town leaders came forward with large loans and substantial purchases of the Company's stock. The Flint Road Car Company, which began with $2,000 in borrowed capital, was incorporated in 1893 with $150,000 capitalization. Durant's threats having achieved their objectives, the company stayed in Flint.

DURANT RIDES THE HORSELESS CARRIAGE

The automobile is such a fixture in American life that it is difficult to imagine a time when it didn't exist. But when Durant was making his first fortune, the horseless carriage was an exciting prospect for the tinkerer, the inventor, and the engineer--and a highly risky enterprise for the investor. The early autos were individually crafted machines, developed by inventors and sold to the wealthy. Because of the poor public roads in the United States at the time, the early cars offered bumpy rides, frequent mechanical failures, fewer luxuries than the top-of-the-line horse drawn carriage, and a "sense of adventure" that didn't translate into an equation for mass production.

But Billy Durant, after an initial period of skepticism, saw the unlimited commercial possibilities of the automobile. Brilliant and, at the time, unheralded inventors (Karl Benz and Daimler in Germany; Panhard and DeDion in France; the Duryea Brothers, George Selden, and Hiram Maxim in the United States) were working "to perfect a stationary gasoline engine and then reduce it in size so that it could fit into a carriage."[4] For every technical breakthrough, there were a hundred failures. For every hundred technical breakthroughs, ninety-nine men lost their life savings. The mythology of free enterprise, with its attempts to justify unlimited wealth for the successful entrepreneur based on the high risks involved, was rooted in this period of impressive individual contributions and all-too-rare reward for one's labors.

By 1904, Durant had taken over the financially troubled Buick company, correctly assessing that its powerful and technically advanced engine, in conjunction with his own brilliance in sales and marketing, could catapult Buick to a dominant position in the fledgling industry. As *Scientific American* reported in January of that year: "The period of experiment is over, and the growing confidence of the public in the automobile is resulting in a remarkable growth in the industry."[5]

Durant began by recapitalizing Buick with $500,000 in stock of questionable value. The inflated stock was sold based on "inventions not yet patented for business reasons," that is, assets that didn't exist. The practice was so unethical and usually calamitous to the investor that the Michigan state legislature soon passed laws making it illegal.[6] Through innovation and deception, Durant had built Buick, with sales of almost 9,000 vehicles in 1908, into the largest producer of automobiles in the country--larger even than Ford.

The Automobile Worker and the Labor Process: From Skilled Craftsman to Assembly Line Worker

Henry Ford was the manufacturing genius of his time. He dramatically improved auto assembly by developing first the stationary assembly line, in which teams of workers moved from car to car, and then the moving assembly line, in which the car was transported from worker to worker, each one assembling a minuscule part of the total product. Ford refined the manufacture of standard parts and developed the strategy of building virtually identical cars in large numbers. These economies of scale made the mass auto market possible.

While Ford's manufacturing brilliance was unquestioned, and was amplified by the mythology of his "$5 a day" benevolence, in fact, the transformation of auto assembly from skilled workers doing a complex combination of jobs to semi-skilled workers carrying out simple and repetitive tasks at breakneck speed set the basic conditions for the class conflict in the auto industry--a conflict which rages to this day.

The evolution of the labor process in the automobile industry and how it was used to degrade and oppress the auto worker is a fascinating and critical subject itself, one that fortunately has been treated in depth in David Gartman's *Auto Slavery*. Based on that study, however, two aspects of the story deserve emphasis.

First, the destruction of the skilled workers and their unions.

> Early auto workers were not fresh recruits to industrial labor. Most had experience with similar work in other [bicycle and carriage] industries. They were usually second- or third-generation industrial workers, thoroughly imbued with the requirements and culture of the factory....
>
> Most of Detroit's early auto workers were organized into strong craft unions....The largest and strongest of these were organized by the metal-trades workers, iron molders, machinery molders, patternmakers, metal polishers and machinists....Judging from the reports of labor strife in the early shops, these unions were active in the auto industry.. ..Employers everywhere began to see union efforts to regulate output and production methods as a major obstacle to their quest to cut costs and increase profits....Employer associations launched a nation-wide open-shop drive around 1903 to break the unions....By

> 1907, the Employers Association of Detroit had won a total victory for the open shop. The craft unions were crushed, leaving the workers of the budding auto industry unorganized for thirty years.[7]

Second, the replacement of skilled workers with semi-skilled mass production workers. While the skilled craftsmen's unions were broken, even as individuals they had too much independence for Ford and Durant. Because the workers had skills that were transferable to other industries, if they didn't like their working conditions, they took a walk. Gartman argues that the move towards greater and greater division of labor served not only the objective of economic efficiency, but also that of subjugating the workforce:

> "Dividing and subdividing operations," Ford said, "keeping the work in motion--these are the keynotes of production....The net result of the application of these principles is the reduction of the necessity of thought on the part of the worker and the reduction of his movements to the minimum."[8]

And in case Ford's contempt for the workers seemed unintended, he clarified his thoughts, arguing that his process allowed him to render his workers unskilled, "or to put it more accurately, [they] must be skilled in exactly one operation which the most stupid man can learn in two days."[9]

The conscious decision to "de-skill" the workforce and to reduce the worker to an interchangeable part in the production process allowed Ford and Durant to consolidate their influence in the early auto industry and created the conditions that would eventually lead to the formation of the UAW.

While Durant allowed Ford to refine the process of auto production and adopted most of his methods, Durant conceived of himself as a salesman, a stylist, a promoter. He understood that the auto was not just a financial investment, but a highly personal consumer decision that warranted more variety, pizazz, luxury, and product differentiation--a whole line of makes and models. Thus, it was Durant who tried to organize a "United Motors" of many car companies. Under Durant's plan, each company would have kept its individual product identity but would have been able to reduce costs through shared parts purchases and consolidated marketing and management staff. In 1908, after Durant tried unsuccessfully to engineer a merger of Buick, Ford, and Reo, he formed General Motors out of a merger of Buick and Oldsmobile. In the same year, the newly created GM bought out Leland's Cadillac, Champion Ignition (which later became AC spark plugs) and the Oakland Motor Company (which later became Pontiac).

DURANT'S FIRST DEFEAT BY THE BANKERS

Durant's conception of a "General Motors" was farsighted, but his execution was plagued by the uncertainties of the times and his own errors in judgment. The only consistently profitable company in the new GM was Buick. While Durant focused his energies on recruiting top staff, developing innovative marketing schemes, and acquiring the rights to new technological breakthroughs, his financial management was sloppy and his systems of accounting and inventory control were a shambles.

Durant used his charisma and confidence to attract new investors but was wary of the large bankers, whom he viewed as parasites and termed "the barracudas of Wall Street." He understood that, in their conservatism, many of the major banking houses had underestimated the growth potential of the nascent auto industry, and he wanted to take advantage of their misassessment by expanding aggressively--with his own capital and that of banks he believed to be less meddlesome--to prevent banks he perceived to be domineering from moving in. In 1910, GM made profits of $10 million on sales of $49 million, but Durant's strategy of eluding the control of hostile bankers by continued expansion made him more dependent on the "friendly" banks from which he already had outstanding loans.

Prudent expansion was replaced by wild speculation. A $7 million investment in John Heany's tungsten filament lightbulb (which was to have been a competitor to the J.P. Morgan backed General Electric bulb) proved a fiasco. Watered-down stock deals--Durant himself was not above the shady dealings he ascribed to the "barracudas"--and a sudden drop in Buick sales brought Durant's precarious empire, by 1910, to the verge of collapse.

These policies had disastrous effects on the lives of the GM workers. As Buick sales declined, Flint, which had boasted that the Depression would never set foot inside its city limits, was jolted out of its euphoria:

> Employment in Durant's works had tripled in just two years, but now 15,000 carriage and automobile workers faced lay-offs. Increasing numbers sat helplessly in the tent cities and shacks...without jobs, without savings, and without hope of public relief.
>
> The shock reverberated for years; in 1910, Flint, Michigan, home of motordom's greatest capitalistic venture, elected a Socialist mayor. The resentments would last a lifetime, the bitterness handed from father to son.[10]

It wasn't just anger at individual wheeler-dealers like Durant that would lead the workers to elect a Socialist mayor. It was anger against a system that produced enormous wealth, but not for them; a system that sanctioned wild speculation by manufacturers, investors, and bankers, which produced disastrous consequences for their lives. This class anger was reflected in significant electoral support for the Socialist presidential candidate of the time, Eugene V. Debs.

Two years after its formation, General Motors was on the verge of disintegration. After virtually every bank in the country had refused to loan Durant any more money, a consortium of bankers was summoned by the Boston and New York investment houses of Lee, Higginson, and Company and J. and W. Seligman to preside over GM's avalanche of debt. Meeting in the director's room of the Chase National Bank in New York, the bankers first leaned towards the cannibalization of the company, but they finally decided to grant GM a loan of $15 million--under very harsh terms.

First, they "discounted" the loan, which meant that while GM would have to pay back $15 million at 6 percent interest, the bank would, in actuality, only give GM $12.75 million. Second, the bankers voted themselves a bonus of $6.17 million in preferred stock, for a total profit of 62 percent! Third, the bankers put GM in receivership and nominated a new board of directors, with the express goal of removing Durant from leadership.

The syndicate set up a new leadership group, with Charles Nash as president and Walter Chrysler as the head of production. General Motors had been saved, but at Durant's expense. According to Durant: "The $15 million loan finally offered had outrageous terms which I was forced to accept to save my 'baby' born and raised by me, the result of hectic years of night and day work."[11]

DURANT AS THE FATHER OF CHEVROLET

Stripped of his fatherhood, Durant went out and made another "baby." Still holding the title of vice-president at GM, but exercising no power, Durant set up an independent company--Chevrolet. He got the name from a famous race-car driver of the time, Louis Chevrolet, whom he hoped to use as the figurehead for the new venture. But when Durant changed the original idea from a luxury model to compete with the Cadillac to a lower-priced model to compete with the Ford, Louis Chevrolet's pride and design sensibilities were offended. He sold his name and his stake in the new venture to Durant.[12]

Durant's assessment of the Chevrolet's proper niche in the market proved to be right on target. While the Chevrolet was more expensive than Ford's Model T, it was lighter and more powerful. And Ford couldn't build enough cars to satisfy the demand for a low-priced automobile. By 1913, Chevrolet had sold 13,000 units and, by 1916, sales had soared to 70,000. Durant was now ready for his next move--taking back control of General Motors.

While Durant was taking great risks, creating a whole new company from scratch and making a success of it, the bank trustees in control of GM were being far too conservative. Although they had instituted long-overdue financial controls, in general, the bankers had played it too close to the vest and had badly underestimated the growth of the auto market. In 1910, the year of Durant's removal from power, Buick and Ford had each sold 30,000 cars. But by 1916, while Buick sales had increased to 124,000, Ford sales had jumped to 735,000. In Durant's last year, GM sold 21 percent of all the cars bought in the United States; at the end of the bankers' five-year trusteeship, GM's market share had fallen to 8.5 percent.[13]

Durant, based on his phoenix-like performance at Chevrolet, was able to convince some of GM's largest stockholders, many of whom were still personally loyal to him, that if he were back in power, GM would make much larger profits and pay the dividends the bankers were hoarding. Durant surreptitiously accumulated large blocks of GM stock, buying at depressed prices and exchanging Chevrolet stock as an incentive.

But Durant realized he couldn't beat the bankers by himself. His own backers at Chevrolet convinced him to enlist the support of the powerful du Pont family of the Wilmington, Delaware, chemical empire. In the years preceding the United States' formal entrance into World War I, the du Ponts were making enormous profits selling gunpowder and dynamite to the Allied Powers, but they were also looking for long-term investment opportunities. They assessed that GM stock was undervalued, and that with Durant's dynamic leadership and their greater business sophistication, the profit potential was very attractive. Pierre S. du Pont and his top financial advisor, John Raskob, agreed to bolster Durant's bid to take back control of General Motors.

On September 16, 1915, five years after his removal from power, Billy Durant swaggered into the board of directors meeting of the General Motors Corporation. Backed by the muscle of the du Ponts, his pockets bulging with stock certificates, Durant made his now-famous announcement to the stunned bankers: "Gentlemen, I'm in control of General Motors today."[14] He had come to reclaim his baby. The bankers, unprepared and out-organized, were forced to relinquish control.

Of course, as with many power struggles among the wealthy, everyone got richer. To soften the blow for the bankers and to prove to his new allies that the GM corporation had far more dividends than the bankers had been willing to distribute, the Durant team immediately issued a dividend of $50 a share on stock that was selling for $135 a share. For Raskob and du Pont, who had just come on the scene with an initial purchase of only 3,000 shares, this translated into an immediate $1.5 million profit their first day on the job. Meanwhile, the men who produced the GM automobiles still labored for less than $3 a day.

DURANT'S SECOND ADMINISTRATION AND FINAL DEFEAT

In 1915, Durant took over a company that had failed to invest in its plants, failed to expand technology and production to keep up with an expanding market, and was in danger of becoming a second-rate competitor to Henry Ford. Durant's second term at the head of the corporation produced several breakthroughs:

– Through a complex legal maneuver, rather than Chevrolet becoming incorporated into GM, GM was taken over by Chevrolet. "David swallowed Goliath," as business analysts described it at the time.

– In 1916, GM formed United Motors, a subsidiary of parts suppliers such as Delco, Remy Electric, and Hyatt Roller Bearing. Alfred P. Sloan, the next major figure in this story and the president of Hyatt at the time, was appointed by Durant to serve as president of United Motors and a vice-president of GM.

– In 1918, Durant, despite objections from most GM Board members, bought with his own money a fledgling refrigerator company that would later become Frigidaire.

– In 1918, GM was reorganized so that Chevrolet became part of GM. The five basic divisions--Chevrolet, Cadillac, Oldsmobile, Buick, and Oakland (which later became Pontiac)--were in place.

– In 1918, GM bought out the Fisher Body Works and brought its founders, the Fisher brothers, into the GM management team. This followed Durant's pattern of integrating the best parts and supply manufacturers, and their top executives, into the growing GM empire.

– In 1919, GM formed the General Motors Acceptance Corporation (GMAC), which facilitated credit purchases of GM vehicles.

General Motors, with its five divisions in place, its parts suppliers and financing arm--and even its refrigerators--under one corporate umbrella, was truly the house that Durant built. And yet, by 1920, Durant, once again, was evicted from his own house.

When Durant first brought in the du Ponts, he saw them as allies against the banking group but also as people with little knowledge of, or interest in, the intricacies of running an auto company. Thus, while he supported Pierre du Pont's appointment as chairman of the GM Board, he didn't perceive him as a threat.

In 1917, when a falling stock market left GM short of cash for needed expansion, John Raskob, as Pierre's chief advisor and now a GM board member, wrote a private memo to the du Pont board of directors urging them to buy $25 million of GM stock on the open market. He advanced two arguments to support this move:

1) The investment would help consolidate the du Ponts' control of the corporation. As Raskob argued: "With Mr. Durant, we will have joint control of the companies. We are immediately to assume charge and be responsible for the financial operation of the Company."[15]

2) GM was an excellent outlet for the enormous profits that the du Ponts were making through their dynamite and gunpowder sales. Realizing that the war, and the war profits, would eventually end, the du Ponts saw GM not just as a good investment, but--with their $25 million investment securing their control--an excellent market for du Pont products. In the famous statement that later became an important piece of evidence in the antitrust suit that forced du Pont to let go of its GM holdings, Raskob argued: "Our interest in the General Motors Company will undoubtedly secure for us the entire Fabrikoid, Pyralin, paint and varnish business of those companies."[16]

Heeding Raskob's counsel, du Pont invested the $25 million. And later, in 1920, when John Raskob, now the head of the GM finance committee, proposed ambitious expansion plans that even Billy Durant felt were over-extending the corporation, Raskob convinced du Pont to buy $25 million more in stock to finance his scheme.

As the stock market rose and fell in 1920, Durant and the du Ponts engaged in stock market speculation in which they artificially drove stock prices down and then raised them in order to turn over paper profits. These maneuvers once again drove GM close to financial collapse. This time, the du Pont interests turned against Durant. They secured a new ally and brought a new force into the GM management battles--the banking house of J.P. Morgan with its powerful partner, Edward Stettinius.

With Durant's own personal finances and those of the corporation in a state of chaos, and the real possibility of Durant, the du Ponts, and all the other large investors losing their fortunes, a coalition of the Morgan and du Pont interests forced Durant to resign. They agreed to pay off his massive stock debts and leave him some money in the form of GM shares, but they effectively stripped him of all influence and authority.

In twelve years, from 1908 to 1920, Durant had organized a coalition of struggling companies into the second largest auto manufacturer in the country, a corporation worth $350 million, employing 100,000 workers in thirty-five cities, and selling $600 million worth of motor vehicles annually.[17]

One can imagine Durant's sense of outrage. He had built the corporation practically from the ground up. He had begun his journey, along with Henry Ford, Henry Leland, and the other auto pioneers, when there was no auto industry. He had conceived bold ideas, raised the capital, taken the risks, hired the workers, designed and marketed the products, and made and lost fortunes many times over in the process. And in the end, here was Durant, vanquished, driven out of the Promised Land, not by another auto man like Henry Ford, but by the du Ponts, whose claim to fame was producing gunpowder, and by the arrogant bankers of the House of Morgan, who produced nothing--except profits.

While Durant's anger was well justified, in the hardball world of business profit and loss, his view was one-sided. Even his greatest admirers had to admit that Durant had contributed to his own downfall. A genius and a maverick, he was also an unscientific gambler who rebelled against capitalism's ruthless rules, ignoring its "house odds" that built in fortunes for the few and downfall for the many. Durant had run GM as a one-man show, attracting strong, dynamic men, but soon driving them to quit, as they learned you could work *for* Billy, but not *with* him.

Durant played checkers with his cronies while he made top executives wait. He had his hair cut by a barber while he held business meetings with bankers. But despite these endearing--or maddening--idiosyncracies, Durant's methodology was fundamentally unsound. He kept shoddy records, made most of his deals in his head, and worked on hunches that were frequently brilliant, but just as often disastrous. He defied the basic rule of capitalism, that you go into business to make a maximum return on your investment. For the Alfred P. Sloans and the modern corporate managers, profits are the goal, and the product is just a means to amass those profits. For Durant, the product--the automobile--was the goal, and profits were secondary, a means of buying more inventions, building more factories, and expanding the production of automobiles.

Billy Durant was in love with the automobile and wanted to build General Motors into a manufacturing colossus. At this, he succeeded masterfully. But because he couldn't master the rules of finance, he was eventually destroyed by those who could.

Durant was not alone in his defeat. Many of the early twentieth-century entrepreneurs and inventors who founded their own companies ended up watching from the sidelines as the scientific managers and high-powered bankers drove them out in the ruthless transition to the modern corporation.

In 1920, while the headlines focused on the great battles of the industrial managers, the workers still labored in isolation and anonymity. After the breaking of the skilled craft unions, there had been an effort to form an auto workers union. As early as 1891 there had been an International Union of Carriage and Wagon Workers, affiliated with the Knights of Labor. As the carriage industry was supplanted by the fledgling auto industry, and many former carriage workers transferred their skills into auto, the union attempted to make the transition, changing its name and its organizing mission to the Union of Carriage, Wagon and Automobile Workers and attracting 13,000 members by 1916.

But the bitter intercraft rivalries of the AFL condemned the effort to failure. Other craft unions demanded that the union drop the "autoworkers" from its name, and when its leaders refused, the AFL suspended it. In the postwar period of the Palmer raids against radicals and communists and the bitter in-fighting among the more conservative AFL unions, the now-independent Auto Workers Union was no match for Ford or GM. The 343,000 auto workers at the time had to labor without union protection.[18]

Durant left General Motors with no power and no car company, but with a sizeable fortune, which he lost during the Great Depression. He made several unsuccessful efforts to form other ventures, and spent his last years in Flint, Michigan, where he owned a restaurant, famous for "Billy's homemade spaghetti sauce," and operated a bowling alley until shortly before his death in 1947. Durant's fall from the pinnacle of power was used as an object lesson to reinforce the ideology of profit maximization and was drilled into the consciousness of an entire generation of GM executives by his successor--Alfred P. Sloan.

NOTES

1. Ed Cray, *Chrome Colossus: General Motors and Its Times* (New York: McGraw Hill, 1980), p. 20. This is the best single work on GM's history and has provided a factual foundation for much of my analysis.
2. William Serrin, *The Company and the Union*, (New York: Alfred A. Knopf, 1973), p. 78. Serrin, formerly a reporter for the *Detroit Free Press*, is a labor writer for the *New York Times*. This book, subtitled *The "Civilized Relationship" of the General Motors Corporation and the United Auto Workers*, is still influential among dissident autoworkers. Serrin's reportorial critique of the GM-UAW 1970 contract negotiations was ahead of its time, and helped shed light on the union's subsequent problems.
3. Lawrence R. Gustin, *Billy Durant: Creator of General Motors* (Grand Rapids, Michigan: William B. Eerdmans, 1973), p. 41. Gustin's excellent biography of Durant was drawn upon by Cray and Serrin and helped provide the framework for this chapter.
4. Cray, p. 23.
5. Cray, p. 28.
6. Gustin, p. 78
7. David Gartman, *Auto Slavery: The Labor Process in the American Automobile Industry, 1897-1950* (New Brunswick, N.J.: Rutgers University Press, 1986), pp. 36, 37. This book fills a long overdue void in the literature about twentieth-century industrial capitalism and provides an essential piece of the puzzle for those attempting to understand the auto industry. Another important contribution in this field is Harry Braverman's *Labor and Monopoly Capital* (New York: Monthly Review Press, 1974).
8. Gartman, p. 48.
9. Gartman, p. 48.
10. Cray, p. 90.
11. Cray, p. 96, 97.
12. Serrin, p. 83.
13. Cray, p. 132.
14. Cray, p. 139.
15. Cray p. 153. Also see Serrin, p. 85.

16. Cray, p. 153
17. Cray, p. 182.
18. Roger Keeran, *The Communist Party and the Auto Workers' Unions* (New York: International Publishers, 1980), p. 32.

Chapter Three

ALFRED P. SLOAN'S BLUEPRINT FOR GENERAL MOTORS

The Auto's Ascendancy and GM's Domination (1920-1980)

Alfred P. Sloan was president, then chairman of the board of the General Motors Corporation for thirty-three years, from 1923 until 1956. However, his decisive influence on the direction of the corporation actually spans six decades--from the end of the Durant era until the beginning of the Roger Smith era in 1981.

Sloan was the most impressive and influential industrial manager of the twentieth century. He took Billy Durant's bold ideas and adapted them to the ruthless exigencies of capitalism. By his own proud self-description, Sloan was the father of the modern, scientifically organized corporation. Politically reactionary, fitting the classic stereotype of the financial man who genuinely believes that his greatest social responsibility is to maximize profits, Sloan was a brilliant administrator. Anxious to raise practice to the level of theory, and determined to make his mark on history, Sloan created a foolproof administrative system that, like the auto-assembly process itself, could mass-produce interchangeable parts, in this case GM executives.

If Durant's ego drove him to prove he was irreplaceable, Sloan's ego drove him to produce a system in which he was himself the platonic form, stamping out successor after successor in his image. GM's awesome manufacturing, designing, marketing, and financial success, on the one hand, and its historical refusal to tolerate any government, union, or societal restrictions on its behavior, on the other, can be traced directly to Sloan's influence.

After graduating from MIT with a degree in electrical engineering, Sloan took his first job with the Hyatt Roller Bearings company in Trenton, New Jersey. John Wesley Hyatt was one of the many inventors-turned-parts-manufacturers whose bearings went into the axles used in Fords, Buicks, and Chevrolets. When Sloan was appointed general manager in 1899, Hyatt was on the verge of bankruptcy. But with advanced engineering ideas, upgraded technology, aggressive sales campaigns, and a generous helping of his father's money, young Alfred constructed a thriving enterprise "with 3,800 production workers on a piece-work basis, its $4 million in annual sales based on the automobile industry's fortunes."[1]

In 1916, Durant approached Sloan about selling Hyatt and becoming part of the burgeoning General Motors network through its subsidiary, United Motors. Sloan realized it was prudent to accept Durant's offer, for then, as now, the machinations of auto manufacturers represent a constant threat to auto parts suppliers. As Sloan assessed the situation:

> More than half of our business came from Ford, and our other big customer, General Motors, dwarfed the remainder. If either Ford or General Motors should start making their own bearings or use some other type of bearings, our company would be in a desperate situation.[2]

So at forty-one, Sloan, whose sole understanding of the auto industry came from making a tiny part of the axle, sold Hyatt to GM for $13.5 million, assumed the presidency of United Motors, and became a GM vice-president.

Sloan's rapid rise to power took place because his unique management skills were urgently needed to repair the main weaknesses of the GM corporation. In 1920, after the Morgans and du Ponts had forced Durant out, the fundamental question remained: Who could run GM? Sloan, never short on confidence, was sure he knew the right man for the job.

But Sloan also knew that he was not respected enough in business circles to assume the presidency directly. The formal title would have to go, at least for awhile, to Pierre S. du Pont.

> Du Pont...was the one individual in General Motors who had the prestige and respect that could give confidence to the organization, to the public, and to the banks, and whose presence could arrest the demoralization that was taking place.[3]

Sloan, however, was well aware of du Pont's limitations.

> There was only one drawback. Mr. du Pont had no intimate knowledge of the automobile business. I happen to be of the old school who thinks that a knowledge of the business is essential to a successful administration.[4]

Therefore, a leadership team was developed to solve these problems. Pierre du Pont was elected chairman of the board and president; a four-person executive committee consisting of du Pont, Raskob, J. Amory Haskell, and Sloan would oversee all major decisions; and between meetings, both Sloan and Haskell would have the authority to act for the president in his absence. By 1920, Sloan had become acting president and had the authority to begin his administrative reforms.

SLOAN AND GM'S THEORY OF CORPORATE PROFITS

When Sloan took over, he inherited a corporation with "just about as much crisis, inside and outside, as you could wish for, if you liked that sort of thing."[5] Sloan proceeded to solve the problems one by one through the following measures:

1) *Establishing financial order.* Durant had justified his acquisition of so many products and inventions with the rationale that the auto industry was in a period of extreme technological flux and that, by buying several engine designs or several patents for ignitions, he was protecting GM against the future technological innovations of its competitors. But, in fact, Durant paid far too much for far too many of these inventions. He diversified unscientifically and did not institute financial controls to evaluate the profit or loss of many of the corporation's divisions. Many of those divisions were losing money, with only Buick and Cadillac making consistent profits.

Also, when Sloan took over, the corporation was plagued with rampant cronyism. Disagreements about investment priorities on the financial committee were solved by giving everyone the money they wanted or, if there wasn't enough money available, the corporation simply issued more stock. Only when auto sales declined and company stock issues were received with skepticism did management panic and begin to address its financial problems.

Sloan's task was to *force* financial priorities on GM. He demanded that each GM division be organized on a profit-making basis and evaluated on its percentage of return on investment. Sloan set the goal of achieving a 20 percent net return on all invested capital. Thus, if a division boasted a $10 million profit, but $100 million had been invested, the rate of return was too low. In short, each division, and each new project, would not only have to pay its own way; it would have to compete with other uses of that capital that might achieve a higher rate of return.

2) *Establishing accurate accounting and statistical records.* When the banking consortium called in the GM board of directors in 1920, the company's books were a shambles. Durant's individualism carried over to the way he ran the company's finances--half the "records" were in his head. He couldn't produce sales figures, stock

certificates, inventory statistics or profit-or-loss statements for individual divisions. So, even if the corporation agreed to institute a policy of judging its work by return on investment, without accurate accounting methods evaluation was impossible. One of Sloan's first reforms was to institute scientific and accurate record keeping, which was the essential foundation for the modern, scientifically managed corporation.

3) *Setting policies for strategic investment.* Sloan felt it was essential to establish scientific rules to determine how GM should invest its assets. He asked: "What is the relative value of the project to the corporation as a whole, based both on return on capital and the need of a particular project in supporting the operations of the corporation?"[6]

Sloan argued that investment decisions, such as building new plants (or *dis*investment decisions, such as plant closings) should be based on comparing how much profit that investment could make relative to other uses of the money. It is significant that no criteria of social responsibility, separate from profit maximization, were included in his management check list.

4) *Establishing production and inventory controls.* When Sloan took over, Durant was frequently building far too many cars based on blindly optimistic "gut feelings" about future demand. (Similar to when Lee Iacocca took over at Chrysler decades later, GM was producing cars first, then pressuring the sales staff to sell them.) Reports from dealers were lagging far behind changes in market conditions, so that GM production was often out of step with actual demand. Sloan tightened production schedules and instituted far more accurate methods of determining consumer demand, thereby saving millions of dollars that had previously been tied up in unsold inventories.

5) *Centralizing authority.* GM now prides itself upon giving individual division heads great autonomy but, when Sloan took over, the company was in a state of laissez-faire chaos, practicing "decentralization with a vengeance," as he described it. Before allowing decentralization and initiative, GM had first to establish strong centralized controls.

Sloan established a formal organizational chart based on the German staff-and-line model. A centralized staff, responsible for long-range planning for the entire corporation, had to be established. Only then could individual line managers take the initiative based on those objectives and plans.

Second, Sloan had to create a "team" of managers who saw their first allegiance as being not to their individual divisions, but to General Motors as a unified corporation. Otherwise GM would continue as a loose amalgam of individual and competing fiefdoms. Sloan tells the story of how haughty Buick managers, angry that their division was the only consistently profitable one, would hide money from the central office and force the GM treasurer to beg for funds for the rest of the corporation. Over a period of years, Sloan successfully developed product men in Detroit and financial men in New York who were not Cadillac or Chevrolet men, but General Motors men.[7]

6) *Organizing the GM product line.* It was Billy Durant who understood that GM could eventually overtake Ford as the industry leader by developing a diversified product line to compete with the Model T. But, as with most of Durant's ideas, it took Sloan to implement it in a way that was scientific and profitable.

When Sloan came to power, many GM divisions were competing with each other for the same market share. Sloan reorganized the GM product line. Beginning with the least expensive and moving to the most expensive, the GM lineup would be Chevrolet, Pontiac, Oldsmobile, Buick, and Cadillac. There would be no duplication of price or model. Sloan referred to this as "a car for every purse and purpose."

In all of these organizational changes, Sloan was up front in his main objective--profit. Every corporate decision, every discussion of safety or quality or labor relations was governed by the goal of maximizing GM's return on investment. While Durant saw profits as a vehicle to allow him to build more cars, Sloan saw cars as a vehicle to make more profits--and it was Sloan's view that prevailed. As Sloan explained:

> Competition is the final price determinant, and competitive prices may result in profits which force you to accept a rate of return less than you hoped for, or for that matter, to accept temporary losses....Nevertheless, no other financial principle serves better than *rate of return* as an objective aid to business judgement.[8]

By placing General Motors on a disciplined, scientifically managed path, Alfred P. Sloan positioned GM to take advantage of the dramatic growth of the U.S. auto market over the next six decades. Under his leadership, by the beginning of the 1930s, GM had surpassed Ford as the nation's largest producer of automobiles.

> Even during the Depression, when sales dropped 70 percent, General Motors never failed to earn a profit or pay a dividend. Between 1927 and 1957, General Motors averaged an annual profit of 173.2 million dollars, the largest of any corporation in America.[9]

Albert Bradley, Frederic Donner, James Roche, Richard Gerstenberg, and Thomas Murphy, who followed Sloan as GM's chairmen, had to exercise judgment and initiate policy, but they did so within the strictly established management guidelines that Sloan had dictated. Even after his death in 1966, Sloan's basic system endured.

THE SOCIAL LEGACY OF ALFRED P. SLOAN

For the socially conscious reader, the history of GM in the eras of Durant and Sloan is quite enjoyable, as long as the discussion stays within the confines of management thought processes and values--car models and sales, cost estimates and profit measurement, corporate reorganizations and leadership battles. But as soon as broader social questions are raised--automobile safety, air pollution, product durability, workers' health, safety and job security, civil and community rights--the historical antagonism of GM management to any and all of those concerns becomes evident. In the interest of social justice and historical accuracy, a broader set of criteria must be brought to bear in evaluating Sloan's legacy.

Sloan's Influence on GM Management Behavior

Both industry analysts and assembly line workers can attest to GM's reputation as a harsh employer. As with all major components of GM's corporate behavior, that too can be traced directly to Sloan's influence. His principle of maximizing the profits of the corporation, and that of each of its divisions, is not in itself remarkable. But GM's ruthless and unwavering application of that policy over the decades has placed enormous pressure on plant managers, foremen, and assembly line workers. As each plant manager, superintendent, general foreman and foreman realizes that his upward, or *downward*, mobility will be determined by the profitability of his particular operation, the pressure to maximize the bottom line is passed on to those below. And at the bottom of this pyramid are over 350,000 GM production workers who are engaged in a daily battle to keep up with the nonstop pressure of the assembly line.

GM's Historical Opposition to Corporate Social Responsibility

This profit pressure has also pitted GM management against the interests of the auto consumer and the broader public. For example, in 1927 Henry Ford, after seeing one of his test drivers thrown through a windshield and severely injured, ordered the installation of the newly developed safety glass in all his models. Sloan considered following Ford's lead. He acknowledged that the installation of safety glass would provide far greater protection to the purchasers of GM products, but rejected it as a bad business decision.

> However, irrespective of accidents or no accidents my concern in this problem is a matter of profit or loss....You can say perhaps that I am selfish, but business is selfish. We are not a charitable institution--we are trying to make a profit for our stockholders.[10]

This was not an isolated incident. Sloan believed in profit not merely as an economic motor but as a religious principle. He would brook no interference from unions, consumers, or government. In *Chrome Colossus*, his history of General Motors, Ed Cray chronicles a long series of incidents that reinforce this theme:

– GM's fierce opposition to the workers' right to union representation and its aggressive, if ultimately unsuccessful, efforts to crush UAW organizing drives.

– GM's refusal to repair the lethally flawed Corvair even *after* Ralph Nader's *Unsafe at Any Speed* was published, and its ill-fated campaign to slander Nader that boomeranged and helped pass the National Traffic and Motor Vehicle Safety Act.

– GM's opposition to laws mandating seatbelts, impact-resistant bumpers, airbags, pollution controls, and fuel economy standards, as well as any legislation that would place restrictions on a corporation's right to close down plants.

While Sloan claimed to be a strong advocate of entrepreneurial ingenuity, he refused to accept the challenge of pursuing profits within socially responsible limits regulating corporate behavior. As such, it is not surprising that Sloan was an unabashed opponent of the New Deal. When Roosevelt decried the destructive behavior of the "economic royalists" and supported collective bargaining through the Wagner Act, Sloan condemned even minimal government regulation as a move toward a "sovietized America." Sloan, along with the du Pont family, formed the American Liberty League in 1934, an extreme right-wing organization dedicated to defeating Roosevelt for reelection. But despite his letters to GM workers warning them that a vote for Roosevelt would produce "class strife and economic shackles on management which could break the company," Roosevelt was reelected with 61 percent of the vote.[11]

Sloan learned his lesson and withdrew from such overt interference in the political process (preferring to exercise power behind the scenes). However, the corporation's historical antipathy to any form of government regulation lives on at General Motors to this day.

SLOAN AND THE UAW: FROM CLASS WARFARE TO SOCIAL COMPACT

For over a dozen years, from 1920 when he assumed power to the beginning of the Franklin Delano Roosevelt presidency in 1933, Sloan and the GM executives were well aware of labor discontent but quite successful in defeating any attempts to bring in a union. By 1935, however, the historical playing out of many unsuccessful strategies for organizing the autoworkers, along with a distinct left turn in the nation's political mood, changed the balance of power between capital and labor in the auto industry.

Throughout the 1920s and early 1930s, AFL unions had attempted to organize autoworkers through a coalition of craft unions amalgamated into "federal unions." Jurisdictional fights among the craft unions and the AFL's conciliatory stance towards the employers doomed the strategy to failure.

The first effort at an autoworkers' industrial union, the Auto Workers Union, after initial leadership from the Socialist Party, was led by the Communist Party during the 1920s. The Communist Party correctly criticized the timidity of the AFL leadership, but instead of working to build a movement from below, they formed their own "revolutionary unions" under its Trade Union Unity League. While attracting many dedicated workers, the concept of a "revolutionary union," as opposed to a trade union, could not possibly unite the vast majority of auto workers. Although they led several important but unsuccessful strikes, the independent AWU isolated the most politically radical workers from the more trade union oriented majority, and allowed the AFL to red-bait the idea of an industrial union as synonymous with the CP's revolutionary union strategy.

Franklin Delano Roosevelt, a mild reformer in his first term, moved to curb some of capitalism's worst excesses and impose minimal standards of behavior on the corporations--whose shortsighted greed and anti-social behavior had helped bring about the Great Depression. In 1934, Roosevelt pushed through the National Industrial Relations Act (NIRA) that declared "employees have the right to organize and bargain collectively through representatives of their own choosing."

Initially, many of the nation's half million auto-workers believed that the law would provide government support for union organizing drives and soften employer opposition. But, in practice, neither Roosevelt nor the NIRA offered much protection:

> The auto manufacturers defied [the NIRA] with impunity. They fired unionists, employed private detectives and spies, established company unions and refused to bargain with the federal labor unions. On January 31, 1934, [AFL auto organizer] William Collins reported to the AFL Executive Council that employer intimidation was so great that he could no longer persuade workers in Detroit, Flint, Lansing and Pontiac to attend meetings. The fledgling federal labor unions in Michigan were, in his words, "destroyed."[12]

Thus, by 1935, coalitions of AFL craft unions, revolutionary unions led by the Communist Party, and government reform strategies led by FDR had all failed to bring collective bargaining to the auto industry. The failure of those strategies, however, generated an openness to new ideas and new coalitions among the key participants. Some AFL leaders who recognized the futility of coalitions of individual craft unions became advocates of industrial unions which would unite all auto workers, skilled and unskilled. The Committee on Industrial Organizations,

(CIO), which would later become the Congress of Industrial Organizations and split with the AFL, was formed in 1935. It was led by United Mine Workers president John L. Lewis and provided money, staff, and political legitimacy for the industrial union drive in automobile manufacturing. Many gifted organizers affiliated with the Communist and Socialist parties. They had laid the groundwork for industrial unionism, through a decade of prior organizing. They were able, if only temporarily, to subordinate their differences, and provided a day-to-day leadership of the movement that was every bit the equal of the corporate brain trust.

While Alfred P. Sloan claimed that GM was a model employer and the best-laid plans of the UAW-CIO would meet little enthusiasm from his satisfied workforce, nonetheless the corporation took a few precautions to keep out the union in case the workers did not agree with his assessment. The government's La Follette Committee revealed that from 1934 to 1937, GM had paid $836,764.41 to detective agencies and had established "a far flung industrial Cheka" [secret police] that included "fifty-two Pinkerton detectives who reported on union activity in GM plants."[13]

Despite GM's best efforts, an industrial union of autoworkers was an idea whose time had come. Events moved rapidly. The UAW's founding convention was held in April 1936 and, by December 30 of the same year, the union was involved in the now-legendary Flint sit-down strikes. With its new president, Homer Martin, its first vice-president, Wyndham Mortimer, and a young man named Walter Reuther on its executive board, the UAW felt it was time to take on General Motors.

On December 30, 1936, several hundred autoworkers occupied GM's Fisher Body One and Fisher Body Two plants, plants containing the valuable dies from which all standardized parts were constructed. The corporation was able to obtain an injunction from Judge Edward D. Black which would permit the police to forcibly evacuate the strikers. Fortunately, CIO attorney Lee Pressman disclosed that Judge Black owned 3,365 shares of GM stock, then valued at over $219,000. Black was charged with obvious conflict of interest and the injunction was temporarily lifted.[14]

For forty-four days, the sit-down and the strikes in other GM plants became the focal point not just for the UAW, but for the industrial union movement. Brigades of women, led by Genora Johnson (now Dollinger) and Dorothy Kraus, brought food to the sit-downers, organized the picket lines, and battled the police. Flint police threw tear gas grenades and shot bullets at the strikers; the sit-downers hurled car hinges propelled by massive homemade slingshots back at the police. At daily meetings, thousands of striking workers discussed events and planned policy in a "town hall" spirit of direct democracy.

The story of Flint has been told well by others and is not to be told here.[15] In terms of "the bottom line," however, on February 11, 1937, the auto workers finally evacuated GM's plants--but not before the union was recognized and a contract had been won. Roy Reuther, one of the organizers of the sit-down, described the scene when the men finally evacuated the plants:

> When the boys came out, I never saw a night like that and perhaps may never see it again. I liken it to some description of a country experiencing independence....We had a procession down to Chevrolet and Fisher Two. Women came greeting their husbands--some of the families being together for the first time since the strike began--kids hanging on to daddy with tears of joy and happiness. When they came out there was dancing in the streets. It was a seething sea of humanity--a joy--fears were no longer in the minds of the workers.[16]

There are many lessons from the early UAW period that have direct bearing on the Van Nuys story and today's UAW. Three factors in the UAW victory deserve emphasis:

First, the UAW was able to resist GM's proposal to negotiate the contract one plant at a time. Since the

GM strike was spontaneous in its inception, beginning with strikes in both Atlanta and Cleveland before spreading to Flint, GM proposed ending the sit-down through a series of local agreements. Victor Reuther, an active participant in the Flint strike who later went on to become the union's education director, explained:

> When GM proposed this "divide and conquer" tactic Homer Martin, the UAW president at the time and a weak-willed man, wanted to agree, but John L. Lewis said "Over my dead body" and sent Homer out on a speaking tour to get him out of the picture. Had we allowed GM to negotiate one plant at a time the strike would have been defeated. We understood that each individual local was no match for the power of concentrated capital. That was why we formed the UAW in the first place, to create a national, industrial union in the auto industry.[17]

Second, the UAW was able to defeat a company-organized back-to-work movement among the workers. There is some mythology that virtually all the workers occupied the plant, when in fact no more than several hundred were inside while thousands waited outside. The corporation formed an organization, The Flint Alliance, as an alternative to the union. As Victor Reuther describes it:

> GM had for some time, been promoting an anti-union back-to-work movement of "loyal employees" through the Flint Alliance...and mounted an elaborate PR campaign to appeal to business and religious groups in the community to support the non-union workers who, it was charged, would suffer from more days of idleness. The reactionary group branded the UAW leaders Communists and outside agitators.[18]

The UAW had to organize the support of the many workers who were not in the plant, had to win the support of many small business people and religious leaders, and had to convince GM that it was the *exclusive bargaining agent* for the workers. Through the victory at Flint, in which GM recognized the UAW as the sole bargaining agent for its members, and the years that followed when the UAW worked to consolidate that victory, GM backed away from attempting to form company unions or "cooperative" factions of unions to advance their aims. In recent years, however, as will be discussed, GM has reinstituted such tactics in the Van Nuys situation, which makes the Flint example quite relevant today.

Third, the UAW successfully defeated GM in the political arena. The sit-down itself and the famous decoy plan--in which UAW organizers purposely allowed informers to believe they would attempt to seize the Chevrolet Nine plant (thus diverting GM security police), only to seize the more strategic Chevrolet Four plant which was their objective all along--testified to the workers' tactical brilliance. Nonetheless, if the organizing drive had been reduced to a simple trade union battle between the fledgling UAW and the mighty General Motors, the corporation would have won through brute force.

Fortunately for the strikers, GM had actively campaigned against both newly elected Michigan Governor Frank Murphy and newly reelected President Franklin Delano Roosevelt. GM's active intervention in the political arena and its view that the likes of Murphy and Roosevelt were bringing America to the brink of socialism did little to ingratiate the corporation with the governor or the president.

The strikers, conversely, carried out a politically sophisticated strategy of allying with Murphy and Roosevelt while not depending upon their support:

> Throughout the strike the Socialist press tried to correct the autoworkers' "illusions" by relentless criticism of the government and repeated warnings to labor not to "expect

> that the President, class representative of the capitalist state, will fight its battles." The Communists also warned against the folly of relying on the Roosevelt administration, "a capitalist government."[19]

The criticism from the left, within a union movement that was clearly sympathetic to Roosevelt, put some pressure on him to deliver, or to risk greater Socialist or Communist influence. Similarly, while the workers were aided immensely by a governor who had strong reservations about sending in troops to evacuate the workers, they were also aware that Murphy had been Mayor of Detroit when his police, backing up those of the city of Dearborn, had been involved in the killing of four Unemployment Council protestors in front of a Ford plant in 1932.[20] When the UAW organizers heard rumors that Murphy was leaning towards sending National Guard troops into the plant, workers in Fisher Body Two sent him the following appeal:

> Governor, we have decided to stay in the plant. We have no illusion about the sacrifices which this decision will entail. We fully expect that if a violent effort is made to oust us, many of us will be killed, and we take this means of making it known to our wives, to our children, to the people of the State of Michigan and the country that if this result follows from the attempts to eject us, you are the one who must be held responsible for our deaths.[21]

The troops were not called. The UAW workers' strategy was aided immensely by the benevolent neutrality of both Roosevelt and Murphy, but they were able to win that help through an independent political stance that kept the pressure on. They created events that impacted the politicians' decisions and did not limit their influence to simply "working from the inside." By out-organizing GM, both among the auto workers themselves and in the broader political arena, the UAW was able to force a major modification of GM's behavior, and to win recognition. As Alfred Sloan was later to lament:

> It appeared that the UAW was able to elicit the support of the government in any great crisis. The government's attitude went back as far as the 1937 sit-down strikes, when we took the view that we would not negotiate with the union while its agents forcibly held possession of our properties. Sit-down strikes were plainly illegal--a judgement later confirmed by the Supreme Court.
>
> Yet President Franklin D. Roosevelt, Secretary of Labor Frances Perkins, and Governor Frank Murphy of Michigan exerted steady pressure upon the corporation, and me personally, to negotiate with the strikers who had seized our property, until finally we felt obliged to do so.[22]

From the victory at Flint to the end of World War II was a long and complex period in the union's history: factional battles between President Martin and the architects of the Flint victory; a short-lived coalition consisting of rank-and-file activists, the Reuthers, Socialists, and Communists to defeat Martin; and a sharp intraunion battle between forces allied with the Reuthers and forces allied with the Communist Party that raged for almost a decade, ending with the consolidation of the Reuther caucus and the decisive defeat of the Communists by 1947.

While this period has been the subject of considerable study and debate by labor activists and historians, it seems that the Communists' effort to portray Walter Reuther and his allies as "the right" and Reuther himself as "the bosses' boy"--as the factional literature of the time claimed--had little basis in fact. In the wartime debates about piecework, it was Reuther who opposed it and the Communist Party which advocated it. In the union's agreement to a wartime no-strike pledge, it was Reuther who attempted to restrict its implications and walk the difficult line between the needs of the war effort and the rights of the autoworkers, whereas the Communist Party attempted to enforce it categorically and uncritically as part of its application of "the United Front Against Fascism." And on the war itself, it was Reuther who moved slowly but consistently to support the war against the Nazis, whereas the Communist party line of strong support (1935-1939), complete opposition (1939-1941), and strong support once again (1941-1945) shifted so many times and with such rapidity that its members suffered from whiplash.

The area that needs further discussion and serious reevaluation, however, was the role of the UAW and the CIO in allowing government investigating committees and big business to haul workers--Communist and non-Communist--in front of "investigating committees" such as the House Committee on Un-American Activities to charge them with the crime of their political beliefs. Similarly, at the 1941 UAW Convention, the union passed a resolution barring from office "anyone who was a member or subservient to any political organization, such as the Communist, Nazi, or Fascist organization."[23] Since there were no organized Nazi or Fascist groupings challenging for power in the UAW, this was clearly aimed at the Communists. The effort to politically prohibit both members of the Party and those "subservient" to it, accepted the premise of the government investigators that political affiliations and even one's political beliefs were essentially a crime.

The Reuthers' decision to walk over the line between sharp policy debates with the Communists as part of an electoral strategy to defeat them and supporting efforts to bar them from UAW office succeeded in defeating the Communists as an organized force, but not without a price. For no matter how much many workers disagreed with particular CP policies, many of the most dedicated union activists in each plant were Party members or sympathizers. The effort to forcibly remove them from the UAW body politic could not take place without tearing the union apart local by local, compromising the integrity of the union, and disclaimers not withstanding, bringing the union closer to the ideological and political orbit of corporate America.

Moreover, as was shown, the belief of non-Communist labor leaders that big business would welcome non-Communist militancy while repressing Communist militancy was naive. In fact, big business used the entire postwar red-baiting period that is now abbreviated as McCarthyism to attack the Communists, first and foremost, but all of organized labor as well. As C.E. Wilson, head of General Electric at the time argued: "The problems of the United States can be summed up in two words, Russia abroad and labor at home."[24]

The result of two years of intense red-baiting and labor-baiting was the passage of the Taft-Hartley Bill in 1947:

> The Taft-Hartley law reinstituted injunctions, gave courts the power to fine for alleged violations. It established a 60-day cooling off period in which strikes could not be declared. It outlawed mass picketing. It provided for the suing of labor for "unfair labor practices." It denied trade unions the right to contribute to political campaigns. It abolished the closed shop...and authorized employer interference in attempts of his employees to join a trade union. It prohibited secondary boycotts. It authorized and encouraged the passage of state, anti-union, "right-to-work" laws.[25]

Given labor's heroic role in the war, both on the front lines and in the factories, this was a quite a double cross. The key to its passage however, was its highly popular anti-Communist provision, section 9(h), which provided for the filing of non-Communist affidavits by unions:

> No benefits of the act [the National Labor Relations Act] would be accorded to any labor

> organization whose officers had not submitted affidavits within the preceding 12 months showing that they were free from Communist party affiliation or belief.[26]

Many anti-Communist labor leaders, who had contributed to the postwar red-baiting, attempted to support the intent of the law's anti-Communist provisions while opposing Taft-Hartley in general. Such ambivalent views, however, contributed to the passage of the law. Ironically, while the anti-Communist provisions of Taft-Hartley were ruled unconstitutional in 1959, its anti-labor provisions last to this day.

The UAW, which had grown through a rough-and-tumble period in which internal fights and political debates were accepted as part of the difficult reality of union-building had itself become caught up in the cold war. In 1949, the UAW supported the initiative of CIO President Phillip Murray to lift the charters and expel eleven International unions from the CIO for being "Communist dominated."

Alfred P. Sloan saw these events in a positive light:

> The following year [1948] our labor relations were dramatically changed for the better. That year saw the defeat and discrediting of the Communist element in the United Auto Workers and the beginning then of somewhat greater stability in the union's internal affairs.[27]

The Postwar Collective Bargaining Relationship: "The Treaty of Detroit"

While Sloan and the UAW were looking for greater stability in the relationship, it did not come without a great deal of struggle. In 1945, shortly after the war's end, Walter Reuther, a UAW vice-president and head of its GM division, had the following negotiating polemic with Harry Coen, GM's assistant director of personnel:

> Reuther: Unless we get a more realistic distribution of America's wealth, we don't get enough to keep this machine going.
>
> Coen: There it is again. You can't talk about this thing without exposing your socialist doctrines.
>
> Reuther: If fighting for a more equitable distribution of the wealth of this country is socialistic, I stand guilty of being a socialist.
>
> Coen: I think you are convicted.
>
> Reuther: I plead guilty.[28]

In fact, despite the hyperbole of negotiating rhetoric, both GM and Reuther understood that socialism was not at issue. By 1945, the UAW was not attempting to challenge GM's basic rights to manage, let alone the system of capitalism itself. But it was demanding that GM allow the autoworkers to enjoy the more traditional "fair day's work for a fair day's pay."

In 1945, after a 113-day strike, the UAW won a pay raise of 18.5 cents per hour. The raise was far less than the 30 cents that Reuther had said the workers deserved, and the strike was criticized by R.J. Thomas, the UAW president at the time, as "starting six weeks too early and ending a month too late." Still, the strike established both Reuther and the UAW as a force to be dealt with and convinced GM that Flint was not a one-shot effort.

In the 1948 negotiations, Reuther and GM's Charles Wilson agreed upon a wage formula in which wage increases would be tied to increases in productivity as well as protected from inflation through a cost of living allowance. GM was so pleased with that contract and its promise of greater labor stability, that in 1950 it proposed a five-year contract which the union accepted.

Fortune magazine called the contract "The Treaty of Detroit," saying "GM may have paid a billion for peace [but] it got a bargain." The article continued:

> General Motors has regained control over one of the crucial management functions-- ...long-range scheduling of production, model

> changes and plant investment. It has been so long since any big U.S. manufacturer could plan with confidence in its labor relations that industry has almost forgotten what it felt like.[29]

The "Treaty of Detroit" lasted for almost thirty years. While there would be strikes, walkouts, polemics, and at times direct confrontations, the corporation came to accept the union's legitimate concerns about raising the standard of living of its members--if not as an ethical proposition, at least as a fact of life to assure industrial stability. Over the next decades, UAW members won step-by-step increases in wages, medical and dental benefits, supplemental unemployment benefits, and retirement benefits after completing thirty years at hard labor.

Reuther referred to the auto plants as the "gold plated sweatshops"; and while the union never was able to revolutionize the working conditions of its members, it did place significant restrictions on the breakneck pace of the assembly line. Reuther proved to be every bit the match for Sloan and was a resourceful fighter for the welfare of "his men."

Alfred P. Sloan, looking back on the early confrontations with the UAW, and with the perspective of the "Treaty of Detroit" explained the evolution of his thinking:

> What made the prospect [of the UAW victory] seem especially grim in those early years was the persistent union attempt to invade basic management prerogatives. Our rights to determine production schedules, to set work standards, and to discipline workers were all suddenly called into question...it seemed to some corporate officials as though the union might one day be virtually in control of our operations.
>
> In the end, we were fairly successful in combatting these invasions of management rights. There is no longer any real doubt that pricing is a management, not a union function.

> So far as our operations are concerned, we have moved to codify certain practices, to discuss workers' grievances with union representatives, and to submit to arbitration the few grievances that remain unsettled. *But on the whole, we have retained the basic power to manage.*[30] (Italics added)

William Serrin, in *The Company and the Union*, summarizes the historical relationship that evolved after years of more direct confrontation:

> What the companies desire, and receive, from the union is predictability in labor relations. Forced to deal with unions, they want to deal with one union, one set of leaders, and thus they have great interest in stability within the UAW and in a continuation of union leadership. They also want the limits of bargaining clearly understood and subscribed to.
>
> "GM's position has always been, give the union the money, the least possible, but give them what it takes," says a former negotiator. "But don't let them take the business away from us." The union has come to accept this philosophy as the basis of its relationship with the company: it will get money, some changes in work procedures, usually nothing more.
>
> "We make collective bargaining agreements," Reuther once declared, "not revolutions." Both the union and the companies, a mediator says, have one goal: "They want to make cars at a profit."[31]

This view captures an important part of the "civilized relationship" that developed in the postwar years, but it underestimates the union struggle that was necessary to achieve and maintain that relationship. Though GM certainly wanted "stability," it had first attempted to achieve it through a "far flung industrial Cheka" and the immediate dismissal of union sympathizers. It was only after the union's ascendancy that Sloan could argue matter-of-factly: "The issue of unionism at General Motors is long since settled. We have achieved workable relations with all the unions representing our employees."[32]

Sloan could argue, after the union was a *fait accompli,* that his initial worries that the union would attempt to interfere in all GM's management decisions were unfounded, since now he understood that it would *only* be in the areas of wages, benefits, job classifications, and working conditions that the union would exert its influence. But at the time the men were barricaded in the Fisher Body plants, issues of wages, benefits, working conditions, job classifications, and, of course, union representation itself were considered tantamount to socialism if not communism. It was only after losing those areas of exclusive management control that GM sought to argue that those were "legitimate" arenas of union influence.

In the Van Nuys case study, we will see almost fifty years later another situation in which a union local attempted to expand the definition of union rights and restrict the authority of management rights--an effort to apply the confrontational model of the early UAW to a different historical period. One lesson of the Sloan model of GM behavior is that GM is immensely practical: it stakes out its position and fights as hard as it can to win, which it usually does. But when it loses, it quickly adjusts to the new conditions and moves to rationalize any union victories as "consistent" with company objectives in order to prevent any further union inroads.

If there was a "Treaty of Detroit," it was only because first there had been a war, one in which the UAW had fought GM to at least a standstill. And if the postwar labor relations were characterized by greater industrial stability and the attenuation of class conflict, that was at least in part because the UAW's collective bargaining achievements were the envy of unions throughout the Western capitalist world. As will be detailed later, there were some serious weaknesses to that strategy, weaknesses which the corporation would later exploit. But without recognizing the enormous ingenuity and valor that were necessary to achieve many of the UAW's victories, history is reduced to a checklist in which labor's accomplishments are taken for granted and only its errors are perceived three-dimensionally.

The 1960s and 1970s: The UAW Begins To Fall Behind

In the 1960s a new wave of social protest and political radicalism surfaced, and this time it was not centered in the factories or led by the old left, either communist or socialist. The UAW's response to the civil rights movement and the anti-Vietnam War movement indicated some problems that would become more pronounced in the late 1970s.

On the civil rights issue, the UAW was far better than most unions. Reuther was a prominent leader of the 1963 March on Washington and the UAW was a strong advocate of the critical civil rights legislation of the 1960s. The UAW supported a great deal of Martin Luther King's agenda and, while some in the civil rights movement perceived King to be quite moderate, in the context of the political reaction of the 1980s, the fundamental radicalism of King's brilliantly crafted strategy is far more evident. In retrospect, his nonviolent confrontational tactics involving mass demonstrations, boycotts, and sit-ins were only "moderate" compared with the even more militant forces of the time.

One arena where the more revolutionary views of the black movement found strong support was the auto factories in Detroit, especially in the Chrysler plants where outmoded equipment and the most brutal of working conditions were commonplace. Groups such as the Dodge Revolutionary Union Movement (DRUM) and the Eldon Avenue Revolutionary Union Movement (ELRUM) defined both the company and the union as the problem (if not the enemy), launching wildcats, work stoppages, and machinery takeovers to achieve their goals. On the one hand, their one-sided rejection of both "trade unionism" and the UAW as a whole were ultraleft and strategically dead-ended. On the other hand, their efforts to spotlight the concerns of the black workers and to expose the oppressive nature of shop-floor conditions posed a challenge to the established UAW leadership.

UAW Secretary-Treasurer Emil Mazey had little tolerance for the new groupings of black workers:

> He said the black revolutionaries represented the most dangerous radical thrust since the 1930s and was instrumental in having 350,000 letters sent to Detroit-area UAW members accusing DRUM of being a hate organization whose purpose was to divide the working class on racial lines.[33]

Three years later, in 1973, when political radicals with roots in the black liberation movement became active in UAW locals, a wildcat strike, one of many at the time, broke out at Chrysler's Mack stamping plant. A group of workers, believing they were utilizing the tactics of the UAW founders, occupied the factory--which the press attacked as a "plant hijacking." Police entered the plant and removed the workers:

> The next morning, workers who wanted to keep the strike going were confronted at the plant gates by Douglas Fraser [then head of the UAW Chrysler Department], Irving Bluestone, Emil Mazey and other top UAW executives, backed up by a force of nearly 2,000 older or retired UAW loyalists. There was some fighting with local militants, but the sheer size of the union force guaranteed that the strike was over.
>
> It was a bitter day for many UAW members around town who remembered the fierce organizing drives of the thirties and [who] had once led the same kind of flying squads to keep factories shut down....The inspector of the local police precinct thanked Doug

> Fraser personally for his help and said it was great being on the same side.[34]

Many of the black workers who initiated those actions look back self-critically, not about some of the tactics employed but, rather, about the general strategic perspective from which they were derived. The incident, however, reflected the alienation on the part of the top UAW leadership from the growing anger of many black workers at the bottom. Many of these workers were experiencing directly the limits of the contractual agreement and the brutality of shop-floor working conditions compounded by racist practices. They perceived the UAW leadership as unable to respond to their problems and threatened by their protests which violated the Treaty of Detroit.

The union had an even greater problem coming to terms with the Vietnam War. The Vietnam War was not the responsibility of "southern racists" but was the liberal's war, the Democrat's war, the war of presidents Kennedy and Johnson. While the UAW was never a hawkish force like the George Meany wing of the labor movement, nonetheless it gave enough support to Lyndon Johnson's policies to be in the camp of the war's supporters. David Halberstam, in *The Reckoning*, tells a story of a Passover *seder* at which Walter Reuther, confronted by Leslie Woodcock (Leonard's daughter) and Barry Bluestone (Irving's son) on his support for the war, attempted to explain his position:

> Walter Reuther said..."Let me, if I can, explain why I have not come out against the war." The UAW, he said, has debated the issue at great length, and feelings were very high. "But because we have major negotiations coming up soon--a very delicate time--there is strong feeling that this is not the time to break ranks with the President on this issue."
>
> Even as he was finishing, Leslie Woodcock was screaming at him. "You've said it, you've finally said it!"
>
> "What do you mean?" Reuther asked.

> "For fifty cents an hour in the pay envelope," she said, "you'll let thousands of Vietnamese and Americans die in the war."
>
> Roy Reuther, normally the gentlest of men, shouted at her, "That's not what Walter meant!"
>
> "That's exactly what he meant," she said.[35]

A study of the UAW during that period, however, would indicate that was not exactly what Reuther meant. Reuther was a social unionist, and never reduced his world view to a narrow contract perspective. The problem, however, was that the UAW leadership became too dependent upon the liberal wing of the Democratic party for its strategy of social activism. Thus, they believed that an open break with Lyndon Johnson on the war would jeopardize not only contract demands but their leverage on other issues as well.

Paul Schrade, the UAW West Coast regional director from 1962 to 1972 explained:

> In April 1967, I spoke out against the war at a rally at San Francisco's Kezar Stadium along with Coretta King and many others. The press picked up on it, knowing the UAW had not opposed the war, and gave my participation a lot of play.
>
> At the next meeting of the International Executive Board, Walter called me on the carpet. He said I was too far ahead of the membership, that we couldn't afford to do it. He argued that in his responsibility as president of the union, virtually every negotiating move he made, because of the centrality of the auto industry, involved the President of the United States. He said he tried to talk to Johnson about the war, but Johnson blew up at even the mention of any criticism.
>
> Walter brought in Leonard Woodcock to the meeting. Now Leonard was my friend, but he was the spiritual and intellectual leader of the hawks on the board. He would even quote Dean Rusk to us.

> I told Walter that I opposed the war out of conscience, but also because many of our members and their sons would die in the war if it wasn't ended. Walter paused, and said he thought that was a good point. But he repeated that I was making a big mistake, and that he didn't like it one bit. But, to his credit, he never demanded that I stop speaking out. There were few unions where that type of dissent--at least at the top--was allowed at the time.[36]

Whereas in the union's early years Reuther and the UAW leadership had worked closely with both John L. Lewis and F.D.R. but felt able to criticize them and disagree with them on an issue by issue basis, over the years the union's political independence declined--increasingly restricted by the limits of Democratic Party liberalism.

The UAW was confronted with new challenges in the 1960s and 1970s--social movements that were not of its making. It attempted to adjust, to catch up, with varying degrees of success. The issues raised by the civil rights movement and the anti-war movement indicated some problems in how the UAW as an institution would be able to adapt in the social arena.

In the contractual arena, however, the GM/UAW relationship proceeded without major incident into the late 1970s. The relationship remained stable in the period of the consolidation of many auto companies into a Big Three, the oligopolistic pricing policies of the industry set by GM, and the control of the world auto market by American firms. Under those conditions, the Treaty of Detroit was a workable model.

In the late 1970s, however, events that had been long in the making ended the American century twenty-five years early. International competition replaced American oligopolistic control and the Big Three could no longer be guaranteed even the American domestic market. For years, auto workers on the shop floor had repeated the legendary bargaining position of Walter Reuther: "Gentlemen, we understand that it is your pie, but our members are demanding a larger slice." Seemingly overnight, that posture was no longer adequate. The pie itself was in danger. Significant institutional change would be needed both at GM and at the UAW. The Alfred P. Sloan period had finally come to a close. The Roger Smith era in GM's history had begun.

NOTES

1. Ed Cray, *Chrome Colossus: General Motors and Its Times* (New York: McGraw Hill, 1980), p. 150.
2. Alfred P. Sloan, *Adventures of a White Collar Man* (New York: Doubleday, 1941), p. 93.
3. Alfred P. Sloan, *My Years With General Motors* (Garden City, New York: Doubleday, Anchor Books, 1972), p. 46. One cannot begin to understand General Motors from an historical perspective without a careful reading of this classic. Sloan talks as if he is lecturing a freshman in "GM 101," but, in so doing, his brilliant insights into management strategy and his straightforward defense of management objectives provide a rare insight into the man and the corporation he shaped in his image. All other notes abbreviated as Sloan refer to this book.
4. Sloan, p. 47.
5. *GM Annual Report*, 1986.
6. Sloan, pp. 135, 136.
7. Sloan, p. 138.
8. Sloan, p. 160.
9. William Serrin, *The Company and the Union* (New York: Alfred A. Knopf, 1973), p. 105.
10. Cray, pp. 270, 271.
11. Cray, pp. 281-283.
12. Roger Keeran, *The Communist Party and the Auto Workers' Unions* (New York: International Publishers, 1980), p. 103.
13. Jerold S. Auerbach, *Labor and Liberty: The La Follette Committee and the New Deal* (New York: Bobbs Merrill, 1966), pp. 112, 113, as quoted in Keeran, p. 150.
14. Victor Reuther, *The Brothers Reuther* (Boston: Houghton Mifflin, 1976), p. 149.
15. See Reuther, Chapter 13; Keeran, Chapter 7; and Sidney Fine, *Sit Down: The General Motors Strike of 1936-1937* (Ann Arbor: University of Michigan Press, 1969).
16. Reuther, pp. 170, 171.
17. Interview with the author, June 2, 1986. Also see Reuther, p. 148.

18. Reuther, p. 161.
19. Keeran, p. 165.
20. Keeran, pp. 72-74. Murphy denied any responsibility, "wiring the Young Communist League that he was blameless, since the murders occurred outside of his jurisdiction." Still, what came to be called "The Ford Massacre" no doubt contributed to his unwillingness to call in the police against the Flint sit-downers.
21. Reuther, p. 168.
22. Sloan, pp. 460, 461.
23. Keeran, p. 223.
24. Richard O. Boyer and Herbert M. Morais, *Labor's Untold Story* (New York: United Electrical and Machine Workers, 1982), p. 345.
25. Boyer and Morais, p. 348.
26. Charles J. Morris, ed., *The Developing Labor Law* (Washington, D.C.: Bureau of National Affairs, 1971), p. 44.
27. Sloan, p. 463
28. Serrin, p. 162.
29. Serrin p. 170.
30. Sloan, pp. 475, 456.
31. Serrin, pp. 156, 157.
32. Sloan, p. 476.
33. Dan Georgakas and Marvin Surkin, *Detroit, I Do Mind Dying* (New York: St. Martin's Press, 1975), pp. 43, 44.
34. Georgakas and Surkin, p. 231.
35. David Halberstam, *The Reckoning* (New York: William Morrow, 1986), p. 348.
36. Interview with the author, July 6, 1987.

Chapter Four

THE HIGH-TECH WORLD OF ROGER SMITH:

The Period of Rising International Competition (1981-Present)

When Roger Smith took over the reins of General Motors in 1981, there were rumblings in the business press that GM was a ponderous giant, unable to move with the decisiveness and flexibility needed in a competitive world economy. Despite its declining sales and market share, GM still controlled a whopping 63 percent of the U.S. market for North American made cars, and 45 percent of *all* cars, including the imports. With its dealer networks intact, and its enormous capital reserves, GM was in a strong position to turn things around. But Roger Smith took over when the rules of the game had changed. No longer was it a simple competition with Ford, a head-to-head battle with one major competitor at a time. As Smith described the "old days":

> It's like the story of the two guys being chased by a bear. One of them stops to put on his tennis shoes, and the other guy says, "Why are you putting on your tennis shoes? You can't outrun a bear." "I don't have to outrun a bear," the other guy says, "I just gotta outrun you."[1]

By 1981, the days of just having to outrun Ford were over. The internationalization of America's domestic auto market, the increase in Japanese imports to almost

20 percent of U.S. sales, and the rise of Nissan, Toyota, and Honda had found a lethargic GM designing cosmetic changes in some of its gas guzzlers and priding itself on "downsizing" much of its product line. Industry analysts and consumers were far less impressed. The myopic thinking of past GM executives, one of whom once said, "There's something wrong with people who like small cars," had to be uprooted. It was Smith who led the movement within GM to come to grips with the seriousness of these problems: "At one point, we said, hell, we're not gonna make it unless we do something drastic here."[2]

The first drastic change was to radically reduce the total number of employees. For example, in California in 1982, GM closed its Southgate plant with 4,000 employees and closed the Fremont plant with almost 7,000 workers. (Fremont was reopened in 1985 as a joint venture with Toyota, but with only 2,000 employees.) Those developments were merely symptomatic of a broader strategy. An internal GM document, leaked to the press in 1984, indicated a conscious plan to reduce the total GM hourly workforce by 80,000 jobs--from 375,000 to fewer than 300,000 by 1990.[3]

SMITH'S REORGANIZATION OF GENERAL MOTORS

Smith initiated the first major restructuring of GM's management since the days of Sloan. Sloan had developed the corporation's famous staff-and-line organization and a ponderous committee system to curtail the uncoordinated and subjective decision-making system that he had inherited from Durant. But, when Smith took over, increased competition and declining customer loyalty mandated decisive action in an organization that was taking far too long--over three years--for an idea to move from its conception to its implementation. Smith assured the public that, while he would ask for reductions in hourly personnel, there would be sharp cutbacks in management positions as well.

By January 1984, GM had established two streamlined divisions to replace the previous five: Buick, Oldsmobile, Cadillac (BOC), the big car group; and Chevrolet, Pontiac, Canada (CPC), specializing in smaller cars. This reorganization was intended to break down many of the fiefdoms that had developed in individual divisions, to reduce management cost-per-unit by eliminating duplication, and to reduce the number of layers of management to allow a more direct line of decision making. The goal: a leaner and more flexible GM.

To its credit, GM under Roger Smith, unlike many of the parasitic corporations that accumulate profits through paper transactions and takeovers, has worked to expand the productive capacity of its capital. It has brought state-of-the-art technology to a smokestack industry and has made intelligent new corporate acquisitions that both diversify and enhance its role as an automobile manufacturer. The new, mega-merged General Motors is a model of rational corporate integration.

GM is, and will continue to be, an automobile company. Unlike, for example, American steel companies that are using their holdings to essentially get out of the industry, GM is building a conglomerate with autos strongly in the center. As *Automotive News* explains, cars are still the "cash cows, providing the financial ability for GM to acquire new business interests."[4] The GM of today is a fascinating tapestry of interwoven holdings and acquisitions, outlined below.

1) *The General Motors Assembly Division.* GMAD, with its two subdivisions, BOC and CPC, is the hub of the corporation. In 1986, GM sold 8.8 million vehicles worldwide, with the vast majority, 6.2 million cars and trucks, sold in the United States. GM employs almost three quarters of a million people worldwide (734,000) and its average number of U.S. hourly workers in 1986 was 379,000.[5]

2) *General Motors Acceptance Corporation.* While its car divisions gross the most revenue, GM's most profitable product is money. Through GMAC, GM owns the largest U.S. finance company, with assets of $54 billion. Besides providing additional revenues, GMAC

allows the corporation to offer discounted finance terms to sell slow-moving products, shuffling profits from the car to the financing, then back to the car.

3) *Electronic Data Systems.* EDS, purchased in October 1984 for $2.5 billion, specializes in computer software. EDS programs allow GM to solve many computer problems that could make computer-aided manufacture a high-tech nightmare. In many GM factories, the initial introduction of different brands of computers run by different software programs was producing such a level of incompatibility that computer-aided manufacture was causing more production delays than occurred before it was introduced. Through its corporate purchasing power, GM has forced competing computer companies, which had consciously made their products incompatible with the goal of winning exclusive contracts, to agree to a cooperative manufacturing automation protocol system (MAP). This allows GM and other manufacturers, through the use of a simple coaxial cable, to connect data from previously incompatible systems throughout the plant.[6]

The ability of GM to produce parts, assemble them, check with dealers about inventories, arrange financing, and correct defects in any aspect of this chain is made possible by EDS. As *Automotive News* reported:

> GM is becoming the computer lexicographer for the automobile industry and perhaps ultimately, for the manufacturing world....Ford Motor Company and Chrysler Corp. have already met with GM to create a common computer language for suppliers....It is possible then that EDS could wind up as the provider for the entire auto industry.[7]

4) *GMF Robotics--the mechanized autoworker.* GM's factory of the future, its workerless utopia, will be staffed by as many robots as possible, since each robot displaces two workers. GM is not just leading the way in introducing robots into the U.S. auto industry, it is taking the lead in manufacturing them. In 1982, GM established GMF Robotics, a joint venture with Fanuc,

the Japanese computer firm. Today, GM is running the only profitable robotics company in the United States, primarily because of large orders from its best customer --GM. Through the effective use of its large capital reserves and its acquisition of smaller, high-tech firms such as Technowledge Inc., GM has become, according to Laura Conigliaro, technology analyst for Prudential Bache Securities, "Number one in the domestic auto industry in robots, and number one in machine vision, intelligent robots and intelligent robots that can see."[8]

5) *GM/Hughes.* GM has a long history of acquiring lucrative defense contracts. During World War II, under pressure from Walter Reuther and the UAW, it was able to transform its entire operation from automobiles to defense production. GM's purchase of aerospace and defense giant Hughes Aircraft for $5 billion in June 1985 provided cost-plus government contracts and the promise of highly profitable operations--a hedge against the fluctuations of auto sales. But Hughes may also provide GM with a future advantage over its competitors:

> GM now sees microprocessors as potentially the heart of a car, and looks to Hughes to help develop them into a system that can continuously monitor all of a car's mechanical and electronic systems, diagnose malfunctions, and correct them.[9]

6) *GM/Isuzu and GM/NUMMI: If you can't beat them, join them.* After dismissing the challenge of the Japanese in the early 1970s, GM today not only acknowledges the strengths of its competitors, it has entered into several joint ventures with Japanese firms.

Besides its joint venture in robotics with Fanuc, GM also owns a 40 percent (and controlling) interest in Isuzu motors of Japan and has pressed for a relaxation of import quotas to get more of those cars into the United States. GM has also joined with Toyota at the New United Motors (NUMMI) plant in Fremont, California, to produce the Nova and to learn Japanese management techniques. GM hopes to learn the secret of inculcating greater worker loyalty and productivity through the NUMMI experiment and to spread the gospel of "workplace cooperation" to its other plants.

On paper, these dramatic changes were quite impressive and, for a few years, after initial industry skepticism, GM Chairman Roger Smith was being heralded as a bold innovator and even compared with the legendary Alfred P. Sloan. In 1984, a *Los Angeles Times* profile, titled "GM Chairman Smith's Image Changes from Bumbler to Guru," reflected that view:

> Two years ago, it seemed as if nobody could say a good word about Roger B. Smith ....But suddenly this year, the 59-year-old Smith has become a darling of Wall Street and of academics and management consultants who follow the auto industry.[10]

But, by 1986, the tone of many of the articles had changed again. This time the refrain was more like "From bumbler to guru and back to bumbler," as GM's market share declined and many of Smith's best laid plans went awry. As ominous clouds once again gathered overhead, many GM watchers tried to understand what had gone wrong.

ROGER SMITH'S TROUBLED SECOND ACT

GM's problems began with a growing surplus of cars fighting for market share in a stable domestic auto market. Japanese imports have grown from 11 percent of the American market in 1978 to 21 percent in 1986. And just as GM was trying to adapt to Japanese competition, Yugoslavia's Yugo and South Korea's Hyundai made further inroads into domestic auto sales. GM countered with the Pontiac Lemans, built in South Korea by Daewoo Motors, but it will also have to compete with the Ford Festiva, produced in South Korea by Kia

Motors, and the Mercury Tracer, built in Ford's new plant in Hermosillo, Mexico. A combination of 1.2 million imported cars *not counting Japanese imports* will be joining the competition by 1990.[11]

The competition for the domestic market also includes the growing wave of "transplants," American auto plants owned by foreign manufacturers. For years, the UAW has been demanding "local content" laws mandating that Japanese manufacturers open up plants in the United States. While these laws were not passed by Congress, UAW-generated pressure convinced many Japanese and Korean firms to open U.S. plants. The result: "By 1990, Japanese and Korean car makers will be able to produce 1.6 million cars in North America." [12]

The increased production is leading to what the *Wall Street Journal* refers to as "a gathering glut." "Industry forecasters now warn that within four years, Detroit and the rest of the world could be shipping 15 million cars a year to an American public prepared to buy only 12 million."[13]

While both Ford and Chrysler are effectively rising to the challenge, there are growing signs that GM's master plan is flawed. The first hints of problems were expressed in early 1986 as *New York Times* writer John Holusha gave critical reviews to "Roger Smith's Troubled Second Act."[14] The article summarized three major problems of the GM reorganization--higher per-unit costs than its domestic competitors, declining market share, and possible errors in design judgment--and described a company that had made all the right moves, except selling cars. Almost a year later, this analysis was validated as GM was forced to offer bargain-basement 2.9 percent financing in order to unload enormous inventories of unsold 1986 cars. Industry analysts began to worry about GM's future.[15]

To begin with, Roger Smith may have gotten a little carried away with his high-tech buying spree. GM has spent more than $60 billion on plants, machinery, and new acquisitions, pushing GM's cost-per-unit figures far above those of Ford and Chrysler. While GM president F. James McDonald argued that these are necessary short-term costs to reduce long-term ones, some analysts believe that many of the GM purchases have reflected an infatuation with technology that is not cost-effective. Technical problems in the implementation of a computer-aided production process have produced costly delays and foul-ups. Typical of the problem is GM's vaunted, high-tech Buick City complex in Flint, Michigan:

> The plant has had one of the slowest startups of any auto plant on record and is still not making its rated capacity of 75 Buick LeSabres and Oldsmobile 88s per hour. For weeks, the robot arms that glue and set windshields dropped the glass on the front seat. GM pulled out an entire robotized welding line and let people do the work.[16]

As one anonymous GM executive told the *Los Angeles Times*: "Roger did important things, but he had two weaknesses: He knows nothing about cars and he has mistaken the process for the product."[17]

The "product" referred to is the GM line-up of cars. Despite all of GM's computers, robots, reorganizations, and acquisitions, the bottom line of the auto industry is still putting out a product that the consumer will buy--in a market flooded with competitors. When Alfred P. Sloan first took over GM, his first order of business was to organize "a car for every purse and purpose" and to make sure that each model was distinctive in its price range. In his drive to bring state-of-the-art technology to GM, Roger Smith placed very little emphasis on designing exciting products. Jack Kirnan, a sales analyst at Merrill Lynch remarked:

> [GM's] cars, especially their luxury cars, simply look too much alike. A Buick looks like an Oldsmobile which looks like a Cadillac, and consumers aren't going to pay a lot of money for a car that isn't different from other cars.[18]

These miscalculations were reflected in GM's declining market share. During the late 1960s and early 1970s, until the advent of the imports, GM's share of the U.S. market hovered around 50 percent. Since then, GM's total share has declined from 44.5 percent in 1981, to 42.6 percent in 1985, to 41.3 percent in 1986. Worse, after an earlier sales slump, GM market share plummeted to 36 percent for the first twenty days of August 1986, precipitating GM's emergency rebates in September 1986. GM's strategy with the rebates was literally to "buy" an increasing market share, since defections in consumer preference are very hard to reverse in this era of increased competition. As James Flanigan explained in the *Los Angeles Times*:

> With its enormous financial strength--only $2.5 billion in long-term debt against $29.5 billion in shareholder equity and $5 billion in ready cash--GM can afford to buy a share of the market, for a while.[19]

While harshly criticized and even ridiculed by many industry analysts for stealing future sales with short-sighted financing giveaways, GM's somewhat desperate efforts to maintain its market share had a certain logic to it. Given GM's enormous outlays of over $60 billion since 1979 for capital improvements, it needed extremely high sales volumes in order to spread those costs and reduce cost per unit. The problem, however, was more structural. For as GM attempted to buy a share of the market, a Chrysler executive told *Business Week:* "They have failed to comprehend that their market share is gone forever, forever, forever--even if they do everything right."[20]

Obviously, Roger Smith read *Business Week* as well. For in April 1987, only a month after its front-page article, "GM: What Went Wrong?", Smith began a tour of the country to convince the media and GM stockholders that GM's future was bright. He announced: "GM may be forced to cut car production to boost its profits. Maximizing profits will now be 'the principal bellwether of our performance' rather than market share or sales."[21]

Smith's latest about-face, however, was more symptomatic of the problem than the solution. For to accept lower market share, while perhaps a recognition of reality, would only force GM to spread its massive capital outlays over fewer cars and thereby *raise* cost per unit. GM's constant reorganization plans, and its increasingly contradictory explanations of its strategy were raising serious questions not only about its business acumen, but about its credibility.

In past decades, when other UAW organizers tried to map strategy against GM, there was grudging respect for the corporation: "Whatever GM touches turns to gold." In recent years, however, as UAW activists have tried to base their strategies on GM's projections, there have been growing indications that GM itself doesn't quite know what it is doing.

In 1985, for instance, GM management told the workers at Van Nuys that the sporty Chevrolet Camaro they were building would be taken away from the plant. In a new, state-of-the-art "GM-80" project, the Camaro would be built with an all-plastic body at a specially equipped facility in the Midwest, most likely in Pontiac, Michigan. The news of Van Nuys losing the Camaro by 1988 or 1989 was validated by *Automotive News.* Within a year, however, industry journals reported, and GM management confirmed, that due to unresolved technical problems the project was being indefinitely postponed.

In 1985, GM announced that its much-heralded Saturn project--to compete with the Japanese for the *subcompact* portion of the domestic market--would open in Spring Hill, Tennessee, by 1990.[22] GM argued that its highly controversial "experimental" contract with the UAW--wages at 80 percent of normal levels and far greater management prerogatives--was necessary if it was to be cost-competitive in the low-profit subcompact market. But, by late 1986, before one Saturn car had been built, there were industry rumors that GM was considering converting the project to the production of *compact* cars with luxury accessories--that is, a sector of the market in which GM is already competitive. Some saw this as a conscious deception by GM to win a lower wage package with the promise of competing with the Japanese to build a subcompact, only to later use the Saturn contract as a club against GM workers building compact cars in other plants. Others saw it as another example of GM's inability to make successful plans even a few years into the future.

Business Week reported ominously:

> Some observers say Saturn is already doomed. "The faster they admit it's a mistake the better," says one former GM executive. Rumors persist in Detroit that GM may try to save face by folding Saturn, now a separate carmaking subsidiary, into its Chevrolet or Pontiac Division.[23]

In early 1986, when GM announced an 8.8 percent financing offer to spur lagging sales, many industry analysts criticized GM for unscientific inventory planning, for offering incentives that neither Ford nor Chrysler felt were necessary to move *their* inventories (but were forced to match), and for robbing their own future sales. GM denied those charges, arguing that it was a short-term move to clear excess inventories. But, by November 1986, GM was forced to offer 2.9 percent financing to clean up the inventory problems it had created with its previous incentive plan.

GM's declining credibility is a symptom of a corporation in serious trouble. Dan Luria, senior researcher at the Industrial Technology Institute, is one of many industry analysts who raise fundamental questions about the corporation's long-term future:

> I think that GM is in much worse trouble than it realizes. If you just look at GM's sales of cars and trucks in its North American operations in 1986, the company would show a $300 million operating loss. Its profits for the last year are very deceptive. They come from GMAC financing, a small profit from European operations, $600 million in tax credits, and

> money that the corporation had stashed away in case it had to pay fines for exceeding CAFE (Corporate Average Fuel Economy) standards. GM did not comply with the mandated fuel economy standards but was able to convince the Reagan administration to roll back the mandated levels, so it was able to pocket that money as well.
>
> GM's overall quality is poor, and in the few instances where it makes excellent components, such as constant velocity joints, it makes them too expensively. It isn't a problem here or a problem there; the corporation as a whole has some serious, structural weaknesses that it may not be able to reverse.[24]

GM's erratic behavior and its inability to deliver on its promises is a relatively new development and part of the new conditions that UAW activists must confront. GM makes "danger lists" of plants and then changes the victims on the danger list almost overnight. It announces bold new initiatives, and then has to rescind them. As Pete Beltran, president of UAW Local 645 in Van Nuys, assessed:

> Things have changed dramatically in the past few years. When I came to work for GM, we had a sense that the corporation was all powerful, if not very fair. But, in recent years, many of the workers are getting a frightening feeling that GM doesn't know what it is doing anymore.[25]

The strategic assessment of GM as a confused colossus, agreed upon by business analysts and union organizers alike, became part of the historical context--presenting both problems and opportunities--in which the Campaign to Keep GM Van Nuys Open had to operate.

LABOR RELATIONS IN THE ROGER SMITH ERA

Labor Costs

Since the advent of significant Japanese competition and GM's declining market share, the company's labor relations strategy can be summarized succinctly: massive efforts to reduce labor costs and labor itself in the name of cooperation.

When Roger Smith first took over GM's chairmanship in January 1981, he had every reason to suspect he was walking into an ambush. "In 1980, the company had racked up its first loss, $763 million on sales of $63 billion, since 1921. The next year it reported a modest profit of $333 million on sales of $63 billion, a mere 0.5 percent profit margin."[26]

GM had many problems to address, but the easiest solution to sell to both its stockholders and the general public was to cut labor costs. Certainly, as international competition intensified, labor costs *were* a problem. In 1981, for example, GM's hourly labor cost was $25 (wages and all other benefits) compared with $11 an hour for Toyota. But the "problem" of the UAW wage package that had produced a decent life for over 350,000 auto workers and their families was not discussed in the context of *all* of GM's problems. "High labor costs" were used as an excuse, and the auto workers themselves were used as a scapegoat.

From Concessions to Plant Closings

GM's first step to deal with its hourly wage costs took place in February 1982 when GM management--its appetite whetted by the union wage concessions given to Chrysler in 1979 and 1980--demanded that the UAW reopen the national contract to provide them with similar relief. But because of the opposition of many UAW local presidents such as Pete Kelley, Local 160, Warren, Michigan; Don Douglas, Local 594, Pontiac,

Michigan; and Pete Beltran, Local 645, Van Nuys, California, the majority of delegates at a specially convened UAW-GM subcouncil voted to reject the company's initial demand for contract reopeners. GM then followed with a trump card of its own--announcing the closing of four plants.

Within a few months, as a plant closing at GM's Southgate plant in Los Angeles was actually carried out and stunned workers watched the doors close forever, GM once again demanded contract reopeners. This time, the pressure from General Motors and from UAW president Douglas Fraser for the workers to reopen the contract succeeded.

When the contract--containing $2.5 billion in wage and benefit give-backs--was brought to the rank and file for ratification in the spring of 1982, a network of local officers, calling themselves "Locals Opposed to Concessions," showed GM the depth of membership dissatisfaction by organizing a 48 percent "no" vote. Still, GM got its $2.5 billion no matter how close the vote and, of equal importance, had refined a new tactic in its labor relations arsenal--the plant closing.

From 1980 to 1982, GM's plant closings were management's economic response to plant overcapacity and decreased demand. But GM management soon learned--at first through empirical observation of the workers' panicked response and later by raising those observations to the level of theory--that plant closings were a powerful weapon to enforce union compliance with corporate objectives.

To add indignity to injustice, on the very day the workers narrowly ratified the concessions, GM proposed dramatic increases in executive bonuses. Still, militant UAW presidents, strengthened by the 48 percent "no" vote, were sanguine about beating back the next wave of GM's demands. GM's actions were helping to galvanize a resistance movement. First, the company was making no pretense of being the workers' friend; this was blackmail plain and simple: give us these concessions or we'll close down your plants. Second, the demands were being raised against *all* the GM workers simultaneously through take-aways from the national GM-UAW agreement. Any efforts by GM to continue this strategy over the long term would allow national coalitions of UAW locals, such as Locals Opposed to Concessions, to become even stronger.

Quality of Work Life/Whipsawing

GM also understood the problems of its approach. As a result, under the leadership of Roger Smith and President F. James McDonald, the corporation began to dramatically reorient its labor relations strategy for perpetual concessions: First, it began to camouflage its demands for speedups, layoffs, job eliminations, and plant closings in the rhetoric of cooperation--"Quality of Work Life" and "the Team Concept." Second, it deemphasized demanding concessions at the national level. Instead, it focused on winning them one plant at a time by forcing all the plants in the GM system to compete against each other as to which ones would stay open and which ones would be closed. This plant against plant competition came to be called *whipsawing*.

The lethal combination of demands for job cutting and the new rhetoric of workplace cooperation became most evident at GM's yet-to-be-built but already heralded Saturn project. GM predicts that Saturn will be a workshop of cooperation based on the Japanese model--real or imagined--of workers and management submerging differences and practicing cooperation with the goals of higher quality, greater profits, and job security. But so far, the only specifics of the project are that the UAW has agreed to a substandard wage level and has ceded many hard-fought rights back to the company.

The picture is filled out by the management-oriented publication *Quality Progress* that reports: "General Motors insiders have been cited as saying it will take 75-80 percent fewer man hours to build a Saturn car than to build a traditional automobile."[27] With a 20 percent reduction in wages, an 80 percent reduction in the workforce and dramatic structural reductions in the union's power, it is no wonder that Roger Smith said,

"My fingers used to be longer before I chewed them off waiting to get my hands on Saturn."[28]

But while Saturn has not even produced one car, its influence as a lever against locals at other UAW plants has already been substantial. Pete Kelley, president of UAW Local 160 and an outspoken critic of the union's concessionary strategy argued: "Saturn has become a Trojan horse in our midst. Armed with the threat of plant closings, the company is now playing local against local to see who will meet or exceed Saturn's give-backs."[29]

Victor Reuther, a founder of the United Auto Workers, has become an outspoken critic of the growing cooperation between management and union officials. He has been speaking at many UAW locals, opposing not just concessions, but what he believes is the far greater danger to the union itself--the competition among locals. Reuther explained the problem from an historical perspective:

> In 1937 at Flint, General Motors attempted to negotiate one local at a time, and we were able to resist, even though the UAW was in its infancy and we had not yet won a contract. While there are certainly pressures on the union today, it is unforgivable that certain International officers seem intent on giving away not only our heritage, but a great deal of our power.
>
> General Motors is trying to achieve today what it was unable to achieve in 1937--to turn the UAW into a loose federation of locals competing among themselves. What is even more upsetting to me is to hear some union advocates of this policy invoke Walter Reuther's name to justify their actions. I can assure you that Walter would be on the side of the fighters at the grass roots level who are attempting to maintain this union's traditions.[30]

The process that Reuther describes, while beginning in the workplace, began to spill over into the surrounding communities as well. For as soon as Roger Smith had targeted "cost reductions" as the key to competitiveness, GM began to demand similar concessions from municipal and state governments. A *Los Angeles Times* article by this author described GM's community strategy:

> At Pontiac, Michigan GM wants a tax assessment reduction of 70 percent, where GM property taxes account for 47 percent of the community's tax base. In Warren, GM is demanding a 65 percent reduction; in Flint, 45 percent; in Saginaw 82 percent. If GM does not have its way, there is the threat of closing the plant and moving elsewhere. If GM *does* have its way, then workers in those communities would have to pay up to $400 a year more taxes, or suffer dramatic declines in social services.[31]

While GM tried to win concessions from some communities by threatening to close a plant, it attempted to exact concessions from others with the promise of opening up a new one. Youngstown State University's director of labor studies, John Russo, describes "Saturn-mania"--the GM-orchestrated competition among communities to attract the Saturn project:

> It involved politicians and community leaders offering the world's largest industrial corporation tax abatements and exemptions, utility rate reductions, industrial revenue bonds, new highways and access routes, union free atmospheres and free land and training.[32]

Russo's conclusion raises a frightening specter of GM's power in the Roger Smith era:

> Overall, Saturn's influence on the public consciousness is indicative of just how easily

> global corporations can shape the national economic debate, using sophisticated public relations techniques along with a measure of old-fashioned economic blackmail. Built on the themes of nationalism, modernity, cooperation and technological determinism, Saturn has captured the public imagination and provided a vision of a better economic future if only corporations have their way. This is a Faustian bargain, yet one many communities will increasingly accept unless alternative visions of economic development are seen as attainable.[33]

THE APPEAL--AND THE DANGER--OF GM'S "WORKPLACE COOPERATION" MOVEMENT

One would assume that, in the face of the whipsawing of UAW locals and the blackmailing of local communities, a national coalition of the UAW and threatened communities would arise spontaneously in defense of jobs and community integrity. But GM's efforts, cloaked as they were in the catchwords of "competitiveness" and "cooperation," found support among many officials of the UAW International, liberal intellectuals, and even many assembly line workers.

The company's appeal touched a deep chord among the workers. From the inception of the moving assembly line and the application of time and motion studies to introduce speedup under the rubric of "scientific management," autoworkers have had a deep longing for even the most rudimentary restrictions over management's control of production.[34] The formation of the UAW was prompted not primarily by wage considerations as much as by the unbearable working conditions in the shops.

While the union was able to curtail some of management's worse abuses, as late as the mid-1950s, according to Isaac Ayala, a veteran of the GM Van Nuys plant, "working conditions were still so bad, a young man could grow old in ten years":

> When I first began work at Van Nuys, the line went so fast that at the end of the day even a strong young man just wanted to go home to rest up for the next one. I once called my foreman and asked him if I could go to the bathroom. He told me, "Sure, if you can do it in your shoe while you're working." It took several national strikes and a few local ones, too, until we even won longer breaks, a little less work on each job, and doors on the bathroom stalls. That's right, they used to have no doors on the bathroom stalls so the foremen could check on you to make sure you weren't goofing off. And this wasn't in the 1930s; I'm talking about this very plant in the 1950s.[35]

Ely Chinoy's classic sociological work, *The Autoworkers and the American Dream*, published in 1955, amplifies Ayala's first-hand story of the autoworkers' alienation. In interviews with hundreds of workers, Chinoy discovered that after just a few years in the plant they had abandoned any aspirations for upward mobility, grudgingly came to accept their class position, and tried to compensate for the tedium of the assembly line with consumer goals and the transfer of their dreams to their young children.[36]

Walter Reuther tried to address the workers' longing for even the most minimal input into the work process. He consistently proposed a system of "cross-training and job rotation" whereby assemblers would learn many different jobs and could at least *vary* the tedium. But GM management, threatened by even this small intrusion into what they believed were their "management rights," and opposed to the additional costs of worker job satisfaction, adamantly refused, labeling Reuther a "socialist."

In each negotiation, faced with fierce resistance from management, the UAW was willing to trade off ideas such as cross-training and job rotation for "a more equitable distribution of the wealth," that is, higher wages and benefits.

By the late 1970s, however, when American firms suffered dramatically declining profits and market share, both corporate and union leaders were panicked. "Competitiveness" became the catchword. The UAW leadership focused their attacks on OPEC nations and Japanese imports, and offered wage concessions to help the Big Three cut costs--arguing that if the companies went down, the UAW would go down with them.

Under President Douglas Fraser's administration, the UAW made its first structural move towards the "new cooperation" by accepting a seat on the Chrysler board of directors. While this was justified as "placing a union watchdog on the board" and as a small step towards "workers' control," when Chrysler management subsequently closed ten plants and laid off 57,000 workers, the UAW appeared to be sanctioning those decisions, which made resistance at the local level even more difficult.

When Fraser retired in 1983, a new leadership team emerged--UAW President Owen Bieber and Vice-President for the GM Department Donald Ephlin. It is through Ephlin's strategic writings, usually published in management journals, that the present direction of the UAW can be understood.

Ephlin challenged militant local presidents to come to grips with reality: the industry is in a crisis. He argued that the role of the union is to reverse the decline of the auto industry and help restore its competitiveness--before it's too late. Ephlin criticized GM for an authoritarian management philosophy that had, over the years, produced a "culture of rebellion" among the workers. This prevented the corporation from instituting any plans to become more competitive that would depend upon worker cooperation.

In recent years, however, according to Ephlin, the Japanese challenge has *forced* GM to become more open-minded. The corporation is now more amenable to union input through a negotiated "joint activities" provision in the contract. As Ephlin explained:

> The keynote of the negotiated worker participation programs is to change the self-concept of both management and worker, as well as change the relationship between the parties for the common good. For workers this has meant strengthening their actual capabilities, as well as reinforcing their sense of self-worth and sense of "ownership" in the process. For management it has meant learning to think of production and skilled trades workers as a capable valuable resource rather than a fixed cost of production.[37]

At the level of rhetoric, the idea of worker involvement appealed to many of the workers' deepest desires --greater control over their working environment, greater respect for their input into the productive process, and greater job security through higher quality products which facilitate greater competitiveness in the world market. But as the idea evolved in practice, three glaring weaknesses became apparent:

1) *The company's main objective was not cooperation in the abstract, but union cooperation in their drive to reduce the number of workers.* The management journal *Quality Progress* asked Ephlin: "GM insiders have been saying that it will take 75 percent to 80 percent fewer man hours to build a Saturn automobile. Do you agree?" Ephlin replied candidly: "In today's situation, where we are competing for the very existence of the industry--the only way we can maintain our standard of living and keep our jobs is to improve productivity."[38]

Even many of the more confrontational local UAW leaders are aware that improvements in *corporate* productivity are necessary, and are willing to consider possible job eliminations through attrition as one element of an overall strategy. But when a corporation sets a goal of a 75 percent reduction of its workforce, and, for example, closes down a plant of 7,000 workers in Fremont, California, and reopens it as NUMMI with 2,000 workers, many workers are questioning the corporation's real objectives in the "new cooperation."

2) *Ideologically, the "new cooperation" begins to transform the union into an instrument to advance corporate objectives.* Ephlin and the UAW leadership frame the problem in terms of "competing for the very existence of the industry," and even talk about "when the Japanese first really invaded our market after the second oil crisis."[39]

Wartime imagery of protecting "our" market from a Japanese "invasion" sets the tone for reducing class conflict with the Big Three. Thus, when GM and Ford demanded, in 1986, to be exempted from fuel-economy standards established by the Department of Commerce, the UAW was silent. When all three corporations opposed the air bag and other safety measures, the UAW was silent. When GM launched a national campaign to threaten communities with runaways if they did not lower property taxes and other assessments, the UAW refused to join with local coalitions.[40]

A new lexicon of nonadversarial labor relations has developed. Union leaders talk about how we have to abandon the "old ways" and "bring in the new"--referring to UAW members who see themselves in the traditions of the Flint strikers or even the Reuther years as "dinosaurs."

3) *The "new labor relations" has not been proposed to the local leadership as a strategy, to be debated and discussed, but as a threat with the possibility of a plant closing as the enforcer.* As Pete Beltran explained: "First, the company will make a threat and tell the local leadership that the plant is in trouble. Then the UAW International rep shows up and says, 'What do you want me to do? Things have changed in the industry; that's just the way it is now. Now, if you want to work out a new, cooperative local agreement, I can help you. If you don't, don't blame me if GM closes down your plant.'"[41]

Efforts to have an open debate in the UAW newspaper *Solidarity* have been rejected and, even on the UAW convention floor, policy debate is sharply restricted. Victor Reuther laments:

> You know I am proud of Walter's achievements and the accomplishments of what is

> called the Reuther years. But I am seeing one mistake we made. The administration caucus, which was used as a legitimate weapon in our battle with the communists, was maintained many years after that battle was over. Essentially, a great deal of authority became concentrated at the top. The vehicle of the administration caucus is now used to prevent open debate in the union.[42]

Paul Schrade elaborates:

> After Walter's death, there was an election among the members of the International executive board to fill his vacancy. As a regional director at the time, I was one of the twenty-five members. I supported Doug Fraser who I felt could best carry on Walter's social unionism. While Fraser had come out against the war late, Woodcock was a hardliner on the war and was enamored of the power of GM. When the vote took place it was thirteen for Woodcock and twelve for Fraser.
>
> Despite the significant differences between the two men, the election was not taken out to the local presidents or to the convention, and certainly not to the shop floor. As far as we were concerned, the election was over. We used to refer to the IEB as "the club." The unwritten rule was that we could disagree all we wanted--among ourselves--but we would not take those disagreements outside of "the club."[43]

In 1970, when the UAW was still in a relatively stable position vis-a-vis the auto companies, this undemocratic approach was hardly excusable, but its direct effects were not always felt. In the late 1980s, however, when the industry is in turmoil and the union faces disorientation, there is no one perspective that is obviously correct--except for the undeniable need for the fullest and most widespread strategic debate within the UAW.

While the Roger Smith era is most often analyzed in terms of GM's efforts at technological change, a dramatic and drastic change is taking place in its labor relations as well. The social compact of the Sloan/Reuther era is being replaced by a far more aggressive strategy on the part of the company. In the context of increased international competition, GM feels that it needs to increase the exploitation of its workforce through speedup, job combination, and job elimination and to create new relations between the company and the union based on tying the union directly to corporate objectives. In so doing, GM has unilaterally abrogated the Treaty of Detroit.

These were the historical conditions in which the Campaign to Keep GM Van Nuys Open developed. As five of the six California auto plants closed around them, UAW activists at Local 645 intensified their discussions. How could local unions fight back against the use of plant closings as a management tactic? Was it possible for a UAW local to develop a political coalition to keep a productive plant open without acceding to either massive concessions or corporate-dominated management techniques? At a time when management, acting out of its own class interests, was taking the offensive, was it possible for labor unions to develop some initiatives of their own? And at a time of rampant social Darwinism, could a successful movement against a single plant closing help to push the pendulum back to the left?

In 1982, a small group of UAW activists in Van Nuys, California, began to pose those questions. Having placed that movement in the historical context of both GM and the UAW, it is time to examine the Campaign.

NOTES

1. Debra Whitefield, "New Look at GM: Unconventional," *Los Angeles Times*, Business section, December 1, 1985, p. 1.
2. Whitefield, p. 1.
3. "GM Has Plan To Cut 80,000 Workers," *Los Angeles Times*, February 19, 1984, p. 22.
4. Marjorie Sorge et al., "GM: A New Kind of Global Conglomerate," *Automotive News*, January 21, 1985, p. 68.
5. *General Motors Annual Report*, p. 1.
6. Jonathan Tucker, "GM: Shifting to Automatic," *High Technology*, May 1985, p. 28.
7. Sorge et al., p. 68.
8. James Risen, "GM Sheds Smokestack Image," *Los Angeles Times*, Business section, October 28, 1984, p. 6.
9. Michael Brody, "Can GM Manage It All?," *Fortune*, July 8, 1985, p. 26.
10. Risen, *"GM Sheds Smokestack Image,"* p. 1.
11. James Risen, "A Gridlock in Autos," *Los Angeles Times*, Business section, September 28, 1986, pp. 1, 5.
12. Paul Ingrasia and Doron Levin, "A Gathering Glut," *Wall Street Journal*, February 14, 1986, p. 1.
13. Ingrasia and Levin, p. 1.
14. John Holusha, "Roger Smith's Troubled Second Act," *New York Times*, Business section, January 12, 1986, p. 1.
15. James Risen, "GM Opts for the Quick Fix," *Los Angeles Times*, Business section, August 29, 1986, p. 1.
16. William J. Hampton and James R. Norman, "What Went Wrong at General Motors," *Business Week*, March 16, 1987, p. 107.
17. "GM Offer Hides Bigger Crisis Than Meets the Eye," *Los Angeles Times*, Business section, September 9, 1986, p. 1.
18. James Risen, "GM Opts for the Quick Fix," p. 2.
19. James Flanigan, *Los Angeles Times*, Business section, September 29, 1986, p. 2.

20. Hampton and Norman, p. 110.
21. "GM Continues Its Efforts to Polish Image" *Los Angeles Times*, Business section, April 11, 1987, p. 2.
22. See Anthony Borden, "GM Comes to Spring Hill," *The Nation*, June 21, 1986.
23. Hampton and Norman, p. 107.
24. Interview with the author, February 20, 1987.
25. Interview with the author, January 20, 1987.
26. "Are GM's Troubles Deeper Than They Look?" *Forbes*, September 27, 1982, p. 181.
27. "Launching Saturn: The UAW Perspective on Quality," *Quality Progress*, April 1985, p. 56.
28. "Roger Smith's Campaign to Change the GM Culture," *Business Week*, April 7, 1986, p. 84.
29. Speech at UAW convention, June 2, 1986.
30. Interview with the author, June 2, 1986.
31. Eric Mann, "Labor's Silent Partner Role Harmful to Workers and Public," *Los Angeles Times*, September 1, 1985, Opinion section, p. 3.
32. John Russo, "Saturns Rings: What GM's Saturn Project Is All About," *Labor Research Review*, Fall 1986, p. 68. (The *Review* is published by the Midwest Center for Labor Research, 3411 W. Diversey Avenue, Chicago, Illinois 60647).
33. Russo, p. 77.
34. See David Gartman, *Auto Slavery: The Labor Process in the American Automobile Industry, 1897-1950* (New Brunswick, N.J.: Rutgers University Press, 1986); and Harry Braverman, *Labor and Monopoly Capital* (New York: Monthly Review Press, 1974).
35. Interview with the author, September 1982.
36. Ely Chinoy, *The Autoworkers and the American Dream* (Garden City, New York: Doubleday, Anchor Books, 1955).
37. Donald Ephlin, "Saturn's Strategic Role in Industrial Relations," *Survey of Business*, University of Tennessee, Summer 1986, p. 24.
38. *Quality Progress*, April 1985, p. 56.
39. *Quality Progress*, April 1985, p. 56.

40. Eric Mann, "Labor's Silent Partner Role Harmful to Workers and Public," p. 3. This article quotes Clarence Ditlow, director of the Center for Auto Safety," as saying: "Every time we organize a coalition, someone says, 'Let's invite the UAW.' We do, but over the years, they rarely show up." It also quotes Jim Musselman, an organizer working with Ralph Nader, describing his frustration in attempting to get UAW president Bieber to join a coalition against GM's demands for property tax reductions. "I cannot comprehend how the UAW leadership can dismiss this as a local issue when GM strategy is being carried out in Missouri, Ohio and New York as well, a strategy which threatens the entire industrial tax base of the country."
41. Interview with the author, May 25, 1986.
42. Interview with the author, UAW convention, June 2, 1986.
43. Interview with the author, July 5, 1987.

Part Three

THE CAMPAIGN TO KEEP GM VAN NUYS OPEN

Chapter Five

IT BEGAN WITH AN IDEA

In 1978, the California auto industry, one of the largest centers of production outside of Detroit, had six assembly plants employing almost 25,000 workers at peak production. The main complaint of the workers was, "Stop all this damn overtime," as exhausted GM, Ford, and Mack Truck workers worked nine-hour days and another eight hours on Saturday to keep up with the seemingly insatiable demand. But in 1979, when the second round of OPEC price increases took place, a major structural crisis long in the making finally impacted the American auto industry, and California was hardest hit.

In January 1980, Ford announced the closing of its Pico Rivera plant outside of Los Angeles--permanently laying off over 2,500 workers on two weeks' notice. The president of UAW Local 216, Ron Delia, tried to organize a large caravan to Sacramento to demand that the state legislature intervene to stop the closing, or do something, anything to help. But the UAW West Coast Regional Director at the time, Ralph "Jerry" Whipple, refused to authorize the caravan--claiming it would only "embarrass the Democrats" and give California Governor Jerry Brown's administration a bad name. Instead, Whipple urged the workers to support a UAW-sponsored federal content bill that would demand that Japanese auto manufacturers build plants in the United States.

The Ford local, with little to lose, disregarded Whipple's admonitions and, along with many other local unions, brought more than 250 people to Sacramento, the state capital, for an all-day hearing in front of the legislators. While that number might appear small, considering that over 4,000 workers had just lost their jobs, at that time few auto workers believed that any concerted action could force an auto company such as Ford to reopen a plant it had declared closed.

After spokespeople from Governor Brown's office and individual legislators expressed their condolences, they were able to deflect the workers' anger by asking, "What are we expected to do? Auto sales are down. We can't demand that companies keep unprofitable plants open." No one had any answers to those questions; up until two weeks before, no one had expected they would ever need them. The movement against plant closings in California was still in its infancy.[1]

Within the next two years, Mack Truck closed its only West Coast plant in Hayward, California; Ford closed its other California plant in Milpitas; and GM closed down its Southgate plant with 4,000 workers, along with its Fremont plant that had employed almost 7,000 workers at peak production. Seemingly overnight, GM Van Nuys was the last auto plant west of Oklahoma City--and GM management was telling the workers that the plant's days were numbered.

GM VAN NUYS AND THE SAN FERNANDO VALLEY

The GM Van Nuys plant was opened in 1947 on a vacant piece of land located in the San Fernando Valley, north of Los Angeles. GM came to town with the rhetoric of a young suitor, introducing GM Van Nuys as "your new neighbor in the San Fernando Valley and Southern California."[2]

For many outside of Los Angeles, "the Valley" is best known by the insipid babbling of the stereotypical "Valley girl." Even in Southern California, the Valley is often perceived as a suburban bastion of white flight from the heavily minority inner city. During the 1970s, a group of white parents, opposed to the busing of minority students into "their" community, formed a group called Bus-Stop. While allegedly concerned about "neighborhood schools," the movement had clear racist overtones. An outspoken parent, Bobbi Fiedler, parlayed her role in that movement into a seat in the U.S. Congress. To many minorities in Los Angeles, "the Valley" was a place where they were not welcome.

The Valley has 1.6 million residents, of whom 40,000 are black and 300,000 are Hispanic. Thus, while the outside stereotype of the Valley is "all white," there is a substantial (19 percent) Hispanic population concentrated in the east. Large numbers of Hispanics live in the areas surrounding the Van Nuys plant, in communities such as Pacoima and Arleta (56 percent Hispanic, 14 percent black) San Fernando (67 percent Latino, 7 percent black), and North Hollywood (33 percent Hispanic, 2 percent black).[3]

Up until the early 1980s, there was a relatively small black workforce at Van Nuys. But with the closure of the GM Southgate plant, many workers transferred to Van Nuys, of whom approximately 50 percent were black. Many of the Southgate workers live in the South Central Los Angeles area, the heart of L.A.'s black community, in cities like Lynwood, Maywood, Inglewood, and Compton. They drive over forty miles each way to work, since they do not want to give up their homes and, after having lived through one plant closing, they certainly won't uproot themselves based on the tenuous long-term future at Van Nuys. These workers have ties, through their churches and community affiliations, to L.A.'s black community of almost one million people, just as the Chicanos in the Valley are part of the almost three million Latinos in Los Angeles.[4]

These ethnic demographic figures are critical to this story in that the Van Nuys plants' workforce is more than 50 percent Latino and 15 percent black. The relationship between a predominantly minority workforce and the surrounding Latino and black communities was a major element in the strategy that eventually developed to save the plant.

Van Nuys, along with almost all of the Valley, is part of the city of Los Angeles. Its school board members are part of the L.A. Board of Education (thus, the busing controversy); its city council members sit on the L.A. City Council; and the mayor of Van Nuys, Panorama City, North Hollywood, Arleta, Pacoima, Sherman Oaks, Sylmar and San Fernando is the mayor of Los Angeles. Had the city of Van Nuys been a separate legal entity, or even the San Fernando Valley itself, this narrative might have developed quite differently. But the Valley is a major factor in Los Angeles politics, and events in the Valley are part of the political life of Los Angeles county, an area with almost eight million residents.

The Van Nuys plant itself is a sprawling, two-story structure of 2.5 million square feet, roughly the size of forty-nine football fields. The plant manufactures Chevrolet Camaros and Pontiac Firebirds, some of the sportiest, best selling models in the GM product line.

The Van Nuys plant itself is like a small city. "You name it, we got it here," say the workers. The first shift, with the higher seniority workers, is overwhelmingly male, but on the second shift almost 25 percent of the workers are women. (Fifteen percent of the workforce is female.) The place is loud, as in LOUD, with the sound of assembly lines moving, air guns shooting thousands of screws per minute, people yelling, and radios blaring. If you don't like noise you don't like working in an auto factory.

The people are more substantial than most, for only the strong survive "the line" and the work attracts a confident, outgoing type. The work itself is grueling. When a new hire first comes in "off the street" he or she is usually shocked by the pace of the line. An experienced operator will break in the new worker, but the first day it often feels as if no one but a bionic man or woman could keep up with the line--sixty cars per hour whether you are ready or not.

Unlike some fraternities where the ethic is to paddle the hell out of the new pledge because that what was done to you, there is a tradition of helping the new hires learn the ropes because, for the most part, that was how you made it. Because of those traditions, a large part because of the influence of the United Auto Workers, autoworkers are friendlier and more cooperative than most. If you are fortunate enough to have a good teacher break you in, and most are, then he or she will break the job up into small parts and allow you to learn the job one part at a time. It is discouraging at first to be chasing an unfinished job down the line, only to realize you are just doing one-third of the job while the workers on both sides of you are doing their best not to laugh in your face.

The line waits for no one, and whether you are finished or not it keeps on rolling. If you aren't finished you chase the job down the line, until a few feet later you have bumped into the next worker, who smiles and usually does the job for you as well as his or her own, which makes you wonder how they can do both while you can't even do your part.

"Hey Charlie, keep this rookie out of the hole," he yells to your trainer. "Going in the hole" means not being able to keep up with the line, a good joke for a few days but not something that will be tolerated for too long. After a few days, however, you miraculously learn the job. As the experienced trainer tells you, "Sixty jobs an hour, GM makes sure you get lots of on the job training."

The Van Nuys workforce attracts a stable and reliable type. The work is hard but the pay can't be beat for industrial work and everyone knows it. Every time there is a layoff, people say, "That's it for this place; I'm going to start my own restaurant," or "I'm going to become a clothes designer." But when the callback comes, everybody is back--the would-be real estate agents, freelance writers, custom photographers, and auto mechanics, because, as they say, "You can't beat the money."

This is not to say that many people don't try. Large numbers of workers have something going "on the side." Many attend night school, many have small businesses, many dream of owning their own business and getting out altogether. It leads to a very independent-minded, if not economically independent group.

Virtually all of the workers realize that you can sell a piece of real estate or jewelry or get a travel agent's license, but GM provides you with forty hours of guaranteed work, medical and dental insurance, and even pays you about 90 percent of your salary when you don't work--to which the union activists add, "but only because the UAW forced them to." Most autoworkers see their job, with all its difficulties, as a great opportunity for a working person. "Working at GM gave me a chance to own a home, nothing fancy, I never expected to be a big shot, but enough to support my family, come home at night in one piece, enough to send my kids to the state university, enough to allow me to be a good father and husband."

The street in front of the plant is Van Nuys Boulevard, a busy thoroughfare during the day and a drag strip at night where caravans of lowriders cruise the streets and caravans of police cars follow close behind. On the other side of Van Nuys Boulevard is the UAW Local 645 union hall--a large structure with a big parking lot that serves as an arena for after-work beer drinking, union strike votes, and something new to the local, Keep GM Van Nuys Open rallies. Next to "the hall" is Mi Casita Mexican restaurant--unpretentious but one of the best in the city, feeding hundreds of autoworkers every day and owing its success, if not its existence, to their business. Next door is Avila's liquor store where many workers grab a beer and cash their checks. On the other side of the hall is Opie's, an old bar that has been the home away from home for many autoworkers whose aching bodies and personal problems have found solace there.

This was the scene of the drama in 1982 when GM first threatened the workers with a plant closing. It was a drama that most of them had little desire to become involved in but, like most historical processes of magnitude, one in which they would be forced to participate whether they wanted to or not.

At the time this narrative begins, while the reality of a possible plant closing was no longer something the workers could deny, many of the workers were not ideologically prepared to even grapple with the problem. If a movement was ever to be built to keep the plant open, some significant changes in the workers' consciousness would have to take place.

THE CONSCIOUSNESS OF THE AUTOWORKER IN THE MOVEMENT AGAINST PLANT CLOSINGS

In the early 1980s, as plant closings in auto, steel, and rubber became a common, if painful, occurrence, one might have thought that widespread rebellion would have been forthcoming. Unfortunately, far too many industrial workers had ingested lethal doses of management ideology and had a greater appreciation of management's rights than they did of their own. Based on several hundred discussions with autoworkers in many closed down plants, the following are examples of some of the ideological obstacles to their active involvement.[5]

Denial: When the workers at Ford's Milpitas plant heard that their sister plant in Pico Rivera was about to be closed, a worker explained: "We are lucky to be building the Mustang, and we are going to get the Ford Escort, the hottest seller. The Pico people were stuck with building the LTDs and other gas guzzlers. I don't want to take advantage of their tragedy, but Ford will always keep at least one plant open in California. So it looks good for us." Within two years, Ford Milpitas was closed, without a fight.

Three years after the permanent closure of the GM Southgate plant, former Southgate workers who were fortunate enough to transfer over to Van Nuys, but unfortunate enough to be placed in the most grueling jobs, kept repeating rumors about the reopening of Southgate. They told their foreman: "I can handle this lousy job because in a year or so I'm going back to Southgate." Only when GM finally sold the property in 1986 did the workers' dream of Southgate's resurrection finally die.

At Van Nuys, even when it became the last remaining plant, many workers repeated: "GM will never close us. The Camaro is the *Motor Trend* car of the year; Southgate was an older plant; GM has always liked this plant, GM needs at least one plant on the west coast..."

Resignation: The Campaign began in a period in which two historical trends were quite obvious to the workers: the growing concentration of capital and the precipitous decline of union influence. The deep-seated pessimism of the times had a discernable impact upon the workers. Literally hundreds of Van Nuys workers have repeated, almost verbatim, the following assessment:

> GM is the largest corporation in the world. If it wants to close this place, there's nothing you and I can do to change that. What am I supposed to do, get a heart attack about it? I figure I'll do the best job I can, keep my mouth shut, and not provoke the company and hope we get a few more years out of the place before they pull the plug.

Free Enterprise Ideology: Many of the workers operated small businesses on the side, or dreamed of starting one. A commonly heard analysis was:

> Look, let's say I open up my own restaurant, but business isn't good and I decide to leave. And then everybody starts to get angry and tell me I can't. What about *the owner's* rights in the situation?
>
> I mean, GM has given me twenty years of work and I've made pretty good money. Now if they aren't making enough money here and want to get out, it's their money and they have a right to go wherever they want to make *more* money.

Several union activists refer to this as the "Seven/Eleven complex"--the dream of auto workers to escape from the assembly line and own a small business, a dream which causes them to identify with the aspirations of big business and to deny their actual class position in society.

In 1982, there was only a small group of activists within the Van Nuys Local 645 who saw things from a different perspective and began to strategize about what it would take to keep the plant open--President Pete Beltran and some of the members of the local's Community Action Program Committee (CAP): Mike Gomez, Mark Masaoka, Jake Flukers, Jorge Vargas, Nate Brodsky, and Eric Mann.

Pete Beltran, the first Chicano president of the local, was elected in 1978, corresponding to the time when Chicanos became the largest single ethnic group in the plant.[6] Self-educated, charismatic, a skilled negotiator, and a major figure in the Los Angeles labor movement, Beltran offers his view of the local's history, with particular attention to the author's questions about the local's changing ethnic composition and its political evolution:

> When the plant was first opened in 1947, almost all of the workers were white. But during the Korean war, about 1953, there was a shortage of workers. The workers in the material department had some of the hardest jobs. They had to unload and open boxes from railroad cars, sort the parts from the boxes, and get them ready for the hi-lo [forklift] drivers. The workers were working thirteen, fourteen, or fifteen hours a day. They filed a grievance about excessive overtime but the umpire upheld the company. Still, seeing that they might have a rebellion on their hands if they didn't cut down the overtime, the company asked the guys if they would mind working with Mexicans, men who had been born in Mexico but had been working in the United States for years. The men said it was fine with them, anything to get some people in there to cut down the workload, and that's how Chicanos got into the plant.

Sometime in the early 1950s a guy hired into the plant named Rolando Flores. He was built like a tree stump, with broad shoulders and massive arms. They put him in the body shop, and gave him the hardest jobs, but he made them look easy. One day, Doug Barnett, the employment supervisor asked him, "Where do you come from?" Flores told him, "Nueva Rosita" (in Coahuila, Mexico). Barnett asked him, "Are there any more like you there?" Flores said, "Yes, hundreds." And Barnet said, "Send 'em all over, I can use all of them." And the whole damn village showed up and many of them are still in the plant today.

I hired in at Van Nuys in 1958. When I got there the plant was about 30 percent Hispanic, 65 percent white, and about 5 percent black. In those days, the main issue was getting relief time. At the time, if you can imagine this, you worked four straight hours without a break, and most people could barely get out of their seat after lunch break to come back to the line. When the contract expired, the company and the union tried to sign a new one without break time in it, but the Southgate local and other militant locals helped lead a movement to get us some break time. At the time, Van Nuys was not a particularly militant local.

For many years the leadership of the union was overwhelmingly white, but these were good union men who didn't tolerate discrimination. One of our early presidents was Hank Fowser. Hank was a perfect transition: he was half German and half Hispanic; he looked white but he spoke Spanish. During the civil rights movement in the 1960s, the big West Coast marches were held in San Francisco and our local presidents Kenny Preston and Howard Owens would march, with the encouragement of President Reuther. They took flak from a few of the guys in the plant, but they marched anyway.

I was elected as delegate to my first UAW convention in 1966 in Long Beach, California. At the time, the UAW was one of the strongest supporters of the farmworkers. Cesar Chavez spoke on the organizing efforts in the fields and the whole stage was filled with campesinos' children singing "De Colores" and everyone was crying and we took up a collection right on the spot and raised over $5,000. Those were good days, when you could be proud to be in the union.

The transition to greater Chicano representation in the leadership of the local was gradual and evolutionary. In some locals there were black and Chicano caucuses because the white officers wouldn't allow any other groups to become leaders in the union, but that was not the case in Van Nuys. Many of the white union leaders needed Latino votes, and many didn't speak Spanish and wanted Latinos to run with them on the slate. As they moved up, got jobs with the International, or retired, Hispanics who had gotten experience moved into the vacated positions.

I was elected Shop Chairman [the chief committeeman or shop steward] in 1967. I ran against the first president of the local, Red Melton. When I won, Red said, "What did I ever do to you Pete?" I said, "Nothing at all Red; it's not personal, it's just that things move on sometimes."

Overall, I think it's fair to say that during the 1960s and most of the 1970s Van Nuys was neither a very militant plant nor one where there was a lot of racial tension. That is not to say that we didn't have some strong union people, but with a very liberal West Coast Regional Director, Paul Schrade, from 1962 to 1972, you didn't have to go against the International to be militant. It was only in later

> years, when GM and the International union began to move in the direction of concession bargaining, and when GM threatened to close the plant and we formed the Campaign, that people began to think of us as a militant local.[7]

Mike Gomez was the local's political action chair. (In the UAW, the political action committee is called the Community Action Program, CAP. From this point on, it is referred to as the CAP committee.) He began his activism in the Chicano movement as a college student and had worked in the plant since 1973. Nate Brodsky, the local's GM Unit Chairman, had been working in the plant since 1961. Jorge Vargas, a native of Peru and a member of the Executive Board, came to the plant in 1962. Jake Flukers, a member of the Executive Board, had been in the civil rights movement in Texas before coming to work for GM in 1977. Mark Masaoka had a long history in the Japanese-American community movement, had worked at Ford Pico Rivera, and had been active in the movement to protest its closing before he came over to Van Nuys in 1981. Eric Mann had been active in the civil rights and anti-war movements and had worked at both the Ford Milpitas and GM Southgate plants before coming to Van Nuys in 1982.

These activists began a long series of strategic discussions about whether it was historically possible to organize a movement to save the Van Nuys plant, and whether such a movement had any possibility of winning. Before they began a serious evaluation of *whether* the plant could be kept open, they had to develop an analysis about why, except for the most narrow self-interest of its 5,000 workers, the plant *should* be kept open.

THE ARGUMENTS FOR KEEPING GM VAN NUYS OPEN

It was a sad reflection of the times that any possible movement to keep a plant open had to begin by justifying its existence. Despite public awareness of the devastating consequences of plant closings, management had effectively shifted the debate to where workers had to justify why a corporation should keep a plant open, rather than business having to explain why it was necessary to close it down.

The UAW organizers understood that in all industrial societies plant closings are an inevitable, and at times positive, occurrence. Plants become outmoded, new technology replaces old, new industries replace antiquated ones, market demand rises and falls dramatically, and yes, firms even go bankrupt. The disagreement with corporations like General Motors was over the *political and economic process* by which decisions over plant closings were made: who makes the decisions and who suffers the consequences?

The activists believed that since a plant closing involving factories of several thousand workers has enormous implications for both the workers involved and the surrounding community, it should not be a simple "management decision." A plant closing should only be allowed as a last resort, under strict union and community supervision.

Thus, the theory of the as yet unborn Campaign began in those early CAP committee discussions based on several major premises:

1) Any talk of the American auto industry as a "dying industry" was far off base. With imports growing to 25 percent of the total U.S. market, American firms controlled an impressive 75 percent of the domestic market.

2) General Motors, with all of its many problems, was still the largest single producer of automobiles in the United States, with over 42 percent of the total market at the time the discussions began.

3) General Motors, despite all of the talk about Los Angeles being the "home of imports," still sold almost 30 percent of all cars in Los Angeles, more than any single car company, domestic or foreign. Los Angeles was known as "the freeway capital" and was the largest new car market in the United States. This was not asking a company that produced carriages to continue to do so in the age of the automobile. This was simply asking the

number one auto company to keep one plant open in the number one auto market.

4) GM agreed that the Van Nuys plant was profitable. In fact, the Chevrolet Camaro was the *Motor Trend* car of the year and a high price, high profit vehicle. Also, GM Van Nuys was producing the cars at a high level of quality and cost-effectiveness. (The additional cost factor, the shipping costs involved with being on the West Coast, will be discussed later.)

In other industries, workers facing plants that were being closed attempted to prove that even when a plant showed a loss on the books it was still *potentially* profitable and the "loss" was often a paper transaction to hide real value. While often true, in the management-oriented public mood of the time, attempting to keep open a plant that claimed it was losing money was an unusually hard organizing problem. At least the Van Nuys workers began with a plant that was undeniably profitable, even if the rate of return was lower than GM might want. The public perception of the profitability of the Van Nuys plant would prove to be a major factor in the workers' favor.

The arguments for keeping the plant open were solid and persuasive. If some type of movement could succeed in keeping the plant open, and if GM was forced to stay in Los Angeles and continued to produce both cars and profits into the 1990s, both industry and labor analysts would have to reexamine why GM had threatened to close the plant in the first place. This could encourage challenges to GM's plant closing threats in other communities throughout the country as well.

Democratic economic planning by workers and communities from the bottom up was the objective of the CAP committee activists. That, however, was the easy part. The hard part was to figure out how a single UAW local could even dream of counterposing that goal to GM's goal of closing down any plant that it wanted to, when and where it wanted to.

THE INITIAL STRATEGY FOR KEEPING THE PLANT OPEN

Through a series of strategic discussions, and a process of elimination, the organizers moved in the direction of a boycott threat.

At the state or federal level, the idea of legislative restraints to prevent a corporation from closing a profitable plant was not even in the realm of discussion, let alone political feasibility. State legislation that proposed "advance notice" before a shutdown, according to Pete Beltran, "is not really a law to stop plant closings as much as an effort to provide better treatment for the victims of the closures." And yet, even after the closures of GM Southgate, Firestone, Goodyear, and General Electric, plant closing legislation of any kind was considered too "radical" by the Democrats, let alone the Republicans. The chances for federal legislation were even more remote. In 1982's Reagan-oriented Congress, both Republicans and Democrats were offering carte blanche to business and benign neglect to labor: solutions would have to be found elsewhere.

The concepts of a "worker buyout" or "employee stock ownership program" were not consistent with the workers' objectives. The initial capitalization of an auto company involves billions of dollars to achieve minimal economies of scale and requires a national distribution network. The goal wasn't to take over a plant that someone else wanted to abandon, the goal was to force GM to maintain a profit level lower than it might want.

A few movement activists from outside the local proposed the idea of "converting" the plant to another product. This idea had its roots in the efforts of anti-war and anti-defense industry activists to convince workers in defense industries that there are alternatives to making weapons of war besides facing unemployment. But that model was out of place in this situation. The GM workers didn't want to convert the plant, nor should they have wanted to. They felt it was absurd to think that an already profitable plant in the heart of the largest new-car market in the United States had to be bought out or converted.

From there, the discussions moved to the concept of "the united front." Whatever the particular tactic arrived at, the organizers felt that there was no possibility of taking on General Motors alone. A broad coalition, representing all the groups in the community that would be threatened by GM closing the plant had to be assembled. That coalition would need a confrontational tactic to meet GM's threat to close the plant with a threat of its own. But what was that tactic?

Some workers proposed the idea of a worker occupation, with broad community support, such as the Flint workers had employed in 1937. But the consciousness and mood of the American autoworkers in general and the Van Nuys workers in particular were far removed from those of their heroic predecessors. The Flint strike had been the culmination of a decade of growing confrontation in the auto industry. The workers were not yet in a confrontational mood in 1982.

Moreover, the tactic was inappropriate even if adoptable. In 1937, capturing the Fisher Body plants involved seizing not only individual factories but also the dies from which GM stamped its parts for many other plants, which were of great value to the corporation. But, in the 1980s, a workers' occupation of a closed Van Nuys plant would be denying GM something that it had already discarded.

Continuing that line of reasoning, the organizers wondered: Was there anything the workers had that GM wanted and were there any weapons besides the strike that a broad united front could use against the corporation? Out of the past successes of the Montgomery bus boycott and the farmworkers' grape boycotts came the idea of a GM boycott: while GM might not want the workers' labor, it desperately wanted the Southern California auto market. And if the autoworkers, as the leading force in the united front and the main organizers of the community, could develop a powerful enough coalition, they could deny a significant part of that market to GM. Through months of discussion, a preliminary consensus was reached: (1) *the main strategy would be a broad united front between the workers and the community against General Motors;* (2) *the main tactic would be the boycott;* and (3) *the main objective of the movement would be getting a long-term commitment from GM to keep the Van Nuys plant open.*

At the time, the social conditions for *any* of these options, let alone the boycott, did not exist. But the backgrounds of many of the organizers in the civil rights, community, and anti-war movements brought a fresh perspective to the discussions.

The labor movement at the time worked within the narrow confines of a self-fulfilling "realism." Too often, when union members proposed innovative tactics with which to fight the company, union officers would consult the contract, look up particular clauses and subsections, and solemnly explain, "It can't be done." But the CAP organizers had not begun their political development in the school of the postwar social compact between management and labor. They had been active in the successful mass movements of the 1960s and early 1970s.

They, along with millions of other Americans, had fought for voting rights and civil rights for black Americans *before* the Civil Rights Act of 1964 was passed. They had fought for Chicano, Afro-American, and Asian Studies departments on college campuses at a time when those demands were won. They had marched against the war in Vietnam, and some had organized against it in its early stages when polls showed that the vast majority of Americans supported the war. For some, direct experience and, for others, historical memory included the scenes of a once-defiant President Nixon falling from power and a once-omnipotent United States army retreating from Vietnam.

The idea of a boycott beginning in the union movement and spreading to the Chicano and black communities seemed a long shot even to the organizers themselves. But the UAW activists had the capability of conceptualizing an idea that had not yet come into being. They could visualize a small movement growing into a large movement, a mood of apathy and defeatism changing into one of confidence and activism. They were able to make a political assessment of social forces and develop a plan to bring those forces into direct confrontation with General Motors. It was hard work, and work that was in no way guaranteed to succeed. But that was the essence of *organizing* and it was that perspective that gave a vitality and optimism to the early plans of the CAP committee.

In the spring of 1982, after the announced closures of the GM plants in Fremont and Southgate, the CAP organizers, based on their strategic discussions, proposed to President Beltran that the local initiate a Keep GM Van Nuys Open campaign. At the time, the strategy was very vague; the committee had only a few people; and the project was hardly considered a "plum" in the union, since almost no one even dreamed the union could keep a plant open against the company's wishes. Beltran, who was expert in the methods of guiding new and potentially controversial ideas through the local, advised: "The project is very important, but go slow. I don't want any leaflets going into the plant about plant closings."

The organizers argued, "But how can we organize people if we don't talk about the possibility of a plant closing."

Beltran replied, "Look, obviously with five other plants closing, many of the workers understand the possibility. But if the union puts out a leaflet talking about a possible plant closing, the company will accuse us of starting a rumor. And if they ever do close the plant, they will claim it was the union's fault for planting the idea and undermining productivity. Let's wait until the company makes a threat; then we can react."[8]

Beltran had other concerns as well. As a former shop chairman and a skilled negotiator, he was thoroughly conversant with the union contract. At first, he had concerns about the "legality" of the Campaign. "According to the contract, GM has the right to close the plant under the management rights clause. So how can the union demand that GM keep the plant open?" Contractually, Beltran was right. The GM-UAW agreement stated:

> The right to hire, promote, discharge or discipline for cause and to maintain discipline

> and efficiency of employees is the sole responsibility of the corporation....In addition, the products to be manufactured, *the location of plants*, the schedule of production, the methods, processes, and means of manufacturing are solely and exclusively the responsibility of the corporation.[9] (Italics added)

The organizers argued that taking on the management rights clause would therefore have to be part of the strategy. While accepting that GM had the contractual power to close down the plant--a contractual provision they believed had to be changed--they asserted that the workers had to build a coalition powerful enough to deter GM from exercising its contractual "right."

Beltran had become a highly successful president by mediating the needs of many different and frequently contradictory constituencies within the local. A Chicano who has openly identified with the aspirations of the Latino community, he was very popular among whites and blacks as well--a president for all the workers. Unlike some local UAW officers whose concerns are limited to narrow trade-union issues, Beltran was very sympathetic to activists in the peace and anti-intervention movements, as well as to insurgents within the union movement. But he also had little regard for their effectiveness, having seen many projects initiated by movement organizers, especially those with explicitly left politics, come to nothing.

In 1982, when the handful of CAP members were speculating about a successful boycott against General Motors, Beltran listened to the scenario with a healthy skepticism and viewed its advocates as he would the baseball team or the recreation committee--as a "constituency" that needed to be placated. The CAP organizers understood Beltran's doubts, and realized they would have to move cautiously and step-by-step to build the credibility of their strategy.

Beltran gave the plan a cautious go-ahead. Nate Brodsky, in reaction to what he felt was the negative image of "plant closures" rhetoric, proposed a "Keep GM Van Nuys Open" project of the CAP committee with

Eric Mann as its coordinator. The question was, what would be its first move?

THE WATERS PLANT CLOSING BILL: A LABORATORY IN DEMOCRATIC PARTY POLITICS

Almost on cue, a made-to-order first step developed for the movement at Van Nuys--the Waters Plant Closings Bill. Maxine Waters, an outspoken member of the California State Assembly, whose district included many workers from the closed down GM Southgate, Goodyear, and Firestone plants, introduced a bill to protect workers from some of the worst excesses of plant closings. In its original form, it required employers to provide one year's advance notice before closing a plant; mandated a state agency to hold community-impact hearings before companies closed; and required companies to provide minimum severance pay and benefit extensions for the workers.

The Van Nuys organizers were excited about the bill, not because they believed its benefits were so generous, but because its provisions could help unions that actually wanted to prevent a plant closing. Advance notice would provide unions and community groups with the opportunity to at least try to reverse the decision. Community-impact hearings could prove an important mechanism for coalitions to pressure elected officials to impose sanctions that might deter a company from closing. The Waters Bill was a rare effort to encourage a democratic industrial policy and was, for a change, a piece of legislation that activists could get excited about. It would expand the scope of organizing work, not just try to alleviate the impact of a closing.

The coalition organizing support for the bill, the Los Angeles Coalition Against Plant Shutdowns (LACAPS), called for a bus caravan to Sacramento, the state capital, to create pressure for the bill's passage. The Van Nuys organizers saw the caravan as a perfect intermediate step for an eventual campaign. It could involve some new members of the local without having to begin by taking on GM directly; if the bill passed, it would provide legislative support for tactics they expected to use in the future, and the lobbying process itself would give members of the local's executive board their first involvement in a movement against plant closings, where they could learn from the experience of activists from plants that had already been shut down.

On June 16, 1982, fifteen members of the Van Nuys local took an all-night bus ride to join more than 500 members of churches, community groups, and labor unions to rally in support of the Waters Bill. The bill was to come before the Assembly Ways and Means Committee, which had to pass the bill before it could be presented to the full Assembly for a vote. When the delegation arrived, the LACAPS leaders were informed that back-room negotiations had chopped the advance notice from one year to six months. Dick Kukowski from the Van Nuys local remarked, "In the ten hours we drove on the bus, the politicians had already taken away six months." Then they were told that, in order to pass it through committee, the community-impact survey had been scrapped altogether as "too costly." Democratic politicians reassured the group, "We don't want to give the Republicans anything to hang their hat on." When an angry Mike Gomez demanded, "Who made these decisions for us?" the group was told by a legislative aide: "The Democratic leadership felt this was the best way to pass the bill. You may not like how this stuff works, but remember, politics is the art of compromise."

But the worst was yet to come. Workers from the closed down General Electric, Firestone, Goodyear, and GM Southgate plants poured their hearts out in moving testimony, thinking that their eloquence was necessary to generate more support for the bill. Then, after perfunctory speeches by many Democrats on the committee (where they had a twelve to nine majority), the Democrats moved to send the bill back for "further study"--a euphemism for killing it.

Prior to the vote, the Democrats had told the demonstrators that it was the Republicans who would try to kill the bill, which was why the caravan had been organized. But, in fact, it was the Republicans, who made no pretense of supporting the bill, who were pushing for the vote. Knowing full well that many of the Democrats did not plan to vote for it, they wanted to expose the Democrats' intentions to more than 500 labor supporters. The Democrats, in turn, did not want to go on record against the bill, so they agreed among themselves to kill the bill procedurally so they could blame the Republicans.

The crowd was furious and started yelling "Sell-out! Sell-out! Why the hell did we drive all the way up here if you'd already decided to kill the bill?" A candid Democratic assemblyman explained to several UAW participants, upon the promise of anonymity, the behind-the-scenes reality of what they had witnessed.

> Didn't you know that we never planned to pass this bill? Maxine Waters was the only one who even wanted the bill; Willie Brown and the party leadership wanted the bill killed. The party leadership agrees ahead of time which bills are priorities. On these, we are strongly pressured to vote along party lines. On other votes, we are free to vote as we please. The California Manufacturers Association made the defeat of this bill their number one priority. With the gubernatorial elections coming up and Reagan being so popular, we don't want the Democrats to appear to be antibusiness.[10]

On the long bus ride home, many of the Van Nuys workers discussed the lessons of the day.

While many of the CAP members had already believed that the Democratic party was at best a weak friend of working people and at worst no friend at all, it was still shocking to see a liberal Democratic committee kill its own bill in front of 500 union members. Many of the less political workers from closed down plants tried to hide their humiliation. They felt their real-life suffering was used as a pawn by politicians who proclaimed themselves "friends of labor."

Some workers proposed that the local never work with politicians again, period! While that feeling was shared by everyone on the bus, the more strategic assessment was that any future Van Nuys coalition would first focus on churches, community groups, and other local unions--as well as on building a strong base among the local's own members--then carefully and selectively invite in the few political leaders who had proven worthy of the workers' trust.

Many of those who had seen the hard work of the LACAPS staff betrayed also began to draw lessons from the experience. In that LACAPS was essentially a staff organization, it drew its influence by mobilizing other constituencies. It depended heavily on the existing leadership of the Democratic party and many International unions. It could approach those forces not as a force in itself, able to discuss, disagree, and deal, but rather as a broker that was offering "staff services."

The Van Nuys organizers were convinced more than ever that the key lesson of the sellout of the Waters bill was "you need to have an independent political base." They predicted that if it ever came to the closing of the plant, many high level political and union officials, as well as top GM officials, would set the terms of the discussion, and the local and its leadership would be frozen out. In order to prepare for that eventuality and to prevent it from happening, the organizers would have to place great emphasis on expanding their base within the local itself, and to build the coalition around forces that were at least tied to the existing power relationships of the society. At every juncture, the Van Nuys organizers avoided those who they felt had cut a deal on the Waters bill with impunity and would do the same over the closing of the Van Nuys plant. It was a bitter, but instructive, experience.

THE DEBATE OVER SHORT OR LONG LEAFLETS

The CAP committee wrote a two-sided leaflet to the membership, reporting on what they came to refer to as the "Sacramento sell-out." The leaflet told the story of "How the Waters Plant Closings Bill was Killed... But the Movement Continues." The leaflet began:

> Many workers have asked us, "how can our union combat the growing atmosphere of rumors and threats to close the plant?" We see part of the solution in changing the political atmosphere in the country. During the 1930's, when workers were laid-off, there were no unemployment benefits. The first step to building a movement for unemployment benefits was to convince the workers themselves that they had a *right* to them.
>
> Today, the movement against plant closings says that corporations have a responsibility to the workers and communities they exploit. Giant multinationals like U.S. Steel and GM have the obligation to re-tool their existing plants. Workers have a right to demand that these plants stay open and don't run away.[11]

The leaflet was very well received in the local, but one union committeeman (a paid, full-time shop steward representing a "district" of about 300 workers) was incensed, not by the content of the leaflet but by its length. He argued, "These goddamn people can hardly read. When we give them leaflets I watch them and they throw them in the garbage. This isn't college, you know. You guys want to write a goddamn book. You have to learn how to talk to the people on the line if you want to organize them."

His views, expressed so bluntly, represented one side of a long-standing debate about the consciousness of factory workers. The CAP activists disagreed with the tendency of some labor organizers to underestimate the intelligence of the people they are trying to organize. Political ideas are frequently complex, and while it is an essential skill to learn how to break ideas down to their basics, patronizing efforts to oversimplify complex ideas frequently lead to the workers losing respect for their union. Contrary to stereotypes, many autoworkers are highly literate in terms of both formal and self-education. Politically, the leaflet did not begin with an appeal to the workers' narrow self-interest, but to their interest in the broader question of workers' rights to restrict corporate decisions, an issue that would be central to any future movement to keep the plant open.

One exciting aspect of organizing in a union of 5,000 workers is the ample opportunity to test political ideas in practice. In virtually every department of the plant, workers were reading the leaflet avidly, and those who were having difficulty reading were asking questions of the workers who read with facility. The leaflet urged workers who wanted to get involved to contact one of the CAP committee members named in the leaflet. Several new people were recruited into the nascent movement through this tactic.

President Beltran was impressed by both the professional quality of the leaflet and by the positive feedback from many of the high-seniority workers in the plant. He was starting to assess that, if handled carefully, a movement to prevent a plant closing at Van Nuys could become a popular issue within the local. The committeeman who had lectured about the stupidity of the people in his district was voted out of office by them a few months later.

GM THREATENS TO CLOSE VAN NUYS: THE WORKERS GET AN ECONOMICS LESSON

It was hard for the Van Nuys workers to take seriously a discussion of a possible plant closing when they were working nine hours a day and some compulsory Saturdays, as they were during the summer of 1982. Then, in September, after a two-week break for "model change" (during which the plant is re-tooled for the next-year's model), the workers returned to a drastically changed situation.

GM management summoned every worker, in groups of fifty, to a two-hour company presentation about the future of the plant. GM officials, armed with graphs and charts, vividly presented GM's projected sales for the 1980s, followed by GM's actual sales figures. They explained that because of higher interest rates and Japanese imports, GM sales were far below expectation. Management went on to explain that they had at least five "surplus plants" and that, unless sales increased dramatically, those plants would have to be closed. Up until this point, most workers thought this was an interesting, but somewhat academic, discussion. Then management produced a chart showing that GM Van Nuys was on the "danger list" of five plants that would be the first to close.

The GM speakers tried to reassure the workers that all was not lost. If they would only cooperate more with management, cut down on absenteeism, and improve product quality, it was possible that the plant could be removed from the danger list, and another, "less cooperative" plant substituted in its place. This was the first time that GM management had overtly argued that each plant was in competition with all of the others. GM made it clear that some plants would be closed; the only question was *which ones*.

In the presentation, one of the factors by which plants were rated was "labor climate," measured by counting the number of grievances filed by workers: the fewer the grievances, the better the climate. A worker spoke up: "Are you saying that if I file a grievance I may, in some way, be contributing to the plant being closed?" The GM spokesman replied: "Not necessarily. We are simply saying that in plants where there is a more cooperative attitude and when more problems can be solved without resorting to the grievance procedure, our unit costs are lower and our competitive position is stronger." The point had been made.

Many of the workers who had previously worked at Southgate were very outspoken. One worker said, "Look, at Southgate you told us the same thing. We killed ourselves for you and you even gave us 'quality hats' (company paid baseball caps with the emblem, "Southgate workers make a quality product") for doing such a good job. And look up on that chart. You have Southgate rated as one of the best plants for quality and you still closed it down. So no matter how hard we work, it looks like you just want to get out of California, and there is nothing we can do to change the fact that our plant is in California."[12]

REGIONAL DISINVESTMENT IN CALIFORNIA: WHAT EXACTLY IS THE PROBLEM?

The captive audience meetings were, for many workers, the first time they had taken the threat of a plant closing seriously. But their hard questions about alternatives to the company's presentation posed a challenge to the Campaign organizers. Generalized statements about "workers' rights" would not suffice. The disparity between GM's plant capacity and its sales was substantial and the corporation was subject to some very real cost pressures in the international arena. In order to win the confidence of many of the workers and to plan a strategy based on economic reality, the organizers had to explain why all these plants were closing in California and what GM's business reasons were for disinvesting its capital from the West Coast. After a great deal of study and a careful reading of the *Wall Street Journal* and the *Automotive News,* the organizers came up with some answers.

GM's main objective was cost-cutting and at the manufacturing end the key word was "consolidation." Its goal was to reduce inventories through "same day" or "just-in-time" inventory systems, whereby parts manufacture, assembly, and shipping of the assembled car occur very close geographically. While GM previously manufactured most parts in the Midwest and assembled them in outlying "satellite plants" such as Van Nuys, the corporation's new plan was to close down its West and East coast plants, build state-of-the-art assembly plants in the Midwest, and ship the completed vehicles to dealer networks throughout the United States. Through reducing inventory costs, GM hoped to save tens of millions.

In terms of this master plan, the main liability of the Van Nuys plant could be summarized in two words: "shipping costs." Although the exterior of the plant had been built in 1947, its infrastructure had been continuously re-tooled and upgraded. In the corporation's presentation, every plant in the GM system was rated by "amount of dollars needed to bring it to state-of-the art." This was their index of modernity, and surprisingly, the GM Van Nuys plant was rated quite high in that category, higher than many plants in the Midwest.

But the problem remained: "shipping costs." GM argued that it was inefficient to manufacture parts in the Midwest, ship them to Los Angeles to be assembled, and then "back-ship" assembled cars to Chicago, Detroit, or New York. It would be cheaper to ship all fully assembled cars from a Midwestern hub. Throughout the years, the press would repeat the shipping cost argument in most articles about the plant. A typical version was expressed in a *Los Angeles Times* article:

> The company's decision [about whether to close Van Nuys]...will be based on a variety of factors, not the least of which is the fact that it costs an estimated $70 million a year more to produce Camaros and Firebirds in Van Nuys than in Norwood, Ohio [the other GM plant that produces those models]...Because of that figure alone it would seem that GM executives in Detroit would almost surely shut down Van Nuys, not Norwood.[13]

In past decades, shipping costs had not been as serious a problem. Before higher energy costs, the charges for shipping automobiles and parts via railways and trucks were far less a cause for concern. Also, in the absence of foreign competition, shipping costs could be more easily passed on to the consumer. GM, as the price leader for the industry, could set prices high enough to absorb any additional costs.

Besides, decentralized assembly did and still does have certain advantages. For markets close to the dealers, individual orders can be filled more quickly. On the West Coast, having plants in Fremont, Southgate, and Van Nuys gave GM greater flexibility. That is still the case but, as of now, GM feels those advantages are outweighed by their disadvantages.

The organizers formulated the problem as follows: Should the problem of GM's shipping costs be resolved by closing down the plant, or by forcing GM to accept a lower rate of profit? They decided that any effort to buy into GM's "challenge" to make the plant maximally profitable would be a disastrous strategy. They argued that the plant was clearly modern and efficient, that the Camaro was a best-seller, and that GM was still making substantial profits from the plant. The fact that those profit levels were not as high as GM might want was not a justification for closing the plant. Otherwise, every plant would be forced to compete with every other on the issue of "profitability," and as fast as one plant made local concessions--which was the whole thrust of GM's presentations to the workers--another threatened plant would just match them, and the cycle of blackmail would continue.

While this point of view would become refined over the years, even in its early stages the Campaign was on a theoretical and practical collision course with Alfred P. Sloan's principles of unchallenged management rights and unlimited profit maximization. As the first round of trying to counter GM's arguments, the most active union workers found this rationale convincing. Perhaps most importantly, by GM posing both the threat *and* the challenge, the basis for initiating the Campaign was set--no longer would the union leadership have to worry about being accused of crying wolf.

GM ASSERTS ITS MANAGEMENT RIGHTS AND ELIMINATES 500 JOBS

While the workers were trying to digest GM's threat, a new problem developed. In October 1982, GM management arbitrarily rescinded its "tag relief" system.

Tag relief is a process whereby, in order to give everyone on the assembly line a twenty-minute break without stopping the line, a group of specialized "relief operators" learn seven jobs and "tag" each worker for a break in sequence without any interruption of production. Since tag relief was part of the local contract, the company, in the view of President Beltran, had no right to remove it arbitrarily.

GM management argued that because of decreased demand, they needed to cut down car production, and that under the management rights clause they could do whatever was necessary to achieve those objectives. Shutting down the line altogether for a mass break (and the resultant layoff of 500 workers) would help them deal with their glutted supply of cars in the field.

Since the overwhelming majority of the 500 workers who would be lost were recent transfers from the already closed Southgate plant, the reaction was strong. Several of the CAP organizers proposed that instead of getting rid of 500 workers, GM move to a four-day work week during the downturn in sales. This would keep everyone working and, under the supplemental unemployment plan, pay workers about 90 percent of the fifth day's wages. A petition supporting this plan was circulated in the plant. Over 500 workers signed it in one day.

Pete Beltran took the company to court and was able to win a temporary restraining order to stop GM from laying people off. GM then went to a higher court, and within a few days was able to get the order overturned. GM then told the union that its only recourse was to strike, knowing full well that workers in a plant threatened with a closing would be reluctant to use that option.

Although the combination of organizing the workers on the line, developing legal tactics, and attracting media coverage neither won the four-day work week nor stopped the elimination of tag relief and the layoff of 500 workers, in the course of this unexpected battle, the movement to keep the plant open took another step forward.

Many of the former Southgate workers, who had not known what action to take when Southgate was closed, became involved in the petition campaign and the court hearings. Kelley Jenco, who would soon become a leader of the campaign, explained how she first became involved:

> When Southgate closed down, all they talked about was job training. But the only ones who got any jobs were the union officials who got paid to give us job training. When I got to Van Nuys, here was a president who was willing to fight. So I took out a lot of the petitions and got some of my Southgate friends involved. When I was walking around with the petitions they would say, "Hey, Kelley, I didn't know you were involved in the union." And I said, "Neither did I, but it's about time."[14]

This was the organizers' first effort at formulating demands that tried to come to terms with market conditions without totally caving in to them. GM said it had a problem--overproduction. The local came up with a solution--the 32-hour work week--which addressed the problem, but from the workers' point of view.

During the tag-relief incident, political disagreements in the local that would later erupt into open conflict began to surface. While some of the elected committeemen were supportive of the proposal for the four-day week and the grass roots petition initiative it brought forth, others opposed its "out of channels" origins as an affront to their authority, and even saw its demands as an affront to the authority of the corporation. These committeemen were "strict constructionists" of the union contract. They argued that "layoffs are part of this business and Beltran is just grabbing for headlines taking the company to court." Off the record, some were heard to argue that it was not a big blow that we lost 500 jobs since "most of them are Southgate people," and many of them are black.

The efforts by one faction of the committeemen to split the local between "Van Nuys workers" and "Southgate imports" in order to justify the company's position would be a harbinger of their later efforts to encourage the Van Nuys workers to directly compete with other GM plants in the concessions sweepstakes. The tag-relief struggle was only the beginning.

NOTES

1. This version of the events is based on discussions with Mark Masaoka, a former Ford Pico Rivera activist who became one of the founders of the Campaign.
2. Rebecca Morales, "Made in L.A.: Automobile Manufacturing in Southern California," Graduate School of Architecture and Urban Planning, University of California, Los Angeles, Summer 1986, p. 9.
3. All figures are based on 1980 Federal Census data. Valley statistics were provided by the Van Nuys Chamber of Commerce.
4. Figures are based on the 1980 Federal Census, with 1987 extrapolated update. Figures were corroborated by James Wisely, demographics consultant to California state legislators.
5. I have worked at the Ford Milpitas plant, the General Motors Southgate plant, and for the past five years, at the GM Van Nuys plant. As could be expected, I spend a great deal of time talking with and listening to autoworkers. While many of the opinions expressed in this book are clearly my own, the efforts to summarize commonly held views are not based on my own predispositions, but rather my effort to really understand the mood and the thinking of the people I have worked with. Throughout the book, the vast majority of statements by autoworkers are footnoted. When they are not, however, the conversations and quotes are based on my own memory and my own notes of discussions with assembly-line workers.
6. The terminology of race and national background that I have chosen to use is as follows: Hispanic refers to "Spanish surname" and all people of Latin American and Spanish descent. It is most often used in demographic material, and is, at times, considered a more "moderate" synonym for Latino. Latino is used by other members of the community to refer to all people of Latin American and Spanish descent--Mexican immigrants, Chicanos, Salvadorenos, Puerto Ricans, etc. The use of Hispanic versus Latino often reflects a different political emphasis. Chicano, as commonly

used, refers primarily to people of Mexican heritage who have been in the United States for a second generation. Thus, it is possible for a Mexican immigrant to be a Mexicano, while his children are Chicanos. In fact, many Chicanos have lived in the United States for over a century. For the purposes of this book, I will use Latino, Chicano, and Mexicano as the main terms and use Hispanic primarily in reference to demographic data, since that it how it is categorized.

7. Interview with the author, February 22, 1987.
8. Throughout this case study, statements by UAW activists pertaining to the Campaign that are not footnoted are based on my first-hand participation in those meetings.
9. *Agreement Between General Motors Corporation and the UAW*, September 21, 1984, paragraph 8, "Rights of Corporation," p. 13.
10. This conversation took place when a group of UAW members angrily confronted one of the Assembly people, among whom was Mike Gomez and the author. As was stated in the text, the "inside" story of the Democrats' strategy of killing their own bill was given with the promise of anonymity.
11. "Our UAW Local is Fighting to Save our Jobs: How the Waters Plant Closings Bill was Killed...But the Movement Continues," leaflet to the general membership, June 1982.
12. I attended several of these meetings and took careful notes. The GM presentations were very helpful, in that in addition to their threat of a closure, they provided valuable information that indicated, to our surprise, that even with GM's concern about the issue of shipping costs, the plant was far more viable (that is, profitable) than we had imagined.
13. "Plan Could Save GM's Plant at Van Nuys," *Los Angeles Times*, Business section, November 5, 1986, p. 1.
14. Interview with the author, February 15, 1987.

Chapter Six

THE CAMPAIGN BECOMES OFFICIAL

In November 1982, as soon as the judge's restraining order had been overturned, GM was free to lay off the 500 workers. But the corporation decided to go one step further and laid off the entire second shift of 2,500 hundred workers. The following Saturday, at a meeting of more than one thousand workers to discuss unemployment benefits and other details of the layoff, Beltran told the Campaign organizers: "I told you to wait until the threat was clear. Well now GM has slapped us in the face with the tag relief, has laid off the second shift, and is openly talking about closing down the plant altogether. It's time to act. Let's announce the Campaign publicly."

When the leaders of the local's Community Action and Community Services committees told the laid-off workers that they were planning a coordinated strategy of both activisim and service, more than one hundred of them volunteered to become involved in that work. Community Service members provided laid-off workers with referrals to social service agencies; negotiated with landlords and other creditors; and provided a place where workers could come for advice with new problems as they arose. Little did they know how severe the problems would be.

The UAW has a contractual "supplementary unemployment benefit" (SUB) for its members that had protected the income and family stability of hundreds of thousands of auto workers over the years. But the benefits are not guaranteed; they are funded by hourly contributions from both workers and management, which are put into a national SUB fund. Because of several years of high unemployment among autoworkers preceding the 1982 layoff, the SUB fund was very low. Workers' benefits, supposed to last fifty-two weeks, ran out in five to six weeks.

Men and women who had been taking home $400 per week received $320 for the first ten weeks (thanks to their SUB benefits), then saw their income drop precipitously to $160 a week in unemployment benefits. Despite their relatively high pay compared with other industrial workers, most of the autoworkers with children had minimal savings, if any at all. With rents or house payments of $600 or more, the layoff placed many workers in a desperate situation.

One worker came into the community services office in the union hall in late December. Christmas was coming, he had no money to buy presents for his children, and his landlord was threatening to evict him. Practically no one was hiring, and most of the jobs available for factory workers paid less than $5 per hour. He asked if he could borrow $500 from the union. The volunteers explained that the local couldn't possibly give loans like that with 2,500 members laid off, but that they would try to negotiate with his landlord and to get some presents for his kids. The man began screaming, became violent, and threatened to attack them for not giving him the money. Finally, he just broke down in tears. He felt worthless, and destroyed, and afraid that his family would be put out on the street before the holidays.

In another instance, several laid-off workers who were single parents from South Central Los Angeles heard that the local was distributing government surplus butter and cheese. They called to say that they needed the food, but wondered, if they drove the forty miles to the union hall, whether the union could provide them with gas money to get home. The early foundation of the Campaign was built on the experiences of these laid-off workers.

DECEMBER 4, 1982: THE WORKERS BECOME ORGANIZERS

The threat was apparent, the anger and desperation of the workers were growing, but there was, as yet, no real movement. The organizers of the Campaign realized that a great deal of education was necessary to explain the strategy of keeping a plant open and to transform workers' consciousness from that of loyal union members to spokespeople, activists, and organizers. With those goals in mind, the CAP committee called an all-day strategy conference. The executive board authorized lunches for one hundred workers, and John O'Gara, a sympathetic board member and the president of the retirees joked, "The day you get a hundred of our people to give up a Saturday for a union conference, I'll cook the lunches myself." The day of the meeting, O'Gara observed, "I'm glad nobody held me to my bet": more than two hundred workers had shown up.

The first objective of the conference was to explain to the workers that, while the Van Nuys movement was in its infancy, they could learn from the experience of other union leaders who had already organized efforts to stop their plants from being closed. The Van Nuys movement was trying to improve upon, not reinvent, the wheel.

Ron Delia, the former president of the closed-down Pico Rivera plant, warned the workers that he had disregarded the danger signs. In his case it was understandable, since Ford management had assured him the layoff was only temporary and, besides, there had been no precedent of Ford closing plants. He urged the workers, "Don't wait till the company gives you two weeks' notice to get organized. Take this layoff as your advance notice. The time to organize is now!"

Dick Presto, once shop chairman at the closed-down General Electric plant in Ontario, California, told of the United Electrical Workers' highly respected, but ultimately unsuccessful, battle to keep their plant open. They had formed a coalition with the mayor, the city council, and local business people in an effort to buy the plant from GE. Presto said: "You don't need a union to make concessions. If you want to give things away, just go to the company yourself; they'll be glad to take whatever you offer. But if you want to fight, you have to diversify your tactics--press conferences, church-based initiatives, demonstrations--so that the company is on the defensive." Presto emphasized: "We began our organizing when GE announced the closing. If we had had more time we might have won. You have a great opportunity to learn from our accomplishments and mistakes, but the main thing is to begin your campaign now."

The workers then gathered into groups of ten, with a discussion leader chairing each group. The organizers knew that too often people come to meetings, listen to fiery speeches, and then go home alone with their doubts unexpressed. By working in small groups, the organizers could solicit ideas and opinions and get people committed to a process that they themselves were helping to shape. Out of those discussions, the conference reached consensus on two important points:

1) *The idea of the boycott.* There could be no movement without a credible strategy. The workers were convinced that the threat of a boycott of GM products in Southern California could be enough of a deterrent to make GM consider keeping the plant open. A strike was not feasible; after all, GM was not sure it wanted the workers' labor anyway. The boycott, on the other hand, not only reflected the workers' anger ("If GM closes down this plant after all the years I've given them, I'll never buy a GM car again"); it appealed to their sense of strategy: "If GM closes down both Southgate and Van Nuys and leaves Los Angeles with no auto plants and more unemployment, why shouldn't the public boycott them?" Mark Masaoka presented the

first market figures to make the case for the boycott that were later used by this author in a *Los Angeles Times* article:

> Last year [1982] more than 450,000 new cars were sold in the Los Angeles area and GM was first in sales, with more than 126,000. GM sold over 250,000 new cars in California and well over a half-million in the Western states....We intend to convince GM that its marketing strategy for Southern California must include production in Los Angeles. That pressure might take the form of a boycott of GM products if the company closes down the last remaining plant in the nation's largest new-car market.[1]

Even the most elementary market research reinforced the viability of the strategy and convinced the workers that the plan had a chance to succeed.

2) *The necessity of a broad, community-based coalition under the leadership of the local.* The workers voted that the first public action of the Campaign was to stage a march and rally on March 1, 1983, to demonstrate community support. GM would not fear a boycott just by auto workers. The Campaign had to show GM that it could convince a significant number of Los Angeles consumers to support a future boycott.

THE CHRISTMAS EVE DEMONSTRATION: THE WIND BLOWS OUT THE CANDLES

Most of the organizers left the meeting elated. They had come up with a workable plan and convinced more than one hundred workers to get involved in the Campaign as organizers. But Jake Flukers, an executive board member, was not satisfied. Jake argued that March 1 was too far away. He proposed a Christmas

Eve candlelight vigil to publicize the plight of the laid-off workers at Christmas. Most of the organizers shared Jake's sense of urgency but argued that, in taking on a giant like General Motors, they wanted the first rally to be large and successful. They doubted that many workers would come out to demonstrate on Christmas Eve and feared that, at such an early stage in the Campaign, a poor turnout would hurt its credibility. But Jake felt it was a moral issue and was not to be denied. Jake announced that he was going to hold his vigil anyway. As Christmas Eve approached, he said he had more than fifty people lined up.

Most of the CAP members told Jake they wouldn't be able to attend his rally but wished him good luck. But when Christmas Eve came, each one of them, against his or her better judgment, offered excuses to family and guests, left the dinner table, and drove out to the plant. It was one of the coldest nights anyone could remember in Los Angeles. The street was dark, the plant was closed down, and it looked either abandoned or haunted. Nobody was there. Finally, out of the shadows came Jake, holding a box of candles. While none of the fifty workers showed up, the ten most active members of the CAP committee stood out there in the freezing cold. Jake kept trying to light the candles, but the wind kept blowing them out. All of a sudden everyone burst out laughing. Then, on that dark and abandoned street, a lone reporter from one of the local radio stations showed up. The demonstrators, after telling her with a straight face that she had just missed over a hundred of their fellow workers who had come to the vigil, went on to explain the demands of the Campaign.

Jake appreciated that most of the CAP members who argued the strongest against the vigil showed up anyway. Out of the trial and error process typified by the Christmas Eve vigil came the type of political friendships that were essential to the long-term viability of the Campaign.

THE MARCH 1, 1983 RALLY: A MOVEMENT IS BORN

The laid-off workers became organizers. They went to churches and synagogues, labor unions, and community groups, giving presentations and asking people to attend the rally. The idea of workers trying to stop a plant closing *before it happened* was very well received. Many of the workers concluded that much of labor's isolation is self-imposed. Unions too rarely make the effort to articulate their cause to a broader public through face-to-face efforts to win allies.

But the organizers' greatest worry was the response of the Van Nuys workers themselves. Many of the workers on the first shift still did not take the threat to the plant seriously: they were still working, after all. The second shift workers were facing so many problems and were feeling so isolated and powerless that some predicted that they too wouldn't turn out in large numbers. The rally was scheduled for 3 p.m. on a weekday so that the first shift would just have to walk across the street into the union hall right after work.

The organizers leafleted the first shift every week and began a phone campaign to the homes of the laid-off workers. Dozens of organizers, speaking English and Spanish, called workers and their spouses at home to fill them in on the latest rumors and to convince them that the rally was an important tactic to try to save their jobs. Based on the responses, they placed each worker into "yes," "no," and "maybe" categories and hoped that 75 percent of those who said they would "definitely" come would actually show up. As one organizer observed, "The easiest way to say "no" is to say "yes."

A week before the rally, torrential rains swept Los Angeles. Every day there was a downpour and every day the organizers assured themselves that the clouds were getting the rain out of their system. But as the rains continued unabated they became increasingly apprehensive and spent even more time on the "phone trees."

On the day of the rally it rained so hard that cars were floating down the street. In the union hall at 9 a.m., the mood was morose. "You know what those bastards at GM did," said Nate Brodsky. "They sent the whole first shift home after one hour. We've lost the whole first shift." (Under the contract, once employees show up for work, GM is obligated to pay them for four hours. Past practice had been that even if there were no parts in stock or the assembly line couldn't run because of a mechanical breakdown, GM *never* sent the workers home before those four hours were up.) While the torrential rains were not of GM's making, the decision to send the workers home after one hour was clearly a tactic to hurt the movement.

Some of the organizers considered calling off the rally in an effort to avert a disaster. But then the phone calls began. "Is the rally still on? My car won't work, but I'm going to walk over with my kids." "You better not cancel that rally. Even if I have to swim, you can count on me." By noon, more than one hundred workers had showed up--three hours early. By three o'clock, more than seven hundred people, many of them soaking wet, packed the union hall. The organizers started hugging each other: the movement was off to an impressive start.

THE CIVIL RIGHTS MOVEMENT MEETS THE LABOR MOVEMENT

From the inception of the Campaign, one of the key strategic elements was the support of the Chicano and black communities. The Van Nuys workforce is more than 50 percent Latino and more than 15 percent black. The organizers felt that the mobilization of those communities was both possible and essential in terms of getting GM to take the threat of a boycott seriously. But in order for that idea to win the day, it had to overcome many political obstacles in Local 645.

In the context of the Campaign, when many organizers talked about the exciting strategic possibilities of involving the black and Latino communities, some workers cautioned, "Don't talk about Chicanos and blacks; it will only turn off the whites and cause divisions. Just say that we are all in this thing together." The organizers countered that there had to be a way to make the politics of race a central issue in the Campaign, without losing sight of the truth that the workers *were* all in it together, and without making the whites feel that they were being excluded or even targeted. The leaflets for the March 1 rally articulated a strategy of unifying the concerns of class, race, and gender within the Van Nuys workforce:

> The United Auto Workers union has a long history of opposing racial and sex discrimination. Our plant is over 50% Chicano and Latino. The vast majority of the nation's 12 million Chicanos live in the Southwest. By closing down Fremont and Southgate (while Ford closed down Pico Rivera and San Jose--both over 50% Chicano) there is a movement to drive Chicanos out of the auto industry and the UAW which we strongly oppose.
>
> For black workers--especially after GM closed down Southgate whose workforce was over 50% black--our plant is one of the last remaining decent-paying industrial jobs. After that, laid-off minority workers will face unemployment at twice the national average. For women workers, many of whom are single heads of households, GM's threat to close our plant would reverse the affirmative action gains of the 1960s and the 1970s--when women had to fight to get into the auto industry in the first place.
>
> We are workers of all nationalities--White, Black, Latino, Asian, women and men. We are proud to be auto workers, proud to be members of the UAW. We are tired of the constant threats, tired of the rumors, tired of

> the lay-offs. The 2500 of us who are working want to know if we will be working tomorrow, next month, next year. The 2500 of us on lay-off are tired of wondering if we will be called back, for how long--until the next rumor, the next threat, the next lay-off.[2]

The rich social practice of the Campaign created many opportunities to solve problems in the process of carrying out the work. At the March 1 rally, Reverend Joseph Bagneris, the president of the Pacoima Ministers Association and a leader of the black community in the San Fernando Valley, was the opening speaker. A legendary preacher, he told the Van Nuys workers a story of a drowning man who reached out for help, but each time his rescuers pulled his arm or leg to drag him to shore the limb came off in their hands. Finally, his exasperated rescuers warned him, "Look brother, no one can save you if you don't stick together." He told the workers that he was deeply moved by the spirit of labor unity he felt at the rally, and he pledged to organize more community support. But, prophetically, he warned that the community would never stay involved if the workers could not stick together to lead their own movement.

While all the workers were captivated by Bagneris, the black workers were especially proud, punctuating his remarks with, "You tell 'em, Rev!" and "Preach, brother, preach!" Chicanos and whites had been the most visible and politically influential groups in the plant, and many of the black workers had felt underrepresented and culturally isolated. But, as the Campaign developed, the highly visible role of many black leaders in the city in defense of *all* the Van Nuys workers both encouraged the black workers and had a significant impact on the consciousness of many whites and Chicanos.

Spokespeople from MEChA (Movimiento Estudiantil Chicano de Aztlan), a Chicano student organization at several state universities, emphasized that many of their parents worked at the plant, and that GM and the UAW had provided Chicano working people with the decent wages necessary for a stable family life. If GM ever closed the plant, however, the community would have no other choice but to boycott.[3] The sense of the plant as an integral community institution, and the particular commitment of minority communities, were being established.

Suddenly, in the middle of the rally, the torrential rains stopped and the sun came out. The crowd yelled, "Let's march," and seven hundred people marched down Van Nuys Boulevard chanting, "Keep GM Van Nuys Open," while little children carried placards saying, "My mommy needs her job back." As the workers filed back into the union hall, the rains came beating down again, and one of the workers said, "I'm not very religious, but that was just like the parting of the Red Sea."

From its inception, the strong community and civil rights quality of the movement made it more of a "cause" than an "issue." A veteran reporter at the rally that day commented: "I left with chills. I hadn't seen that type of spirit since the early days of the farmworkers."

WOMEN IN LEADERSHIP

After the crowd left, more than thirty organizers remained in the union hall, exhausted and exhilarated, to survey the day's events. Jackie Marshall, a laid-off second-shift worker, whose relatives had been active in the Flint sit-down strikes, said, "There are so few times in your life when anything feels worthwhile, but today I felt so much hope, and I don't mind saying, I felt proud of myself and all of us." In that room, that day, at least half of the key activists were women. Kelley Jenco, Jackie Banks Cash, Jackie Marshall, Patti Baker, Teresa Huerta, and Dorothy Travis were among more than twenty women whose work had been critical to that phase of the Campaign. Kelley Jenco, one of the Campaign's leaders, explains how she became involved in the movement:

After having worked for five years at the Southgate plant I was laid off in October 1981. There were strong rumors that the plant was going to close altogether, which it did the following April. Within a three-month period I had lost my job, lost my home, and ended my marriage. It was Christmas Eve and I had run up my last charge account to give the kids the best Christmas I could, but it was very dark and depressing. Then General Motors called on Christmas Eve and asked if I was interested in going to work at Van Nuys. Interested? "Can I come in tonight?"

I began work on January 3, 1982, and moved my two kids, Lisa and Joe, to the Valley. I was happy. I was working ten hours a day, six days a week, and then, in November 1982, GM told us we were being laid off, and again, the plant might be closed. I said, "I can't believe this; they're doing it to me again." At that time, I was working in the body shop. Mark Masaoka came around and was circulating this petition to try to stop the layoff and asked me if I would sign. That's how I began to get involved. I grabbed that petition and went to work.

Of course we didn't stop the layoff, and the next thing I knew I was out on the street again. We had excellent SUB benefits, but they only lasted ten weeks; then it was $160 a week. At the time I had no formal training for another job, but besides, why should I have to look for another job? I liked the one I had. I had always gotten stuck with some of the worst jobs in the plant, but it didn't matter. I loved my job, I loved the people I worked with, and after having been stuck in the house with the kids all those years--my husband had been very angry when I first got hired, which started us on the road to our divorce--my job meant everything to me.

When I first began attending Campaign meetings I didn't understand the strategy too well, but I did understand that the union was fighting back. When I first was laid off at Southgate I went to the local president and said, "What are we going to do about the plant closing?" and he said there was nothing we could do. So I left with my last paycheck in my hand and tears in my eyes. I wondered, is this a union? But at Van Nuys, while I didn't understand all the details, I knew we were trying to take action to save our jobs, and I was glad to be part of it--it was something I *had* to be a part of. It allowed me to come out of my shell, and something I'll look back on with pride and accomplishment. It did more than keep the plant open, it helped me understand myself and get my own life together.

My understanding increased meeting by meeting. The Campaign leaders were very patient and kept explaining the political ramifications of what we were doing, and every day it became a little more clear. But I also learned a lot from the people in the community. Each time I went to speak at a community group or another union I came to understand that it wasn't just happening to us. It's shoes and steel and garment, too. As long as these companies can find someone else to exploit more than they're exploiting you, they're gone.

I never thought the boycott idea was impossible. I had known a guy who was active in the grape boycott with Cesar Chavez and I knew that boycotts worked. My main question was whether we could build the movement and whether people would support us. But each time I went to speak at a union or community group, people were so excited about trying to stop the plant from closing before it was too late that I started to believe

> that if we had to have the boycott, the support would be there.
>
> I also think the Campaign meant a lot to me, and other women, because of the leadership roles we were allowed to play. I remember the first time a reporter from a newspaper called and I turned to one of the men and said, "There's somebody on the phone from the *L.A. Times*," and he said, "Fine, so talk to him." And I thought, "Who me?" But I did talk to him and I discovered that I knew a lot more about the Campaign than I thought. The Campaign allowed the women to be the leaders that we were. We didn't make the coffee and pass out the donuts; we helped to lead the thing and we were good at it. Speaking for myself, it was a wonderful first-hand experience to see people working together, sometimes twelve hours a day, but working on something that we all believed in. It was a great education.[4]

Kelley Jenco went on to become the chairperson of the local's Education Committee where she developed classes for workers wanting to receive a high school diploma, receiving her diploma herself in 1986. Jenco helped reorganize a then-dormant Women's Committee of the local, and was elected to the local's executive board in 1985.

NEW PROBLEMS, NEW SOLUTIONS

Several CAP members proposed another rally in the spring to keep up the pressure on GM. But what would be different about it and what new objectives would it try to meet? At first, the main objective had been to mobilize the membership of the local itself. The organizers had realized that GM's first tactic would be to claim that the Campaign did not have the support of the local. The impressive response from the workers, especially the laid-off ones, silenced that argument. But the long-term strategy of the Campaign was to involve the workers as the main *organizers* in order to mobilize the community as the main *boycotters*. At the first rally several key community leaders attended; but the community as a large, grass roots force was not evident. This time, the goal was to show GM that community support for the Campaign was growing.

Another goal was to increase substantially the media coverage of the movement. The March 1 rally had begun to generate in-depth articles in the print media. The *Reader*, a Los Angeles weekly magazine, ran a full page interview with some of the Campaign leaders, and the *Los Angeles Times* ran a front page Metro section article, "Drive On To Save GM Plant."[5]

The organizers realized that in Los Angeles county, the boycott target area of eight million people, grass roots organizing had to be supplemented by (not *replaced* by) extensive media coverage. The print media were most important for the work with opinion leaders and allowed reprints to be used long after the event. TV coverage of the movement was critical as well, to show GM that no matter how many millions it invested to promote its product and its image, the Campaign could undo a great deal of that with its demonstrations and potential boycott.

In early May, GM announced that it would be calling back the second shift on May 16, the Monday after the scheduled rally. Many of the Campaign organizers were happy about the recall, but skeptical about its permanency. They remembered too well how GM had called back an entire shift of workers at Southgate in the fall of 1981, laid them off two months later, and closed the entire plant four months after that.

But they could also see that, justifiably, many of the laid-off workers were elated about the callback, and that their anger had dissipated quickly after GM's announcement. Some proposed canceling the rally; others argued that the Campaign should take credit for the callback of the second shift and hold a "victory" rally. But the majority of the organizers felt that the first idea fostered a lethal complacency, whereas the second was trying to take credit for a development that was not a product of the Campaign's efforts. The reality was that GM had called back the second shift because market demand had increased for Camaros, not because of the Campaign's activities. But the reality was also that the plant was still in danger and the Campaign was still the best hope of keeping it open. The organizers agreed to go ahead with the May rally, with the theme, "We are glad to be going back to work, but when will the threats stop?"

Once it was explained that the callback did not eliminate the threat to the plant, the community outreach was going very well. After an initial euphoria, many laid-off workers, still eating surplus butter and cheese as they awaited their first paycheck in a long time, understood that the rally was still essential. But new problems within the local had to be solved.

THE WORKERS LEARN ABOUT RED-BAITING

From its inception, the Campaign organizers had tried to enlist the support of the shop-floor committeemen, but with mixed results. Several committeemen were enthusiastic about the Campaign and saw its novel approach as a welcome supplement to their work in enforcing the contract. Many of the leaders of the local's shop committee, however, felt threatened by both the politics and the organizers of the Campaign.

Their differences with the Campaign were a combination of self-interest and union philosophy: they opposed any efforts to directly confront corporate management. Their procompany stance was the product of years of collaboration. The committeemen who were most supportive of the Campaign, such as Mike Velasquez Pete Lopez, and Rick Garcia, were also considered among the most aggressive defenders of the contract, whereas many of the campaign's opponents had used their job as a permanent ticket off the assembly line. They developed cozy relationships with management in which they would "trade off" grievances, getting positive settlements for their political supporters in return for dropping the grievances of workers who were not in their clique. They would travel several times a year to union meetings in Las Vegas and Miami Beach and, under the Quality of Worklife provisions of the contract, would go on trips with company officials to discuss "cooperation." Back in the plant they would accumulate easy overtime with company permission and for some top shop officers their income, through the use of overtime, could almost double that of the average assembler.

While they were threatened by the Campaign, the layoff of the second shift made their direct opposition difficult. The committeemen on the first shift who opposed the Campaign were making $12 an hour, without having to work on the assembly line, while those who were laid off were eating surplus butter and cheese. Directly opposing the Campaign or its organizers would appear too self-serving. But inside the plant, several committeemen began to attack the Campaign as "too radical and not in keeping with union practices."

The conflict escalated dramatically, however, after the March 1 rally. More than thirty worker/organizers, still exhilarated after the last of the crowd had left the union hall, stayed around to sum up the day's events. They grappled with the opportunities and issues raised by the successful rally, including how to respond to the socialist and communist groups that had leafleted and sold their newspapers at the Campaign rally.

Some argued that the local should not allow the groups to sell their newspapers at all, even on the street, because it would associate the Campaign with socialism and communism and turn off many of the Campaign's supporters. Others asserted that the groups had the rights of freedom of speech and press, but the Campaign should have nothing to do with them and should restrict their activities to the sidewalk, which was public property.

One worker argued, however:

> I don't see what's wrong with taking their newspapers. I just saw a film about the women's brigade in the Flint Strike, *With Babies and Banners*. Many of those women who helped to build the UAW said that they used to read socialist and communist papers and, while they didn't agree with everything in them, they learned more about the system and how to change it. I don't see how it would hurt to take the newspapers and see for myself what I think.

Several workers agreed with her view, arguing that just as they read the *Wall Street Journal* and the *Automotive News* without accusations of being capitalists, they should be free to examine socialist literature without accusations of being communists. The lively discussion continued for more than an hour. The Campaign adopted the policy that outside groups could sell their newspapers on the sidewalk, but that during Campaign rallies no groups except the union itself could leaflet in the union hall or its parking lot.

But the discussion did not end in that room. A few people at the meeting who had strong anticommunist views began to systematically spread rumors that all of the workers who had expressed interest in reading socialist literature, and even those who defended their right to, were communists. They proposed that each of the Campaign's twenty-five most active leaders openly admit whether they were socialists, communists, or "Americans." While they picked up little support among the Campaign activists, their "inside information" was seized upon by several anti-Campaign committeemen who then had a more ideological "reason" to justify their opposition.

These McCarthy-like tactics had a destructive impact on the Campaign. The handful of Campaign activists with movement backgrounds--and the greatest interest in socialist ideas--while singled out the most, were also the best prepared for the attacks. "Red-baiting and how to handle it" had been a required course for those in the civil rights and anti-war movements. But for many of the workers for whom the Campaign had been their first political experience, the impact in the short run was devastating.

The main tactic of the red-baiters was to barge into the Campaign office, try to provoke people into a fist fight, and ask people if they were communists or knew that they were being used by communists. Since much of the strength of the Campaign had been the supportive, community-center atmosphere that had been created in the union hall, many workers were discouraged from coming in to work, and the activities of the Campaign ground to a halt.

Temporarily, the Campaign activists retreated to the homes of individual workers, where they held long and searching discussions and began to plan a counter-attack. After a few days, fear turned to anger, as many workers volunteered, "I'm not going to let a few thugs try to destroy all we've worked for."

Many of the workers who had come from Latin America strongly defended the Campaign and their own role in it. The described how, in many Latin American dictatorships, those who opposed the junta or engaged in trade union activity were labeled as communists, tortured, or even murdered. Manuel Hurtado told one of the red-baiters, "I didn't come to this country to be threatened. You have no right to tell me who I should work with and what I should read." Several of the black workers said the "who's a communist game" as they called it, reminded them of J. Edgar Hoover's efforts to undermine the work of Martin Luther King, and they stood up against it. Jake Flukers, one of the initiators of the Campaign, played an important role in defending its politics. Martin Grandy, a worker with seven years in the plant explained:

> If you want to debate communism I would be the first one to oppose it. But I consider myself one of the organizers of this movement and I don't like to see people who are working twelve hours a day to protect my

> job getting attacked for their political beliefs. This Campaign has more different nationalities and political points of view than the United Nations, and if some people in the Campaign believe in socialism, that's their business. I'm starting to get the impression that a few of the committeemen really don't give a damn about capitalism or socialism; they are more interested in keeping their positions than keeping the plant open.[6]

The heart of the issue was whether the Campaign could continue to generate new ideas and strategies, or whether it would begin to recoil into a defensive posture. During this period, Bennett Harrison, a professor at MIT and co-author of *The Deindustrialization of America*, paid a visit to the local, where President Beltran set up a meeting with Harrison and the Campaign activists.

Harrison reported on his recent trip to Europe, where he had studied the approaches of many political parties--Christian Democrats, Socialists, Communists--and the labor unions themselves to issues of plant closings and capital flight. In a long, free-wheeling discussion, the workers asked questions, discussed their own experiences, and compared them to workers in Japan, Mexico, Scandinavia, and Western Europe, all in pursuit of new ideas. Manuel Hurtado observed: "How come when a college professor talks about socialism and capitalism everyone says how smart he is, but when we talk about the same things, people say we are a bunch of communists and threaten to beat us up."

The physical threats were taking their toll. Kelley Jenco explained:

> One night, several women were in the union hall making phone calls to keep people informed about the Campaign. Several committeemen who had had a lot to drink and who hated the Campaign came in. They told us that we "girls" should quit the Campaign, and that since we were single parents it would be a shame if something happened to us and we

> would lose our jobs or get hurt and our kids would be left alone.
>
> My knees were shaking and I had to fight off panic, and then it occurred to me how afraid these guys were of the Campaign. We told them to take their booze and get out of the union hall, and they backed off a little, but we left the hall as soon as we could, and really didn't want to return--which was exactly what they were trying to accomplish. I understood when I joined the Campaign that we would have to fight the company; but fighting our own people and getting threatened in the process--that really hurt.[7]

The Campaign organizers, through late-night discussions with many of their key people, decided to "reoccupy the union hall." Instead of the usual complement of ten activists and five to ten drop-ins working out of the Campaign office, over forty workers showed up each day. After a week of going on the defensive, the Campaign began raising charges of its own. Why were people attacking a Campaign that was trying to keep the plant open, unless they were in collusion with the company? What did threatening people and telling people not to attend the rally have to do with communism? And if some of the leaders of the Campaign *were* communists, why weren't the Baptists and the Catholics, and the other labor unions worried about it? Those who were attacking the Campaign must have other motives.

The willingness of the Campaign organizers to defend their work and to go on the offensive created the conditions for a "unity meeting" with all of the committeemen. Jake Flukers, who was both an alternate committeeman and a Campaign organizer, used his good offices to set up a meeting between the Shop Committee and the Campaign leadership. The two sides sat across from each other in the union hall as if it were a negotiating session between two warring factions.

Many of the committeemen argued that they had nothing against the Campaign, but felt it was an intrusion into their authority. They argued that they were "on the front lines against the company" and yet had never been consulted. Pete Beltran replied that he had brought all the Campaign's activities in front of the executive board which Jerry Shrieves, the shop chairman attended as a member. He argued that, if greater consultation was the only problem, he would personally keep them better informed.

Beltran then asked the committeemen if they would actively support the upcoming rally in May to keep the plant open. Most of them were evasive and noncommittal. The most encouraging development, however, was that Mike Velasquez, an influential first-shift committeeman with over twenty years seniority in the plant, said that in all of his years in the plant, the Campaign was one of the best things the union had ever done and he would continue to support it, 100 percent. Velasquez' testimonial made it more difficult for the Campaign's opponents to polarize the issue as the Campaign *versus* the shop committee.

The peace negotiations, while producing little peace, were another victory for the Campaign. The month-long ordeal had been a growing up process for the Campaign and its organizers. The depth of the personal attacks and the still considerable power of red-baiting within the union movement had dramatically changed the tone of the work--from inspirational enthusiasm to dogged determination. A few of the Campaign's best organizers became discouraged by the ugliness of the attacks and chose to drop out. But the vast majority had confronted and survived a vicious internal battle in the local and had come out stronger and more determined.

While the underlying issues of the conflict did not become apparent at that time, several years later, as this case study will recount, the differences in philosophy and strategy between the two sides in the dispute would emerge full-blown. At that time, however, the Campaign activists were more than happy to move on with their rally preparations.

THE MAY 14,1983 RALLY: THE COMMUNITY STRENGTHENS THE CAMPAIGN

On the day of the rally, the weather was beautiful. The union had made seating arrangements for one thousand people, but as late as 11:30 a.m. (a half-hour before the rally was to start) only a few hundred people had arrived, half of them from the community. Reverend Bagneris approached several of the organizers and said, "I'm sure the folks will eventually show up, but it's funny to me that when they were all laid off they came out two hours early in the rain, and now that the company has called them back they're taking their own sweet time getting here." His observations were on target. That was why the Campaign organizers had paid so much attention to in-depth political discussions with key activists and focused on leadership training. In every movement, large numbers of people will react based on their immediate situation. The goal was to constantly expand the number of workers who understood the movement as a *long-term strategy* and would remain active even when the most overt threats to the plant temporarily subsided.

Although the crowd arrived late, the rally was far larger than the organizers had anticipated--one thousand people. Roughly four hundred were GM workers and their families, and another six hundred were from the community. Eloy Salazar from the Machinists union observed: "Given all the publicity about the second shift being called back, you've built a hell of a solid core in your local." And, of course, what couldn't be shared publicly at the time was that the strong turnout was achieved *despite* organized attacks from within the local.

The rally achieved the objective of demonstrating an impressive show of support from the community. A busload of supporters came from East Los Angeles; another busload of workers came from the shipyard unions in San Pedro more than fifty miles away. A large contingent of black ministers from South Central Los Angeles marched with students from UCLA and laid-off steelworkers from the closed-down Bethlehem steel plant. U.S. Congressman Howard Berman, Assemblywoman Maxine Waters, Reverend Frank Higgins from the Baptist Ministers Conference, and Father Luis Olivares from La Placita Church spoke to the crowd and marched with them down Van Nuys Boulevard, supervised by a caravan of mounted police.

When the marchers returned, Cesar Chavez, the president of the United Farm Workers, addressed the crowd:

> I am pleased to see this union taking the boycott strategy so seriously. General Motors would have you believe that boycotts don't work, but that was what Gallo said, too. Because of the vicious competition in this capitalist society, the boycott can be used as a form of ju jitsu to win your demands. A 5 to 7 percent effectiveness rate, just 5 to 7 percent, can scare the hell out of General Motors and force them to keep this plant open.[8]

After the rally, Chavez told Pete Beltran and some of the Campaign members that too often unions use the threat of a boycott indiscriminately and don't realize the extent of preparation necessary to make it successful. He urged the union's leadership to develop a more scientific plan for how a boycott would actually work in Greater Los Angeles.

The media coverage of the rally exceeded the organizers' expectations. Pictures of the march led by Beltran, Waters, and Chavez became a logo for the movement. The *Los Angeles Times*, *Daily News*, and *Herald-Examiner* all ran major stories. Every television station in Los Angeles covered it extensively, as did the Cable News Network. The *Los Angeles Times* story was the most in-depth analysis and reflected the clarity with which the Campaign had made its point.

Boycott by UAW of GM Threatened

> The United Auto Workers local in Van Nuys threatened Saturday to launch a boycott of General Motors products in California if the world's leading auto maker closes its assembly plant there....To indicate how serious the union is in its campaign, the workers invited Cesar Chavez, president of the United Farm Workers to address their rally....Chavez' union launched a potent boycott against California grape growers a decade ago....The threat of a boycott marked an escalation of an already militant campaign launched by Local 645 to keep the plant open [which] has attracted a broad base of political, union, community and religious support....Attempts by The Times to reach a GM spokesman for comment on the possibility of a boycott were unsuccessful.[9]

Although GM did not respond to the press, the Campaign had achieved a major breakthrough, creating enough media attention that reporters would begin to call GM to ask their response to the boycott threat. If GM's top management in Detroit had not heard about the Campaign prior to May 1983, there was no question that from that day on it had become a cause for their concern.

MAY 16, 1983: THE UAW CONVENTION IN DALLAS

Throughout the early years of the Campaign, a frequently asked question was: "Why isn't your International union doing more to stop these plant closings?" A second question was: "Why isn't your local doing more to get other UAW locals to develop a national strategy against plant closings?"

In answer to both of those questions, Local 645, in addition to its regular elected delegates, sent a five-person delegation from the Campaign to the UAW convention in Dallas which began the day after the rally. The Campaign activists planned to set up a booth to publicize their work, and to use it as a lightening rod to meet other delegates concerned about strategies to stop plant closings.

Their work was helped immeasurably through the work of filmmaker Michal Goldman. Goldman, who was considering a full-length documentary about unions fighting plant closings, agreed to make a "rough-cut" videotape of the May 14 rally. In an impressive display of high-tech electronics combined with old-fashioned perseverance, she managed to direct the film crew on a Saturday, edit all day and night on Sunday, and overnight mail the videotape to Dallas for a Monday arrival. By Tuesday morning, the second day of the UAW convention, the five CAP organizers had set up an information booth and were showing that video to hundreds of delegates. With the help of newly elected West Coast Regional Director Bruce Lee, it was also shown to almost two thousand delegates through dozens of video monitors on the convention floor.

The convention proceedings themselves, however, were very disappointing in terms of the objectives of the Van Nuys organizers. At the International level, the constant theme was the battle against imports and calls for protectionist legislation. While delegates cheered wildly at every verbal assault against Japan, there was no strategy offered with which to confront the Big Three automakers on the issue of capital flight or the widespread problem of whipsawing.

Newly elected UAW president Owen Bieber set a strong tone for demands for higher wages and an end to wage concessions around the theme that the UAW had given enough. While these remarks were cheered by many of the delegates, Pete Kelley, president of UAW Local 160 remarked: "What Bieber isn't saying is how many workers will be left to get the pay raises. They are saying 'No concessions on wages,' but they will let GM get rid of as many of our people as it wants."[10]

Many of the delegates appeared disoriented and dispirited. There was a sense that much more should be done, but few had a clear view of where to go. Unfortunately, the opposition forces didn't offer much of an alternative. Since 1979, beginning with the concessions at Chrysler, there had been considerable disagreement among many local leaders over the strategy of the International union--disagreement that had grown during the 48 percent "no" vote on the GM contract in 1982. The Van Nuys Campaign organizers had hoped that many of those dissident forces would be very sympathetic to a movement that focused on the growing wave of plant closings in the GM system and the danger of another round of closings scheduled a few years in the future.

But at a caucus meeting attended by more than two hundred delegates, the reformers focused their one shot at the International's policies over the issue of "the referendum vote"--the demand to elect International officers through a direct vote of the entire UAW membership, rather than the indirect method of delegate election presently in effect.

On the floor, the debate was lively, but off the mark. The delegates in favor of the referendum vote were trying to argue that the assembled delegates did not really represent the will of the rank and file, and yet they had all been elected by the membership of their own local. More to the point, by focusing on a procedural question--*how* to elect the International officers in a union that everyone admitted was far more democratic than most--they played right into the hands of the International officers by avoiding a major struggle over their *policies*. The fight on the referendum vote had become a ritual in the union and allowed the International officers to let the reformers blow off steam and have a long, essentially democratic debate about how the union wasn't democratic. Then the International could go back to running the union unchallenged for the next three years.

At Dallas, neither the International officers nor the reform delegates raised any agenda debate about a coordinated union strategy against plant closings and the way the Big Three, especially GM, were using plant closings as an instrument of management intimidation. Campaign activist Kelley Jenco, who had come to Dallas hoping to rally local leaders on the issue of plant closings, observed:

> I left the convention very depressed. Even though I had heard a lot of criticisms of the International union, it was hard to believe they could meet for four days and talk about the Japanese and standing up to GM on wages, and not even mention the fight against plant closings. And when they had the band play "Happy Days Are Here Again" I had to pinch myself to see if I was dreaming or having a nightmare.
>
> But I was also very disappointed with the "no concessions" delegates. When we went to their meeting I wondered if we were talking the same language. Many of these guys with secure plants are talking about "no concessions" and "the referendum vote," but they have no program on the issue of plant closings. They know every plant in California has been closed except ours, and yet when I talk to them about the Campaign they seem only vaguely interested because somehow it doesn't affect them directly.[11]

From the perspective of the Campaign organizers, the only positive result of the convention organizing was far greater sympathy from Midwest delegates for a boycott in Los Angeles than had been expected. When the idea of a Los Angeles-wide boycott was first proposed, several critics both within the UAW and the labor movement argued that it was not a good tactic because it would hurt "brothers and sisters" in other GM plants across the country who might suffer layoffs if the boycott was successful. Besides the fact that none of these critics could offer any alternatives, and had done nothing to stop the other five California plants from being closed, their views were not supported by most of the UAW delegates with whom the Van Nuys people spoke. As one delegate expressed it:

> It was great seeing your video. I realize that you're gonna have a heck of a time taking on GM alone, but I don't see much support around here for taking them on together, so you really have no choice. The way I see it, if GM tries to close you down and you try a boycott, most of the locals will support you. They won't help you much, but they'll support you.
>
> As far as your boycott hurting us, I think we can handle it. Since you're boycotting all of GM's products, you'll just hurt each plant a little bit. The main thing is that the other plants will be happy somebody is trying something.[12]

Over the course of the convention, more than two hundred delegates watched the video of the Van Nuys movement, and the Campaign representatives had in-depth conversations with more than one hundred of them. Based on those discussions, they left Dallas convinced that at least in the short run, a united movement within the UAW to keep plants open was not possible. They went back to Van Nuys convinced that setting an example in one region of the country might be the most effective step toward saving their own plant and impacting the UAW as a whole.

NOTES

1. Eric Mann, "What GM Owes the Freeway Capital," *Los Angeles Times*, Opinion section, April 17, 1983, p. 5.
2. Leaflet to the membership for Campaign rally, March 1, 1983.
3. The best coverage of the March 1 rally was provided by *El Popo*, the Chicano Studies newspaper at California State University at Northridge. See the article, "UAW Workers Battle Shutdown," March-April 1983, p. 1.
4. Interview with the author, March 11, 1987.
5. Henry Weinstein, "Drive On To Save GM Plant," *Los Angeles Times*, Metro section, February 28, 1983, p. 1; Jonathan Tasini, "Interview with Eric Mann," *Reader*, March 4, 1983, p. 19.
6. Remarks made at house meetings, May 1983 (confirmed March 1, 1987).
7. Interview with the author, March 1, 1987.
8. Speech to rally, May 14, 1983. Chavez' comments are also recorded in the film, *Tiger By the Tail*, by Michal Goldman.
9. Henry Weinstein, "Boycott by UAW of GM Threatened," *Los Angeles Times*, Metro section, May 15, 1983, p. 1.
10. Interview with the author, May 18, 1983.
11. Interview with the author, June 1983.
12. Conversation with delegate from Norwood, Ohio.

Chapter Seven

COALITION BUILDING: RECRUITING ALLIES AND ANSWERING QUESTIONS

Several years after its inception, the Campaign's coalition was impressive and broad. But the diverse coalition was not easily assembled and, in the process of organizing, many political questions had to be resolved to both attract people to the coalition and keep them involved. Several examples will illustrate the complexity of the process and some of the elements of the Campaign's organizing strategy.

RECRUITING ALLIES

The Involvement of the Black Community

As noted earlier, for many years Van Nuys was overwhelmingly Chicano and white, with a very small black workforce. The majority of the early black workers originally did not come from South Central Los Angeles (where the Southgate plant had been located) but from the nearby communities of San Fernando, North Hollywood, Pacoima, and Lakeview Terrace. But if the boycott threat was to be substantial, significant institutions in Los Angeles' downtown black community had to be involved--a community that was more than forty miles from the plant. While there were 40,000 black residents in the Valley, Los Angeles' black population was 944,000 in 1980 (and an estimated 1.2 million in 1987).[1]

The process of community involvement began in one of the first workshops during the layoff. Each worker filled out a form which included the questions: "What voluntary organizations do you belong to. Can we bring the Campaign to your church, community group or social club?" Dorothy Travis, one of the first black women to enter a skilled trades apprenticeship program and an early activist in the Campaign, proposed talking with her own pastor, Reverend Robert Davis of the St. Peter's Rock Missionary Baptist Church in South Central Los Angeles. When Travis and Eric Mann met with Reverend Davis, he was very sympathetic to the idea of the Campaign, and the boycott. He soon volunteered that before becoming the pastor of the Church he had been an autoworker and UAW member at the Pico Rivera plant, and had seen the impact of the closing on his fellow workers. He proposed that they attend the next meeting of the Baptist Ministers Conference to enlist the support of the group.

In order to address the full body, however, there was a procedure involved. A prospective speaker had to first address the "fraternal relations" committee, make a presentation to the group, and then the committee would recommend to the full body whether one should speak and, if so, for how many minutes.

When Mann began to make his presentation to the group, however, one of the clergy angrily interrupted: "Why should we support all of you? You are all up in the Valley where those folks didn't want to even go to school with our kids. You did nothing to support us when they closed Southgate, but now you come asking for our help." The outrage that he expressed at the idea that a union with any ties to the racist "Bus-Stop" group would have the nerve to ask for their support was legitimate, and had to be addressed before it could be dispelled.

Reverend Davis rose to the Campaign's defense. He explained that while their view of the Valley was virtually all white, in fact, one of his parishioners, Dorothy Travis, had first brought the Campaign to him; that many of the workers were black and Chicano and, from what he knew of the whites in the UAW, they were strongly opposed to racism.

Mann explained that an opposition to racism was a central element of the Campaign and explained that his local worked against Bobbi Fiedler (a "Bus-Stop" founder) in every election. He stated that he had worked at the Southgate plant before it was closed and it was the inaction of the local's president and the International union that had created the negative example that the Campaign was trying to correct. More to the point, almost one thousand workers at Van Nuys were former Southgate workers, many of whom lived in South Central Los Angeles, who needed the Conference's help to prevent GM from closing them out once again.

The fraternal relations members seemed satisfied with those explanations and voted to allow Mann to speak for three minutes. Armed with a better understanding of the legitimate concerns raised in the Fraternal Relations committee, he addressed those issues directly in his presentation to the assembly of more than one hundred Baptist ministers. The Conference's president, Reverend Frank Higgins, was enthusiastic about the cause. He established a special "Keep Van Nuys Open" committee under his leadership, with Reverend William Coleman as its coordinator, that would become a major element in the Campaign coalition.

At the time, Reverend Coleman was the pastor of a small church in South Central Los Angeles, the Good Samaritan Baptist Church. Once a year his church held "Family Day," in which the members of the congregation would entertain each other, with whole families performing gospel songs. Several members of the UAW local were invited, and attended, the most prominent of whom was Nate Brodsky, a Russian Jew by ancestry, but a Baptist by conversion. Brodksy, a gifted singer, sang, "Sweet Hour of Prayer" to an appreciative, if somewhat bemused, audience. Over the years, close political friendships developed between several of the Campaign leaders and those of the Baptist Ministers Conference, and the Baptists became the cornerstone of the Campaign's growing support in the black community--a process that began with the connection between an autoworker and her pastor.

The Involvement of the Business Community

A visible Chamber of Commerce presence in a labor-initiated coalition defied many stereotypes; but the combination of an objective mutual interest and relationships developed with some far-sighted local business leaders made it possible.

Early in the Campaign, one of the GM workers, Ron Sebesta, kept pressuring the leadership to pay more attention to the Chamber of Commerce. Sebesta, a former GM Fremont worker, was business oriented, and felt that the Chamber would give the Campaign both legitimacy in some circles and greater clout with GM. Sebesta contacted Bruce Ackerman, Executive Director of the Van Nuys Chamber. Through their dialogue, Ackerman explained that he did not want to identify too closely with the Campaign or the UAW local and definitely would not advocate the boycott. Still, he initiated a letter campaign from his own members, expressing their concern about the possible closing of the plant. Dozens of letters were sent to GM Chairman Roger Smith by Van Nuys Chamber of Commerce members expressing their concern about the future of the plant.

In 1985, an unexpected turn of events brought the Campaign and local business leaders into even closer alliance. As the plant reopened after model change in September 1985, a hastily installed new paint system caused odors to be emitted into the nearby community. Angry local residents complained to political leaders who in turn asked the South Coast Air Quality Management District (AQMD) to hold hearings on the matter. While many environmentalists felt that AQMD was sympathetic to business and quite lenient on matters of air pollution, GM was justifiably worried. An order to cease production until the problem was remedied could cause production delays of several weeks with an attendant loss of profits.

GM was aware, however, that a pure power play, or a transparently self-interested argument in front of the AQMD might backfire. A more sophisticated approach was in order. GM sent letters to hundreds of local businesses, urging them to attend the AQMD hearings, not on GM's behalf, but on their own. GM argued that if the plant was closed, not only would GM lose profits, but so would local businesses. The plant was not merely GM's private property but, according to a report by the United Chambers of Commerce of the San Fernando Valley which was encouraged by GM, "a vital and integral part of the San Fernando Valley community since its opening in 1947." GM even approached, and coached, several autoworkers to testify as to the personal devastation to them and their families that would result from a closing.

GM won a tactical victory. The corporation was able to win several extensions from the AQMD, built taller smokestacks to dissipate the odor, got experts to testify that while the odor was noxious it was not dangerous, and eventually was able to win a dismissal of the complaint.

But GM had also been forced to make a theoretical concession to the Campaign in the process of winning that short-run victory. As Bruce Ackerman explained:

> GM did an incredible job of community mobilizing. And GM knew full well what it was doing, it was supporting every major premise of the Keep GM Open Coalition, building a powerful case for plant permanency. I have to be encouraged that GM now plans to stay in Van Nuys. For if they try to leave now, there can only be a terrible backlash among many politicians, community groups and business people who came to GM's defense.[2]

David Miller, the President of the United Chambers who was instrumental in preparing the impact report, became an outspoken advocate of the Campaign's objectives. Miller explained:

> Some of my members are uneasy about what appears to be such a close working relationship with a union, especially one as militant as Local 645. But I explain to them that it is a sound business decision. My job is to protect the investments and the businesses of our members, and a plant closure in Van Nuys would be devastating to the business community. In that context, I have the full support of my members.[3]

The relationship with the chambers of commerce proved to be another critical element of the coalition. Like the initial outreach to the black community, it developed out of the initiative of an autoworker who brought his ideas to the Campaign.

Chicanos and Mexicanos:
Building Unity Among the Workers Themselves

While it is often generalized that the plant's population is 50 percent Chicano, in fact, there are many different groups among its Latino population, the most prominent of which are Chicanos and Mexicanos. Understanding that distinction was essential to building a strong movement within the plant.

Chicanos are Americans of Mexican origin who were born in the United States, many having lived and worked in the United States for many generations and many with roots in parts of the United States that were originally part of Mexico. Mexicanos refers to first generation Mexican immigrants, many of whom have worked in the plant for decades.

Walking into the plant, there are many signs of the intermingling of Latino cultures. Workers sell authentic Mexican food made by their wives. After the shift, Van Nuys workers from Oxnard, California, an agricultural community fifty miles north of the plant, sell corn and cucumbers from the back of their pickup trucks. On the assembly line and in the cafeteria, many conversations are in Spanish. The vast majority of the Chicano and

Mexicano workers are bilingual, with Spanish the preferred language of many.

During the second-shift layoff, a dozen workers, most of whom were Mexicanos, led by Manuel Hurtado and Jose Silva, formed a committee specializing in outreach to the Latino community. These workers participated in the Campaign's plenary meetings, which were held in English, and then broke up into their own group that met in Spanish.

The Mexicano workers were adamant that all the Campaign's materials should be provided in Spanish as well as English, but some of the Chicano workers did not agree. For example, when the Campaign buttons were first printed, some buttons said, "Keep GM Van Nuys Open!" and others said, "Mantenga GM Van Nuys Abierta!" One Chicano committeeman who was bilingual said, "Why are we printing some of those buttons in Spanish?" He elaborated:

> When I first got active in the union I used to speak in Spanish at some of the union meetings, and people would say, "Sit down and shut up and learn English." Now I was born in this country and I speak English better than Spanish, but I was just being proud to be a Chicano and I wanted them to hear me speak Spanish. But then I got tired of hearing all that abuse. I don't mind other people wearing the Spanish buttons, but I don't want one. I think it's best for the Campaign if we keep everything in English.

The Mexicanos, however, saw it differently. They argued that they were proud to be part of the Campaign and proud of its democratic structure. Every two weeks the Campaign held plenary meetings involving from 75 to 150 workers, at which all major decisions were made. The Latino activists argued that, in practice, because the meetings were held in English, they were prevented from impacting the overall direction of the Campaign. As Hurtado explained, "I spend all week on the phone getting people to come to the meetings, and then when they get there everything is in English and they walk out. It will be hard to get them back if we don't do something different."

Hurtado, Silva, and others proposed that the local purchase headphones and provide an interpreter at all major meetings of the local. The Spanish-speaking workers argued that their own efforts at simultaneous translation were unsuccessful because few workers were skilled translators and the noise of two languages going at once disrupted the meeting and made them feel self-conscious. Instead, they proposed a United Nations approach in which the workers would wear headphones and a skilled interpreter would keep them informed.

They brought their demand to the executive board of the local. In addressing the board, Manuel Hurtado explained his dilemma:

> This situation is very difficult for me. When I speak in Spanish and someone translates for me, many times I do not feel the translation is very good. People make it too short and leave out many of the points I said in Spanish. When I speak in English my English is not very good, so people think that I am not intelligent and they don't listen to me. At least with the headphones we can understand what is happening and make a contribution to the meetings.

Hurtado, Silva, and Santos Murguia organized more than fifteen workers to attend the meeting and to lobby the board members. The motion to purchase twenty-five sets of headphones and to use union funds to provide translation passed unanimously. The workers were learning that active members could impact the executive board through preparing motions, getting sympathetic board members to present them, and bringing rank and file members to attend the meetings. Even without a vote, an organized membership group could impact the board's decisions. The motion then came before the General Membership meeting the following week, as all motions must, according to the local by-laws; and it was also passed by the rank and file.

In practice, the headphones were not always an effective solution to the problem. At smaller meetings it was not always feasible to find a translator. But at the larger meetings, the headphones were a major breakthrough. For example, at an October 1983 mass meeting that will be described later in the narrative, a long table of Spanish-speaking garment workers and auto workers listened attentively and participated, with help from two professional translators. The headphones had become both a mechanism and a symbol of the Mexicano workers' fight for equality in the coalition.

Relations Between White Workers and Minority Workers: Can Working Class Unity Be Colorblind?

The Campaign organizers tried to walk a difficult line--to highlight the strategic importance of the Chicano and black communities without falling into neglect of the experiences and contributions of the white workers. While the role of minority workers and minority communities was critical, the active involvement of the white workers was also essential if the Campaign was to succeed.

Some of the white workers, a numerical minority in the plant, pointed to the predominance and visibility of Chicano union officials and questioned why the Campaign needed to accentuate the role of minority communities. They felt they had come a long way to understand the commonality of all workers; why place so much emphasis on their differences?

Some political leftists concurred with these sentiments, arguing that, while discrimination was a problem, it was best to downplay issues of nationality within the working class. In particular, they disagreed with placing so much emphasis on the fact that the plant's workforce was more than 50 percent Chicano and 15 percent black. They argued that the threat to the Van Nuys plant was a "class issue," and the plant closing would be an attack on the working class. Highlighting the racial aspects of the struggle would only "divide the working class," they contended.

Other organizers, including this author, argued that, while it could be divisive to place *too* much emphasis on questions of race and nationality or to lay the blame for society's racism on the white workers, racial divisions in the working class already existed and would not go away by ignoring them. They pointed out that, throughout much of the nation's history (and much of the history of the U.S. labor movement), many white workers and their unions had been unwilling to oppose racist practices by the employers, and at times had instituted racist practices of their own in their unions. A reading of the UAW's own history indicated that the union was strongest when it actively addressed issues of discrimination. For example, when the UAW successfully organized the Ford Motor Company in 1941, it did so only after paying far greater attention to the concerns of black workers and promising to "address the blacks' intense dissatisfaction because the UAW-CIO had made such negligible efforts to destroy discrimination at companies like GM."[4]

Learning from that history, they argued that, despite the generally good relationship between Chicano, black, and white workers on the Van Nuys assembly line, any efforts to deny the strategic importance of the civil rights implications of the plant closing (in an effort to placate the real or imagined fears of some white workers) was not educating workers in class solidarity. Worse, it underestimated the political consciousness and open-mindedness of many white workers to the fight against racism. Thus, Campaign literature tried to point out that a closing at Van Nuys would be a devastating blow to workers of all ethnicities; but with Los Angeles unemployment rates at 6.6 percent for whites, 9.5 percent for Latinos, and 12.3 percent for blacks, the special problems of minority workers made the social costs of the plant closing even greater for them.[5]

But the argument for highlighting the civil rights aspect of the Campaign was not made to white workers primarily by pointing out that minority workers were more oppressed than they were; although true, that would tend to downplay their own very real suffering and exploitation and their own valid reasons for fighting back. Rather, the role of minority movements was explained in *strategic terms*, emphasizing that the strength of the Chicano and black communities was essential for workers of all nationalities (including the white workers) to keep the plant open. Thus, the Campaign framed the issues of class and race in a way that would allow white workers to understand the racial and national sentiments of minority workers and to see them as a positive factor in their own struggle to save their plant, their union, and their own jobs.

Based on this outlook, one Campaign leaflet asked: "If you care about the maintenance of 5,000 jobs in the San Fernando Valley, if you care about stopping a plant closing before it happens, it you care about the problems of Chicano and black workers, come to the rally on May 14 [1983]." Several committeemen who were opposed to the Campaign took the last phrase out of context and tried to argue that the Campaign did not care about white workers. They told white workers in the plant that the Campaign only cared about Chicanos and blacks, and told Chicano and black workers who were not active in the Campaign that its organizers were "using" the minority issue to divide the union.

After rereading the leaflet, the Campaign organizers agreed that, given a group of opponents ready to seize upon any unclear formulations, their language had not been well chosen. Pete Beltran was especially concerned that the efforts to reach out to the Chicano community be made in a way that was not seen as excluding the white workers.

In future leaflets, references to concern about the loss of jobs in the Chicano and black communities were changed to: "We are workers of all nationalities, white, black, Chicano, and Asian, and we are all concerned about the civil rights implications of closing down a predominantly minority plant." By specifically mentioning the white workers as part of the working class, and by arguing that it was white workers as well as minority workers who were concerned about the special problems of minority communities, the Campaign was able to reach out to the white workers more effectively. Through dozens of leaflets and scores of conversations initiated by Campaign organizers, many white workers came to believe that greater working class unity could be built by confronting, rather than avoiding, issues of discrimination, race, and racism.

As the Campaign evolved, a certain comfortableness about race and class developed that reflected a political generosity and class consciousness on the part of many of the leaders. Ed Asner ended his speeches with the chant, "*El pueblo unido jamas sera vencido*: The people united will never be defeated." Father Luis Olivares spoke about the historical significance of the Campaign not only for the Chicano community, but also for the working class as a whole, and took particular efforts to commend *all* of the workers for the historic roles they were playing. Reverend Higgins, with strong roots in the black community, told the workers: "You know, I am very angry at General Motors for what they have done to the black community, but I want you to understand that this a human rights issue, a workers' issue, not just a black issue, and I am here to fight for *all* of your welfare."[6]

Many of the white workers came to observe that the emphasis on racial pride and national identity was not a form of exclusion but a way to strengthen the coalition. Moreover, it was not just a self-interested formula, but a social issue that appealed to their best instincts and gave their cause a greater nobility. Nate Brodsky, Kelley Jenco, Chris Dorval, Marty Grandy, Jackie Marshall, Robert Garrett, John Fontes, Ron Sebesta, Nancy Thomas, and many other white workers, became outspoken opponents of racial injustice and played leadership roles in the Campaign.

Throughout the Campaign, the decisive organizing premise was that, in building a coalition as broad as was needed, the contradictions and conflicts between workers and small business owners, between minority and white workers, between Mexicans and Chicanos were not unfortunate obstacles, but were inevitable and objective problems in the society at large. The role of the organizers was to develop equitable policies to resolve those contradictions. The process of understanding peoples' legitimate interests and concerns, and working out the types of compromises necessary to keep people in the coalition, without sacrificing the strategic thrust of the Campaign itself, allowed Baptist ministers, Chamber of Commerce leaders, and Spanish- and English-speaking Latino workers to join together to keep the plant open.

QUESTIONS AND ANSWERS

To win the support of community leaders--people with strong views, strong self-conceptions, and many other causes competing for their limited time and energy--it was necessary to enter into a process of dialogue and even constructive debate. In the process of developing political relationships with opinion leaders throughout Los Angeles, the Campaign organizers came to better understand that "organizing" is a two-way street. In discussions with Father Luis Olivares, Congressman Howard Berman, Reverend Frank Higgins, Professor Rudy Acuña, Chamber of Commerce presidents David Miller and Bruce Ackerman, and many Van Nuys autoworkers, their questions, concerns, and, at times, disagreements helped to modify and refine the Campaign's strategy.

As Campaign activists from the plant returned from meetings with leaders of the Catholic Archdiocese, the Democratic Party, the Mexican American Political Association (MAPA), the National Association for the Advancement of Colored People (NAACP), the International Association of Machinists (IAM), and the United Teachers of Los Angeles (UTLA), a common set of questions began to surface that had to be answered if the movement was to advance.

"You say that GM should practice social responsibility and should not close down your plant. But given Japanese competition, won't too much emphasis on social responsibility keep U.S. companies inefficient, which will only lead to more layoffs and plant closings anyway?"

GM can well afford to stay in Van Nuys, and stay there quite profitably, if not as profitably as it might like. GM, if it ever closes the plant, will argue that it was "forced to" by market factors, specifically shipping costs.

To begin with, if the plant was not profitable, why was GM manufacturing 175,000 to 200,000 vehicles a year? Obviously, there were substantial profits being made at Van Nuys. GM claimed that producing a Camaro in Van Nuys as opposed to a Midwest location added several hundred dollars in shipping costs (a claim the Campaign would later contest as exaggerated). But this was an argument for why *greater* profits might be gained elsewhere, not why it was unprofitable to produce cars at Van Nuys.

If GM wanted to, it could reduce those shipping costs while still keeping the plant open. The more cars sold on the west coast, the less shipping costs are a factor. For example, if a car is assembled in the Midwest and shipped to California, or if the parts of the car are shipped to California and then assembled, the cost to GM is essentially the same as long as the car is sold on the West Coast. The cost problem develops when too many cars have to be "back shipped" from Los Angeles over the Rocky Mountains.

To address this problem, the Campaign has demanded that GM diversify the model mix, that is, make several different car models in the Van Nuys plant. In that way, a greater percentage of the cars produced in the plant could be sold on the West Coast.

Also, the West Coast market, although a highly competitive one, offers significant opportunities for GM sales. The GM Van Nuys plant produced approximately 170,000 vehicles in 1986. In that same year, GM sold over 403,000 cars and trucks in California, and over 646,000 vehicles in the western states.[7] It is hard to believe that GM cannot figure out how to operate one West Coast plant successfully with a built-in market of over 646,000 units.

In short, GM, with all the problems that have been documented, is still a company that declared more than $2 billion in profits in 1984 and 1985, and Van Nuys is a profitable plant in the largest new-car market in the United States. It is not GM's demand for profits, but its demand for *maximum* profits that is being opposed.

"But that reasoning is naive. Maximum profits are not just amassed for personal gain. They are essential to investment and new technology. If every GM plant was restricted by some quasi-socialist concept of "fair profits," there would be no capital formation, no expansion, no technological innovation, no money to cover downturns in the economy or misassessments by management. The bottom line of your Campaign, if extended to other GM plants, would lead to the decline of the corporation."

This point has been raised since the advent of capitalism, and gets closer to the heart of the controversy. Historically, reformers and social activists have demanded strict limits on profits while business theorists have argued that the drive for maximum profits is essential to economic growth. Obviously, high profits can serve certain beneficial objectives, but there is no ironclad formula as to what is "maximum profitability." In fact, in almost every instance, the "maximum" profit a corporation can amass is curtailed by social as well as market factors.

For example, many corporations go into Third World countries and amass such high rates of profit that they abandon production in their own country. When later faced with social revolution abroad and possible expropriation of their assets, these companies, after having opposed the revolution unsuccessfully, try to reach accommodations with the new government. Frequently, an agreement is reached in which the American company, with its technical expertise, is allowed to stay, but only after agreeing to a higher rate of taxation, the training of native management, and a lower rate of profit. These corporations survive and frequently prosper under the new restrictions.

While arguing for maximum profitability, Alfred P. Sloan, an immensely practical man, understood the need for flexibility.

> Competition is the final price determinant and competitive prices may result in profits which force you to accept a rate of return less than you hoped for, or for that matter, to accept temporary losses.[8]

Obviously, while Sloan was referring to the pricing policies of his competitors, there are many other factors that force corporations to "accept a rate of return less than you hoped for," such as regulations governing air pollution, corporate income tax rates, and union wage demands. In the case of Van Nuys, if GM came to believe that the possibility of a successful boycott was a business risk they did not want to provoke, it might decide to accept profit levels that were lower than hoped for but nonetheless quite substantial.

"Obviously it would be better if your plant remained open. But how serious are the consequences if the plant actually closes? What are the social costs of a closing at Van Nuys?"

Endless studies have been done on the impact of plant closings on industrial workers. Their findings are invariably grim. A Bureau of Labor Statistics report, *Displaced Workers of 1979-1983*, surveyed 5.1 million workers who had been on the job at least three years before being let go. The study found that a year later two million workers had not found new jobs; and, of the three million who had, nearly half were earning less than on their previous job.[9]

The Campaign organizers, while utilizing this information when appropriate, did so with great caution. For, in the antilabor political climate of the times, data on the devastating impact of plant closings were used, at best, as an argument for maintaining woefully inadequate services for laid-off workers and, at worst, as an object lesson with which to terrorize those workers who were still employed.

"The worker as victim" was a concept the Campaign came across in all its work and angrily and aggressively worked to combat. As a result, the Campaign consciously, and in retrospect correctly, avoided many discussions of "what would happen if the plant closed." As Nate Brodsky explained:

> What the hell do these middle-class people think is going to happen if the plant closes? That we'll all become yuppies and move to Palm Springs? That General Motors will let us all hang out by Roger Smith's swimming pool? That's why we don't call it a "plant closings movement." The plant is open and we damn well intend to keep it open.

This aggressive posture was adopted by virtually all the Campaign activists, although for some, only after bitter experiences. Kelley Jenco explained:

> During the 1982 layoff, we did a lot of interviews with TV reporters. One guy wanted to come to my house and do a "personal" profile. So I went on and on about the Campaign and how good I felt about fighting back and how I needed my job back and about the boycott. And he asked me a few questions about Joe and Lisa and how we were making out, and I explained how hard it was and then went back to talking about our rallies and marches.
>
> So when the show came on, this guy said, "Here is a story about a poor laid-off woman with two kids who can barely support her family," and I started yelling into the TV, "Hey, that's not what the story was supposed to be about. It was supposed to be about the damn Campaign. That's not what I said."
>
> From that point on, I would never talk to a reporter about any of my personal problems. When reporters would ask, "What will you do if the plant closes?" I would always answer, "The plant isn't going to close. We're gonna keep it open."[10]

In actuality, very few community groups asked many questions about "the social consequences of a closure at Van Nuys." The workers felt that if, by the mid-1980s, with the closure of so many plants in Los Angeles, people couldn't visualize what it would be like for 5,000 autoworkers to permanently lose their jobs, there was little chance they would take action to help the Campaign. But more than that, it was the workers' political decision that an aggressive, confident stance--"the worker as organizer, the worker as fighter, the UAW taking on General Motors," and *not* "the worker as victim"--that would attract the allies necessary to challenge the corporation.

There was one set of figures, however, that the Campaign activists did quote--the economic impact of the closing prepared by the United Chambers of Commerce of the San Fernando Valley. Those figures did not isolate the autoworkers' problems from those of the community but, rather, showed that a closure at Van Nuys would be economically devastating not just to the workers at Van Nuys, but to the entire San Fernando Valley. According to the report, a closure at Van Nuys would have the following consequences:

- The loss of 5,000 manufacturing and white collar jobs with an annual payroll of $157 million.
- The loss of 34.952 nonmanufacturing jobs through the ripple effect.
- Closure of 514 retail establishments.
  The loss of $290.4 million in annual retail sales.
- The loss of $2.3 million in annual bank deposits.
- The loss of $532.5 million in annual personal income.
- The relocation of 108,414 local residents making up 49,858 families.
- The removal of 40,606 children from the public schools.[11]

"We understand that many of the workers are Chicano. But you can't make everything into a civil rights issue. What is the significance of the closure for the Chicano community?"

The Van Nuys plant's workforce is over 50 percent Latino, most of whom are Chicanos. Coalition member Rudy Acuña, professor of Chicano Studies at California State University at Northridge, explained:

> For more than a decade, I have taught Chicano youth at Northridge, many of whom are children of Van Nuys auto workers. I know one worker who was able to send seven children to college at Northridge on his modest wages. Autoworkers are active in improving the public schools, they are active in the Democratic party, and they provide the backbone for many community organizations. The closing of the plant would undermine a critical, stabilizing force in the Chicano community--the Chicano autoworker.[12]

On the economic level, displaced Chicano autoworkers would have a more difficult time finding future employment. While the California unemployment rate for white workers is quite high, 6.6 percent, the rate for "Hispanics" is substantially higher, 9.5 percent.[13]

Politically, the consequences of the closure to the Chicano community would be even more serious. During the United Farm Workers boycott of Gallo wine, for example, the UAW in California and many of its Chicano elected officials played a critical role in the success of that campaign. The Mexican American Political Association has many UAW members, as do most voluntary organizations in the Chicano community. The closing of the Ford Milpitas and Mack Truck plants (as well as the permanent layoff of more than half the GM Fremont workers) in northern California, and the Southgate and Pico Rivera plants in Los Angeles, all of which had many Chicanos in the leadership of their union locals, has significantly weakened the grass roots strata of

Chicano leaders in the state. Stripped of their union base, these talented men and women have survived and at times prospered individually, but have rarely been able to continue their active involvement at the same level, or with the same organizational clout.

But it is not just a question of "Chicanos" in the abstract. The Van Nuys plant is the home of UAW Local 645, one of the most influential union locals in the city. Under Pete Beltran's leadership, the local has supported campaigns to protect the rights of Latin American immigrants, has launched successful organizing drives to organize primarily Latino workers in nearby sweat-shops, and has provided support for virtually every Latino organization in the city. The loss of UAW Local 645 would be a blow to Los Angeles' Latino community of over 3 million people. That is why the organized representatives and leaders of that community have committed themselves to protect the Van Nuys plant and its workers.

"I can understand the significance of Chicanos to the Van Nuys plant, but how can you expect significant support from the black community? I don't see the connection."

In 1985, the twentieth anniversary of the Watts uprisings, almost every Los Angeles television station was clever enough to do a special based on that "angle." The findings were frightening. Black community leaders explained that immediately after the uprising there had been an infusion of government money and social programs--job training, Head-start preschool programs, health care--that had made some actual improvements in people's living standards. However, beginning in the late 1970s, after a brief period of better job opportunities for blacks, there was a significant decline in black employment. The heart of the problem was the closing of heavy industrial plants in South Central Los Angeles--Goodyear and Firestone Rubber, Bethlehem Steel, and the GM plant at Southgate. These companies had provided some of the best-paying jobs in the city for black workers, and the community still has not recovered from those closings.

Many black workers with over ten years seniority, under the terms of the GM-UAW contract, were given "guaranteed income stream" (GIS) income protection benefits when the Southgate plant closed. But a stipulation of the benefit was that workers had to accept employment at any GM plant in the country, or forfeit their benefits. The specter of grown men and women with twenty years seniority being forced to relocate to Wentzville, Missouri, or Shreveport, Louisiana, was explained by one black worker:

> I thought slavery was over. But GM still owns me. I own a house, I have a family, but when GM says "move," I move or I lose my house, my income, and maybe my family. And if I go, I live in an apartment by myself while my family stays back in California. Either way, the pressures on our families are enormous.

As attrition continued at the Van Nuys plant, many workers came back from exile to join other former Southgate workers at Van Nuys. By 1986 there were more than one thousand former Southgate workers at Van Nuys, when both shifts were working, many of whom were black. If Van Nuys is closed as well, they will have suffered through two plant closings.

Reverend Frank Higgins, president of the Baptist Ministers Conference, sees Van Nuys as a test case:

> When Southgate closed down, I don't know why people didn't respond, but they didn't. When Goodyear and Firestone closed down, nobody did anything. But this time, we have organized in advance, and General Motors cannot insult the community two times and get away with it. If Van Nuys closes, the boycott is on. Otherwise, these closings will never stop.[14]

The ability of the Campaign organizers to provide convincing answers to those questions helped to expand the base of the coalition. But for many of the participants there was only one question they needed answered: "*Could the boycott work?*"

NOTES

1. Figures are based on the 1980 Federal Census, provided by demographics consultant James Wisely.
2. Eric Mann, "LA Could Lose Valley Auto Plant, "*Los Angeles Times*, Opinion section, January 26, 1986, p. 3.
3. Interview with the author, June 18, 1987.
4. August Meier and Elliott Rudwick, *Black Detroit and the Rise of the UAW* (New York: Oxford University Press, 1979), p. 101. The UAW later came to be one of the most progressive unions on the issue of race. The point made is simply that racial unity within the union cannot be achieved without a constant vigilance against racism.
5. Figures based on 1985 Los Angeles County unemployment statistics provided by the California State Employment Development Department labor market analyst.
6. Statement at meeting to plan May 14, 1983 rally, UAW Union Hall, February 1983.
7. Market figures provided by *Automotive News, "1985 Market Data Book,"* April 24, 1985. Updated by Christopher Cedergren, Senior Analyst, J.D. Powers and Associates.
8. Alfred P. Sloan, Jr., *My Years With General Motors* (Garden City, N.J.: Anchor Books, 1972), p. 160.
9. Leonie Sandercock and John Friedmann, "Economic Restructuring and Community Dislocation," Graduate School of Architecture and Urban Planning, University of California, Los Angeles, 1985, p. 7.
10. These statements were made in a series of Campaign meetings evaluating community and media outreach in February 1983.
11. Impact report prepared by United Chambers of Commerce of the San Fernando Valley, as quoted in "Community Leaders Rejoice," *Daily News*, November 7, 1986, p. 1.
12. Rodolfo Acuña, interview with Michal Goldman for *Tiger By the Tail*, October 22, 1983.

13. U.S. Department of Labor, Bureau of Labor Statistics. Figures provided by the Department of Employment Data and Research, State of California.
14. Remarks to UAW rally, October 22, 1983.

Chapter Eight

THE GM BOYCOTT: SUBSTANTIAL OR IDLE THREAT?

The essence of the Campaign's boycott strategy was quite straightforward: Since the Van Nuys plant was already profitable and GM's objective in closing it was to achieve a higher rate of profit elsewhere, the goal of the movement was to convince GM management that the closing the plant in pursuit of those additional profits would be a disastrous economic and political decision.

In so many situations, however, threats such as strikes or boycotts are raised but rarely materialize. Since so much of the Campaign focused on one simple question--Could the boycott work?--a great deal of thought went into that answer. For, if opinion leaders in the city who were sympathetic to the Campaign did not believe it was a viable threat, there was no chance that Genral Motors would. What follows is a detailed description of the boycott strategy, divided into four categories: (1) GM's vulnerability to a boycott; (2) GM's weaknesses and the Campaign's strengths in Los Angeles; (3) the economic viability of the Campaign's boycott strategy; and (4) the Coalition's capability of carrying out a boycott if that became necessary.

GM'S VULNERABILITY TO A BOYCOTT

Some products are more susceptible to a boycott than others. Unlike steel, which has no direct consumer market, and unlike ballpoint pens, of which millions are sold but each boycotter can only deny the company a few cents profit per item, automobiles are both significant and expensive consumer products.

Each customer who supports the boycott and actually buys another product instead of a GM model takes away from $500 to $5,000 in profits and will not be available again as a consumer for five years or more.

In past generations, customer brand loyalty was very high; entire families drove Chevrolets almost as a religious principle. But today's new-car buyers are "shoppers," walking along "auto rows" where GM, Ford, Chrysler, Datsun, Toyota, Mazda, American Motors, Volkswagen, and Honda dealers are all competing for their attention. A survey of new-car buyers in Los Angeles indicated that nearly 75 percent of them replaced their cars with a different make and 60 percent spent at least three weeks "seriously looking" for a new car.[1]

Cars are not sold in thousands of outlets, which would make boycotting quite difficult, but in a limited number of dealerships per city. For example, in Los Angeles County there are only 122 GM dealerships, with average annual sales of $15 million per dealer.[2] Several dealers have commented that the vast majority of their sales are made on Saturday and Sunday. Thus, a boycotting group could target a relatively small number of dealerships and put up picket lines just on the weekends in order to achieve its objectives.

Another structural problem for GM that makes it unusually vulnerable is the relationship between the corporation and its dealership networks. The auto dealer is an independent businessman, tied to the GM system through a contract. He is usually very prosperous, often a millionaire. He is wined and dined by GM with big promotional bashes, frequently in Miami Beach or even the Bahamas, since he is the key link between GM and the consumer.

On the other hand, when sales and profits are squeezed, GM puts the squeeze on the dealers. Frequently, GM will announce discounted financing rates to move unsold inventories without consulting the dealers. The mumbled line in car commercials, "dealer contribution may affect total price," means that the dealer was forced to kick in to cover the reduced interest rate. Despite GM's pretense of avoiding favoritism, the largest and most successful dealerships are given a higher percentage of the best-selling cars. Yet, like their less influential cohorts, they are frequently forced to accept "dogs" from GM as the price of delivery of the "self-sellers." GM often forces them to buy "genuine GM parts" (such as Delco stereo systems) with very low profit margins. Dealers who prove uncooperative are threatened with termination of their contracts.[3]

A recent survey of dealer attitudes indicated "all divisions of GM were rated low in many of the dealer satisfaction categories."[4] Thus, increasing pressure against the dealers would exacerbate conflicts within the GM system and cause some dealerships to consider affiliating with other companies or, in the case of the super-dealers who carry many makes of car, dropping the GM affiliation if it proved too costly.

A high priced, high-profit product sold to the general public; a product that consumers only buy on an average of once every five years; a highly competitive industry in which there are over a dozen attractive alternatives to one's product in an era of declining consumer loyalty; limited distribution centers that are highly visible and vulnerable to picketing; and already-existing conflicts with its dealership network that a boycott could intensify: these are some of the structural vulnerabilities that GM would face from any boycott movement.

LOS ANGELES: WHERE GM'S WEAKNESSES AND THE CAMPAIGN'S STRENGTHS INTERSECT

The Campaign focused on Los Angeles County as its target area. Its organizers had no illusions that a GM boycott could become a mass phenomenon in San Diego, Fresno, Bakersfield, or San Francisco. In the 1980s there were no statewide, let alone nationwide, networks for successful boycotts. A boycott would only succeed if the issue was immediate, if the people affected *felt* that they were affected, and if the people in the target area had some sense of commonality and identity. For example, one could theoretically argue that "California" is a target, but the gaps between north and south historically would make that a questionable premise politically. On the other hand, the Campaign organizers believed that, with proper organizational preparation, people in Los Angeles would feel that through closing both Southgate and Van Nuys, GM was attacking "their city."

Given that the Campaign was willing to concede that its boycott possibilities were limited to Los Angeles County, the plan might have been doomed from the outset. But Los Angeles County had several characteristics that made GM unusually vulnerable there:

1) *The Los Angeles new-car market.* General Motors sold 111,542 cars and 41,830 light trucks in Los Angeles County in 1984.[5] Those 153,000 vehicles, selling at an average price of $15,000, constitute the boycott's target--over $2.3 billion in sales in just one year.[6]

Thus, the boycott strategy had a unique advantage--the ability to concentrate its efforts over a uniform media area; a uniform geographic area; and an area that, though enormously large for a city, was still highly concentrated and could be covered with leafleters and picketers with relative ease. For, in fact, GM sold more cars in Los Angeles County in 1985 than it did in the states of Arizona, New Mexico, Oregon, and Nevada combined.[7]

2) *L.A.'s black and Chicano communities.* For a single local that was 50 percent Latino and 15 percent black

to effectively threaten that they would take their concern "to the community," there had to be a large community for that threat to have any credibility. According to the 1980 census figures updated to 1987, Los Angeles County has approximately 8.4 million residents, of whom 3.1 million (37 percent) are Latino and 924,000 (10.8 percent) are black. In a city whose combined Latino and black population was almost 50 percent, the structural possibilities of a successful boycott were evident.

3) *L.A.'s large liberal community.* The boycott strategy targeted liberal geographic constituencies such as Santa Monica and L.A.'s west side as well as liberal organizations thoroughout the city. Los Angeles has two liberal entertainment weeklies, *The L.A. Weekly* and *The Reader;* significant liberal influence within the Democratic party; and many prior contacts who have supported the farmworkers' boycott and other similar causes. There were preexisting groupings in the city who would be favorably disposed towards the boycott.

4) *L.A.'s large student population.* Although the organizers realized that liberal and radical student activism had diminished dramatically in the 1980s, the large numbers of campuses, the enormous student bodies, and the existence of progressive and minority student organizations on each campus provided an important starting point for campus organizing. GM, as with most auto manufacturers, sends out expensive mailings to graduating college seniors in Los Angeles, urging them to make their first car purchase a GM product. The possibility of tens of thousands of Los Angeles area college students subjected to anti-GM boycott literature would in itself be a major deterrent.

5) *L.A. as a major media center.* Los Angeles is the second largest media center in the country. The national attention the Van Nuys movement has received already is partially a reflection of L.A.'s media impact. A sustained boycott of three months or more, combined with national TV and print media coverage, would both bring the charges against GM to a national audience and undo any benefits of the millions of dollars that GM pays to advertise in the Los Angeles market.

The largest new-car market in the United States concentrated in one county of eight million people; a county that is nearly 50 percent Latino and black with a large liberal constituency as well; a large student population and a major media center: those were some of the structural advantages the Campaign had in Los Angeles that were simultaneously GM's weaknesses if a showdown could not be averted.

THE BOYCOTT'S DOLLARS AND CENTS

Those were the exciting political possibilities of the boycott; but even the friends of the Campaign asked; "Where are the numbers?" They agreed that GM would be quite worried about the boycott in political terms alone. But if the boycott was to succeed, it had to have some *economic impact* as well. Otherwise, all the organizing in the world would not hurt GM's bottom line.

To begin with, the monetary damage of the boycott had to be weighed against GM's economic objectives in threatening to leave. GM had made cars at Van Nuys since 1947 at a considerable profit and was continuing to do so, still at a considerable profit. The problem, as GM repeated over and again, was "shipping costs"--which press reports estimated were as high as $400 more per car than at other plants.

When the Campaign was formed, however, and union activists made their own studies of the auto industry, they found GM's claims unbelievable, since anything close to $400 per car would make production at Van Nuys prohibitive. When they questioned members of the press as to where the $400 figure came from, they were told, "General Motors." As they pursued the matter further, however, they found that several industry analysts disagreed with GM's figures.

John Hammond, partner at J.D. Powers and Associates, explained:

> GM can come up with any shipping cost figures that it wants, depending upon how it chooses to calculate them. And while it does cost GM more to produce parts in the Midwest, ship them to California, and ship a completed car back across the Rockies, there are certain factors that mediate that problem. First, GM sends cars to Los Angeles by rail anyway, because L.A. is such a large market. And frequently, GM is able to send Camaros back on those same trains. If Van Nuys was closed, those cars would go back empty, costing GM additional penalties.
>
> Also, no matter where a car is built, there are shipping costs, and a high percentage of them are in the loading and unloading process. If the parts are built in Indiana, sent to Ohio to be assembled, and the car is shipped to New Mexico or Florida, I'm not sure how much cheaper that would be than to assemble it in Van Nuys. GM's $400 figure seems highly inflated.[8]

Dan Luria, senior researcher at the Industrial Technology Institute, placed any possible shipping cost difference at less than $200 and believes even that figure could be compensated for by other efficiencies of the Van Nuys plant:

> GM also has to weigh those additional costs against the profitability of the particular product it is producing. With over 20 percent of the plant's production in the high-end, high-profit IROCs, Z-28s, and TransAms, I would estimate GM's average profit on the entire line as $2,000 per car. In that context, GM at the worst is still making in the neighborhood of $1800 per car. While they of course would want to make the additional $200 per unit, if the plant has other cost advantages to compensate for it, and the threat of a boycott on

top of all that, it might explain why GM has not been so fast to close down Van Nuys.[9]

Thus, from GM's perspective, the "attraction" of closing down Van Nuys was the pursuit of that extra $200 per vehicle. In that the Van Nuys plant produces approximately 175,000 vehicles per year, the total additional profits would come to $35 million. That was what GM *might* gain if it closed down Van Nuys. But what might it lose?

In discussions with industry analysts Dan Luria, Christopher Cedergren, and John Hammond, the following estimates were developed. GM sold over 155,000 cars and light trucks in Los Angeles County (based on 1985 sales figures.) The average price of those vehicles was at least $15,000, far more than the $12,000 per vehicle that Luria estimates nationally, because GM sells a higher percentage of its high-priced, high-profit vehicles in California. Thus, the total dollar amount of GM sales in Los Angeles County is $2.3 billion per year--the target of the boycott.

Of the $15,000 average list price per vehicle, approximately 18 percent ($2,700) is dealer markup. That reduces GM's share to $12,300 per vehicle. After GM subtracts all the costs of production, labor, subcontracted parts, and overhead, Dan Luria estimates that GM ends up with approximately $2,200 per vehicle for fixed costs plus profit.

That $2,200 is the actual "revenue" that GM gets per car, which is distributed into dividends, profits, and the purchase of new acquisitions. Cesar Chavez, leader of the successful farmworkers' grape boycott, estimates that in order for a boycott to be effective, its minimal goals should be a 5 to 7 percent reduction in sales. Applying his guidelines to GM's estimated sales revenue of $2.3 billion per year, a 5 percent effectiveness rate would cost GM sales of $116 million per year and deny GM $17.3 million in fixed costs plus profit. A 7 percent effectiveness rate would cost GM $141 million per year in sales and deny the corporation $24.2 million in fixed costs plus profits. And a 10 percent effectiveness rate, the highest the Campaign could reasonably expect, would cost GM sales of $232 million per year and fixed costs plus profits of $34.6 million.

Thus, the maximum in additional profits that GM might attain by running away from Van Nuys, $35 million, was almost identical to the maximum that the boycott could expect to deny the corporation--$34.6 million.

The Campaign organizers, reinforced by their own study of GM's history and the corroborating opinions of many GM-watchers, became convinced that the significant economic damage that the boycott could inflict, combined with its even greater public relations and political damage, would more than offset any possible gains GM could achieve by closing down the plant.

THE BOYCOTT AS A DYNAMIC PROCESS: COULD THE CAMPAIGN REALLY CARRY IT OUT?

This discussion, so far, has been an analysis of factors, forces, and potential, not a description of a real movement. There have been many times when organizers have given impressive presentations on the potential of a project, only to have it fall flat on its face. The Campaign organizers understood that, while analysis was critical to planning a strategy, it was no substitute for carrying it out.

But within the first few years of the UAW's organizing work, there were exciting indications that, in the somewhat unpredictable chemistry of political events, the Campaign was tapping some very deep historical currents--temporarily submerged by America's swing to the right--that were coalescing into a very powerful movement.

The organizers began to talk in terms of "take-off" and "chain reaction"--what occurs when a series of individual organizing steps coalesce and break through into the popular consciousness. In virtually every constituency that the Campaign had targeted "in theory," in practice the response was usually even better than expected.

Reverend Frank Higgins and Father Luis Olivares became very involved in the movement, even though their churches were far away from the plant. Eloy Salazar, a business agent for a 17,000 member machinists local, took up the Campaign as a personal crusade to "give labor a shot in the arm." By fortunate happenstance, the new congressman in the district where the plant was located became Howard Berman, who previously had been one of the most outspoken defenders of the labor movement in the state legislature. The assemblywoman for many of the former Southgate workers was Maxine Waters, a strong opponent of runaway shops. Professor Rudy Acuña came forth to help with contacts in the Chicano community and on the college campuses; Reverend Dick Gillett helped to form networks of Protestant clergy in support of the movement. Workers reported that in many of their presentations to community groups, members of the audience would ask, "When does the boycott start?"

The organizers had to advise people that their goal was not a boycott, but a commitment from GM to keep their plant open. Apparently, years of plant closings in Los Angeles had set the conditions whereby in many constituencies there was strong sentiment to make the Van Nuys plant a test case, with GM to be the subject of the experiment.

Based on the individual positive responses, the organizers could conceptualize how the chain reaction could work and bring the boycott to the take-off point.

To begin with, the boycott would not have to achieve dramatic inroads in GM sales all at once. It could win symbolic and substantial victories one at a time. On hundreds of college campuses, labor unions, churches, and political institutions, Campaign supporters would introduce motions to ask those institutions to stop all purchases of GM products. Initial discussions with members of the Los Angeles City Council, clergy in the Catholic Archdiocese, and students at UCLA and California State University, Northridge, indicated at least the possibility of a positive response if GM actually closed the plant.

Out of individual victories could come the hoped-for "chain reaction." In this scenario, after GM announced it would close the plant, the International Association of Machinists (IAM) local announces that it supports the boycott and begins picketing at dealerships. Legislators in the state assembly and city council begin to demand meetings with GM officials and begin to introduce motions to support the boycott.

The major newspapers carry stories on the initial wave of boycott activity, which encourages community groups in East Los Angeles to carry out their pledge of support. As picketing clergy, unionists, and auto workers explain the cause to passing consumers, a college student, about to enter a GM dealership to buy a used car, stops to talk with the picketers and agrees to take "first-time buyer" petitions to her campus, where the student council begins a debate about demanding that the entire California State University system drop its contracts with GM. An outspoken state legislator, on campus that day to speak against apartheid in South Africa, also calls for the students to stop GM's attacks on minorities in Los Angeles, and supports the boycott. She then helps to introduce a resolution in the state legislature opposing purchases of GM products.

There was one more factor in this scenario that the auto workers felt would help their cause--GM's historical inability to defend its actions in public. The historical study of GM's behavior, while expanded considerably throughout the course of the Campaign, already indicated that GM would behave in an arrogant and unconvincing way once the media pressure intensified. This was not a Lee Iacocca the workers would be dealing with, but men who talked in terms of "sound business practices" and "unavoidable decisions prompted by declining market conditions." In the battle for public opinion, many preliminary indications were that GM was the company people loved to hate. If GM officials, after having closed both Los Angeles plants, had to ask Los Angeles consumers to reject the boycott appeal of some of the most respected leaders in the city, the confrontation would most likely add fuel to the boycott movement.

This projection was neither hypothetical nor far-fetched; it was simply an extension of actual organizing experiences in the first years of the Campaign. It gave the organizers an exciting picture of how the chain reaction could transform individual organizing successes into a concentrated blow against GM that might be able to reverse a corporate decision to close the plant.

As a report done at the UCLA Graduate School of Management, *A Feasibility Study of a Boycott of General Motors Products in Southern California*, concluded:

> Such a boycott, if carried out in a targeted and scientific fashion, can have severe negative effects on the corporation that will cause it to rethink its closure of GM Van Nuys or suffer the consequences. The consequences of such a boycott will be immediate sales damage to GM's market position among certain key segments and geographic zones. Furthermore, GM's image in the auto trendsetting capital of the United States suffers further damage in an area where the corporation is already being hit hard by imports.[10]

While the early organizing successes of the Campaign convinced both the organizers and their community supporters that the boycott strategy was quite viable, they were confronted with a major problem. If the purpose of all the "preemptive organizing" was to convince GM of the boycott's potential *ahead of time* in order to head off a plant closing, how could the Campaign convey that message to GM in Detroit?

NOTES

1. Peter Olney, Sanja Lappin, William Phelps, and Eric Vincoff, *A Feasibility Study of a Boycott of General Motors Products in Southern California*, Management Field Study Report, UCLA Graduate School of Management, June 1986, p. 17. Hereinafter referred to as the Olney Report.
2. Olney Report, pp. 17, 18.
3. For a discussion of GM's historical tension with its dealers, see Ed Cray, *Chrome Colossus* (New York: McGraw Hill, 1980), p. 400.
4. Olney Report, p. 19.
5. Market figures provided by Christopher Cedergren, Senior Consultant, J.D. Powers and Associates.
6. Olney Report, p. 18.
7. *Automotive News*, market data issue, April 24, 1985, p. 30.
8. Interview with the author, February 19, 1987.
9. Interview with the author, February 20, 1987.
10. Olney Report, p. 48.

Chapter Nine

THE CAMPAIGN MEETS WITH GENERAL MOTORS

In June 1983--shortly after the May 14 rally, the UAW convention, and the second shift's return to work--the organizers of the Campaign held a "where do we go from here" strategy meeting. Pete Beltran raised several concerns.

First, as the discussion of the boycott became more serious it became clear that, both legally and politically, it would not be possible for the UAW local itself to initiate or even formally participate in such a boycott. While many UAW locals supported the Campaign, its organizers knew that even if the plant was closed, the International union would not sanction a local union boycott against GM.

The Campaign organizers approached their closest community supporters with the problem. Interestingly, the community leaders argued that, leaving aside the legality of the situation and internal UAW politics, they had their own stake in the plant and their own commitment to the boycott. In what was both a message of support and a warning, they explained that if GM ever closed down the plant, *they* would initiate a boycott of GM products out of their own self-interest, regardless of the union's response. As Chicano Studies professor Rudy Acuña explained: "The issue has become so significant in the Chicano community alone that, if GM ever closed the plant, just the MEChA's, MAPA, and many of the predominantly Latino Catholic congregations could organize a boycott that would cause plenty of trouble for GM." The community leaders closest to the Campaign established the Labor/Community Coalition to Keep GM Van Nuys Open (hereafter referred to as the Coalition)--an independent coalition that agreed to take responsibility for a boycott if such an action became necessary.

Beltran raised a second strategic problem:

> When you organize a strike, the hard part is not getting your people to go out; the hard part is learning how to bring them back in with a victory. Before the May rally no one was taking us too seriously. But now a lot of the workers are asking me, "What would a victory look like? How can you get GM to agree to a ten-year commitment? You know GM would never put that in a local contract; it would set a dangerous precedent." And I tell them, "Those are good questions; we're working on some answers."[1]

THE COMMUNITY MOVES TO THE FOREFRONT

The organizers concluded that it was essential that GM fully understand the independent political role of the community. Over the years, after having opposed collective bargaining tooth and nail, GM had learned to turn the contract to its advantage, using it to restrict the options of the workers. But a community-based movement, centered in the Chicano and black communities, was a more unpredictable and formidable force that was not subject to the same contractual, legal, or political constraints as was the local.

To implement the community-centered strategy, Local 645 and community leaders decided to call a Labor and Community Leadership Conference to Keep GM Van Nuys Open. The goal was to bring together prominent leaders from all over the city in a coalition so broad and influential that GM would feel compelled to meet with its representatives.

It was hoped that GM would agree to a meeting with the Coalition, at which the group's goal would be to convince GM's top officials to make a public, long-term commitment to the plant of at least ten years, in return for the Coalition's commitment to stop all organizing toward a future boycott. While the agreement would not be legally binding or part of the union's local contract, it was felt that GM would not make such a public commitment unless it was prepared to abide by it, since if GM ever broke its promise and closed the plant, the subsequent boycott would virtually be assured of success.

The organizers realized that once they had announced a big leadership meeting, it had to be successful: a weak showing would be reported back to GM and would eliminate any chance for a meeting with the corporation. Accordingly, before announcing the plan publicly, the Campaign leaders called a meeting of twenty-five carefully selected leaders in the labor movement, and in the black, Chicano, and religious communities, to get their advice and to test the waters. They decided that, if there was a poor turnout for a planning meeting or opposition to the idea among key constituencies, it was better to assess those problems before making a public demand they could not back up.

Twenty-three of the twenty-five people invited showed up, and the other two called to set up another time to discuss the plan. At the meeting, the community leaders were very enthusiastic about the tactic and focused their energies on developing a broader list of one hundred key leaders who were essential. Marvin Katz, a vice-president of the United Teachers of Los Angeles, emphasized: "If we want to convince GM to meet with us, we have to bring out a lot of big guns. If it looks like all we have is the usual collection of liberals in the city, GM will just ignore us."

Over the next three months, the Campaign organizers arranged face-to-face meetings with prominent church, union, and community leaders and received firm commitments from many of them that they would attend. Only after securing those promises did the Campaign organizers announce the upcoming meeting to the media.

Problems developed, however, when a few elected political officials said that even with several months' notice they were not sure they could attend but would definitely send a representative. The Campaign organizers explained that sending staff assistants in their place was totally unacceptable. This was a *leadership* meeting that would be demanding publicly for GM to send one of its two top officials--either Chairman Smith or President McDonald--to meet with the Coalition. If the Coalition allowed politicians to send their staff to represent them, it would open the door for GM to send someone who, likewise, was not authorized to make decisions. The UAW organizers also explained that their 5,000 members were watching carefully as to which politicians took the time to support their movement. With that policy firmly in place, the vast majority of the political officials who were invited confirmed that they personally would be attending.

OCTOBER 22, 1983:
THE COMMUNITY SENDS A MESSAGE TO GM

On the day of the event, as the organizers nervously awaited the turnout, more than two hundred of the most influential labor, community, and political leaders came together to defend the Van Nuys plant. State senators Art Torres and Alan Robbins sat next to immigrant workers from the International Ladies' Garment Workers' Union (ILGWU). Bishop Juan Arzube and Father Luis Olivares from the Catholic Archidiocese; Reverends Richard Gillett and Noble Owings from the Episcopal Church; Reverend George Cole of the Presbyterian Synod; Reverend Ignacio Castuera, district director of the United Methodist Church; and a delegation of ten ministers from the Baptist Ministers Conference led by Reverend Frank Higgins made it clear that the coalition had a strong base among the clergy. Presidents of the International

Association of Machinists, Service Employees, Communications Workers, United Teachers of Los Angeles, and Shipbuilders locals mingled with peace and environmental activists. Chicano student leaders from UCLA and California State University's Los Angeles and Northridge campuses discussed the Campaign with permanently laid-off steelworkers from the Bethlehem plant. In terms of the "chain reaction" element of the organizing, it became apparent that day that the Campaign had achieved a certain status in the city, to the point where it was politically advantageous to be seen as a part of it, and that a comraderie was developing among community leaders who were being energized by the excitement of the movement.

The union hall had standing room only and was jammed with reporters. Bishop Juan Arzube of the Catholic Archdiocese explained that his responsibilities in the Church focused on the Hispanic community. As he moved fluidly between Spanish and English, he also spoke about GM's responsibility:

> GM has said that it plans to close down this plant and move away. But the question is: Are they moving because the plant does not bring them profits, or because they believe they can make *greater* profits somewhere else? I believe the latter is the case. So the issue really at stake is this: Does General Motors have a responsibility to the community that has supported them for thirty-seven years; and does General Motors have a responsibility to the thousands of workers in this plant?
>
> I believe they have such a responsibility. On behalf of this coalition I am calling on GM Chairman Roger Smith to meet with the leaders of the community to uphold that responsibility.

Ed Asner, actor and, at the time, president of the Screen Actors Guild, spoke next:

> I come to you as an old UAW card carrier--a spot polisher and buffer in Kansas

> City and a metal finisher in Chicago. Now, if you called GM today, they would tell you that "*At this time* there are no plans to close the Van Nuys plant." And I would like to believe them. But their long-term strategies seem to belie their assurances. Someone, Oscar Wilde I believe, once said that a cynic is a man who knows the price of everything and the value of nothing. American corporations are cynics--they know only our cost, never our value.
>
> Their profits outshout our dreams. And all too often, their cynicism infects us, it gets to us, and we begin to doubt our own worth. But not here and not today. For our unity and our activism are the powerful reaffirmation of human values and social conscience over cynicism and corporate greed. The people united will never be defeated! *El pueblo unido jamas sera vencido!*[2]

As Asner stepped down from the podium, college students and garment workers, priests and longshoremen, state senators and farm workers took up the chant, "*El pueblo unido jamas sera vencido*" with so much volume and enthusiasm that one of the reporters observed with only a touch of hyperbole: "I don't think you need to send Roger Smith a letter. I think he can hear the message in Detroit right now." On the slight chance that he couldn't, twenty-two community leaders took turns reading an open letter to Chairman Smith asking him to meet with the Coalition in the interest of keeping the plant open and averting a boycott in Los Angeles.

When the program was over, Professor Rudy Acuña observed:

> You know, throughout the '60s we kept talking about blacks and Chicanos getting together; but I'll tell you, in this room today was the broadest coalition I've seen in this city in the past twenty years. Looking around the union hall, for the first time I had the

feeling that if GM was stupid enough to shut down the plant, the boycott could actually succeed.

The press coverage of the Coalition's demand to meet with Roger Smith was excellent. Virtually all the local television stations ran major stories and the Cable News Network coverage prompted encouraging calls to the union hall from UAW locals in other cities. The *Los Angeles Times* ran a feature article, "Factory Becomes Focus of a Cause."[3] *Business Week* ran a full-page article, "A 'Boycott GM' Threat Aimed at Saving a California Plant," which indicated that the Van Nuys model, if successful, would impact the broader labor movement:

> The auto workers' campaign may persuade other unions to react earlier to prospective plant shutdowns or lay-offs. One leader of a 17,000 member International Association of Machinists local says many union leaders are watching the effort, and he predicts that similar campaigns could begin elsewhere if the tactic of rousing community support for a boycott works.[4]

Many labor veterans predicted that while the leadership meeting was an innovative tactic and the press coverage was excellent, GM would never agree to a meeting for fear of legitimizing the Coalition and its boycott threat. While the Campaign organizers acknowledged that possibility, the tactic was based on what they called "hitting the ball into GM's court," that is, taking the tactical initiative.

If GM agreed to meet with the Coalition, it would indeed help legitimize it. On the other hand, since those requesting the meeting included a U.S. congressman, four members of the California state legislature, and prominent clergy in the Catholic, Methodist, Presbyterian, and Baptist churches, a decision by GM *not* to listen to their concerns would antagonize powerful constituencies in California. A refusal to even discuss the matter would also create an even more sympathetic climate for a boycott if it became necessary.

Congressman Howard Berman, whose district includes the Van Nuys plant, engaged in lengthy negotiations with GM Chairman Roger Smith. He was finally able to set up a meeting between leaders of the Coalition and GM President F. James McDonald. As Berman explained:

> Shortly after we sent the letter to GM I was attending the congressional auto caucus [made up of representatives with auto plants in their district], when who should be the guest speaker but Roger Smith. As could be expected, he was trying to ask our help to reduce pollution requirements and other "restrictions" on his operations. After his talk I approached him about the meeting with the coalition. He told me, "What are all those people doing out there, talking about a boycott? That's just crazy, they're just cutting their own throats."
>
> I explained to him that while he might not agree with the boycott, it was a response by people who felt they had no other option and it was in his interest to at least talk with the Coalition. I left that discussion convinced that while he said the Coalition was crazy, it was only the threat of the boycott that persuaded him to send GM president McDonald to meet with us.[5]

JANUARY 22, 1984: FACE TO FACE WITH PRESIDENT McDONALD

On January 22, 1984, leaders of GM met with leaders of the Coalition at the Beverly Hilton Hotel in Beverly Hills. Representing General Motors was its president, F. James McDonald, along with a retinue of his staff and officials from the Van Nuys plant management. Among those representing the Labor Community

Coalition were Congressman Berman, Ed Asner, Bishop Arzube, Father Olivares, Reverend Higgins, California state senators Art Torres and Alan Robbins, California state assemblywoman Maxine Waters, and Pete Beltran and Eric Mann from the UAW.[6] A set of ground rules were agreed upon: half an hour for GM's presentation, half an hour for the Coalition's, and half an hour for discussion.

President McDonald began the meeting with a slide show, the same slide show that GM had presented to the Van Nuys workers a year earlier. It had a chart of every plant in the GM system, ranked by overall profitability. The lowest five plants, although all profitable, were coded in red and placed on a so-called "danger list"--with the Van Nuys plant prominently highlighted at the bottom. Having raised the threat of the closure, McDonald then assured the Coalition that all was not lost. "This list is not cast in cement. I am sure that if the local leadership of the union cooperates with us, tries to cut down absenteeism, raises quality and productivity and creates a more positive labor-relations climate there is still some hope."[7] After his presentation, which took more than his allotted half hour, he opened the floor up for questions.

Coalition members tried to explain to McDonald that this was not a GM press conference over which he was presiding but an effort at a dialogue which *they* had initiated. Despite his strenuous objections and only after angry Coalition members demanded that he abide by the agreed-upon ground rules, McDonald finally consented to listen to the coalition's concerns.

Reverend Higgins fired the opening round:

> I didn't come here to see a slide show. I thought we were going to talk as equals, but you lectured us as if we were children. Let me inform you that I represent over three hundred Baptist churches in Greater Los Angeles, and I can tell you that all three hundred of them will participate in the boycott if you ever close down the plant. I don't buy foreign cars, and I will tell you that if GM

closes down Van Nuys after you already closed down Southgate, we will consider GM a foreign car in Los Angeles.

Professor Rudy Acuña interjected:

Your presentation on corporate profits and plant closings reminded me of General Maxwell Taylor announcing the body counts in Viet-nam--so cold and calculated, as though there are no human beings involved. Now let me tell you something. There has been a long-standing affinity between the Chicano and the Chevrolet, but if you ever close down the plant, I promise you I will do everything in my power to sever that historical relationship.

Assemblywoman Maxine Waters told McDonald:

Your efforts to convince the workers that their future is in their hands is a deception, and you know it. Several years ago the management of the Goodyear Rubber plant convinced the workers that if they only worked harder and turned out more tires per hour, they might save their jobs. People worked sick and worked injured and raised productivity--and then Goodyear closed the plant anyway. We found out later that the central office had already decided to close the plant well over a year before it was announced.

We know that your Detroit office, not local management, and certainly not the workers, makes the decisions on these plant closings, and we are here to let you know that closing down this plant would be a disastrous decision. I want your commitment that you will give a full report of this meeting to your Board of Directors and convey to them the seriousness of our plans for the boycott. Then, if you decide to close the

> plant anyway, you can be held responsible for the disaster.

McDonald was visibly shaken. His advance men had obviously not prepared him for what he had walked into. McDonald said, "I don't understand. When we meet with other community delegations they don't act like this. They are very positive and offer economic incentives for us to keep these plants open."

"We would like to be positive," Waters replied. "Why don't you give us something to be positive about?" She pressed McDonald: "When we go out there to face the press, can we tell them that the plant will be open for the next two years?" McDonald thought for a minute, and said, "Yes." Waters continued: "Can we tell them the plant will be open for three more years?" McDonald said, "No. By 1986 we will have some hard decisions to make and some plants may have to be closed at that time."

After McDonald left, Waters turned to the delegation and said, "Well isn't that interesting. When I propose a three-month advance-notice bill in the legislature, my colleagues say it's too radical. But by organizing this coalition, we've won a two-year advance notice."

At the subsequent press conference, Waters spoke for the coalition:

> President McDonald assured us that at this time the plant would not be closed and predicted that it was safe for the next two years. We informed him that we will continue our organizing so that in the third year, the fourth year, or the fifth year, if GM moves to close the plant, the boycott will be ready to go.

The following Saturday, the leaders of the Labor Community Coalition reported back to a meeting of two hundred active workers at the union hall. It was reflective of both their dedication and political perspective that Father Luis Olivares, Ed Asner, Rudy Acuña, and Reverend Frank Higgins would spend their second day that week on

Campaign activities in order to report back to the workers. But as Ed Asner explained, "How can we represent the auto workers to GM and the press, then go home without reporting on the meeting to the workers themselves? It's their lives we were discussing."

At the Saturday meeting, the workers were both heartened by the news of a two-year extension and angry at what seemed like the endless threat hanging over their heads. President Beltran proposed continuing the Campaign for another two years and was enthusiastically supported.

KEEPING UP THE MOMENTUM: "TIGER BY THE TAIL"

As word of the McDonald meeting filtered into the plant, the workers were very appreciative of the Campaign's efforts and encouraged by the prospects of building the Camaro for at least two more years. But it also became increasingly difficult to keep them involved. While the Campaign maintained a solid core of fifteen to twenty workers at its biweekly meetings, it was having trouble involving new people, and many of the old reliables were going from being activists to being supporters. As Manuel Hurtado, one of the most active organizers explained:

> The people on my line are getting sick of me. They say every time they see me all I talk about is how the plant may close. They say, "Look, in two years, when they try to close the plant, I will get involved again, but right now I don't have time for all these meetings. I want to enjoy myself and spend a little time with my kids."

Other organizers reported similar conversations.

After considerable discussion among Campaign activists in the plant and their counterparts in the community, it was decided to use the short-term lull to produce a documentary film on the movement that could be used to attract greater support when the next round of threats developed. Filmmaker Michal Goldman, who had produced the organizing tape that had been used at the UAW convention, had for some time been interested in producing a more finished documentary that could chronicle the Campaign's history. The Coalition spent the next six months raising the necessary funds for the project; then Goldman went to work.

The result was *Tiger By the Tail*, a powerful film whose name came from a speech by Reverend Higgins who said, "When we sat down to meet with McDonald he walked in there talking to us as if we were children, but he left there knowing he had a *tiger by the tail*." In 1986, the film was chosen as a festival selection at the Global Village Film Festival and also won a blue ribbon for best labor film at the American Film Festival in New York. As a *New York Times* article explained:

> Vying For the Business World's Oscar
>
> Every spring, industrial-film producers vie for their industry's version of the Oscar or the Emmy: the blue ribbon designating a first prize at the annual American Film and Video Festival in New York....
>
> In the employee relations category, first prize went to *Tiger By The Tail*, a 38-minute video about auto workers taking action to keep a General Motors plant in California from closing. Narrated by Ed Asner, the video features interviews and newsreel-type film clips. Its focus is "not workers as victims, but workers as strategists, as organizers."[8]

Goldman's film, while attracting critical praise, was especially valuable in recharging the batteries of many of the workers. Despite the many achievements of the Campaign, at times the seemingly constant efforts to impact General Motors wore the workers down. The film helped to reinforce the social reality of the movement, and as Pete Beltran said, "Every time I wonder if what we accomplished is real, I just go home and watch the film. And each time I end up with chills."

Although in October 1985 the general mood of the plant was still somewhat complacent, the two opening night showings of the film served to reinforce and encourage the most dedicated activists--and attracted a few new faces. As word spread throughout the plant that *Tiger By the Tail* was a "real movie," groups of three and four workers would come across the street to the union hall for daily film showings.

The organizers used the prominent review in the *LA Weekly*, and the resultant publicity that it generated, to schedule film showings at private homes and community organizations. One of the highlights of this outreach work was a film showing at a steelworkers union hall, at which workers from the closed-down Bethlehem Steel plant, striking ILGWU workers, and Hormel strikers on tour from Austin, Minnesota, watched the film and used it to generate a long strategy discussion about new directions for the labor movement.

Coalition organizers used the film showings to launch a letter-writing campaign to GM Chairman Roger Smith in which people informed GM that they would personally join in the boycott if it became necessary. Thus Goldman's film both reinforced the confidence of the Van Nuys activists and served to expand the base of the Campaign.

QUOTATIONS TO CHAIRMAN SMITH

One of the main questions the organizers had to answer after the meeting with GM President McDonald was, "How do we keep up the pressure?" There was a strong sense that they had impacted GM's decision-making process, but with at least two years before the plant might be closed, how could they demonstrate to GM the Coalition's capability for *sustained activity?* If GM was leaning in the direction of taking the boycott threat seriously, and perhaps even changing its original decision, one factor it would watch for was whether the Coalition had merely assembled an all-star cast to talk tough for a few hours, or whether it was part of an organized movement.

New tactics were needed besides demonstrations. Until GM's next overt threat, the demonstration tactic, having already proven very effective, was not appropriate. What was needed was a more low-key but still confrontational tactic, and one that could involve a broader constituency than those willing to demonstrate. Out of that thinking came the "letters to Roger Smith" project.

The Campaign members asked community supporters to sign a form letter to GM that committed the signer to participate in a boycott of GM if the company ever closed down the plant. This both conveyed to GM a growing sense of the boycott's strength and allowed the organizers to accumulate a list of people who could be contacted at a moment's notice if necessary.

Because GM might not be persuaded by even a few thousand letters, the organizers wanted to give GM a vivid demonstration of the "*multiplier effect*." On each letter, the signatory would list the voluntary organizations to which she or he belonged and pledged to bring the boycott to those organizations if it became necessary. Thus, for each hundred letters GM received, it faced the possibility of the boycott at least being introduced to an equal number of *organization*s. The letter ended with the pledge:

> If you ever close down the Van Nuys plant I am prepared to boycott GM products and to urge my fellow workers, neighbors, and members of organizations to which I belong to do the same. On the other hand, if you do make a public commitment to this plant I am prepared to give your products my most favorable consideration.

The Coalition frequently mailed the original to GM and kept a photocopy, with the signatories' permission, for its own records. A few samples of the letters GM received read as follows:

> Marla D., drives 1976 Oldsmobile, two GM products in family, International Association of Machinists Lodge 758, Coalition of Labor Union Women.
>
> Linda D., drives 1974 Audi Fox, two GM products in family, American Lung Association, L.A. Committee on Occupational Safety and Health, 9 to 5 Working Women, National Organization for Women.
>
> Brant R., drives 1979 Datsun, one Oldsmobile in family, Beth Shalom Temple.
>
> John M., drives 1970 Ford, three GM products in family, belongs to United States Cycling Federation, Alcoholics Anonymous, Knights of Columbus.

Just a few of the many organizations that appeared on the letters to GM indicates the breadth of the boycott's potential: United Methodist Church, United Teachers of Los Angeles, Little Tokyo People's Rights Organization, Community Education Network, Adat Ari El Synagogue, Retired Teachers Association, Reseda Women's Club, St. Catherine of Sierra Catholic Church, Writers Guild, California Association of Marriage, Family, and Child Therapists, Screen Actors Guild, Office and Professional Union Local 30, Young Christians for Global Justice, Theta Chi Fraternity, Carpenters Union Local 1913, Harbor Coalition of Unions, West Covina Moose Lodge, Hacienda Kiwanis, Pile Drivers Local 2375, Incarceration Church, NAACP, Mexican American Political Association, Movimiento Estudiantil Chicano de Aztlan, Van Nuys Chamber of Commerce.

Several writers chose to add their own comments. The statements of two UCLA students are indicative:

> Yes, I will boycott and let as many people know about this issue as possible. I teach undergraduates at UCLA and do counseling as well. I intend to use GM's callousness toward the workers as an example of *bad business.*

> I am a UCLA student and you don't want to lose that market. You people are making a big mistake if you don't respond to this campaign.

Sarah C., from Santa Monica, wrote a letter that offered General Motors both the carrot and the stick:

> My philosophy has been to buy American cars, including GM products, since they are well made and support for the American economy means support for workers, communities and the strength of local initiative....But I will join with thousands of others in this area who are willing to boycott GM if your company does not keep the plant open beyond the next year or two.

Rabbi Leonard Beerman of Los Angeles' Leo Baeck Temple wrote Chairman Smith:

> A representative of the United Auto Workers came to our Temple last Friday to speak about the GM Van Nuys plant and the effort being made to keep it open. I think he made a very compelling presentation and it moved a great many of the people who heard him. I am enclosing the letters which they signed at this meeting, and I would be especially appreciative for your response to this appeal since I am also a supporter of the endeavor to keep the Van Nuys plant open.[9]

Another letter sure to command GM's attention was from John Graykowski, Director of the Campaign for

Human Development of the Catholic Archdiocese of Los Angeles, which stated:

> I am deeply concerned about the uncertainty surrounding the future of the Van Nuys plant. I would be most grateful if you would discuss with me what strategies GM is undertaking to assure that the plant will not be closed down....We are reviewing a community proposal to initiate a boycott of GM products in California should Van Nuys be closed. Anticipating that GM is making every effort to keep the plant open I will look forward to reviewing the strategies you are studying to assure this.[10]

In general, the less well-known letter writers received no response, but the more prestigious individuals representing organizations received a form letter. Typical of the argumentation employed by GM was the one addressed to Rabbi Beerman by Van Nuys plant manager Ernest Schaefer:

> Dear Rabbi Beerman:
>
> Your letter of April 21 to Chairman of the Board Roger Smith has been forwarded to me for response....As you know, the automobile industry in the United States is facing a serious competitive challenge from manufacturers around the world. Nowhere is that challenge more evident than right here in California. As a result, all of our facilities and operations worldwide are taking a hard look at the way they do business to determine how changes might be made to improve our competitive position.
>
> Here at the Van Nuys plant, union and management have publicly announced a joint effort to find solutions to the competitive challenge we face. We have asked state and

> local government to become a part of that effort and the response has been very positive.
>
> As with all of our operations, the long term future of the Van Nuys plant will be determined by how successful we are at improving our competitive position, and ultimately, by how well our products are received in the marketplace. At one time or another, every General Motors plant goes through a rather complex and lengthy product allocation process. Over the years, the Van Nuys plant has built many different products. Our current products, the Chevrolet Camaro and the Pontiac Firebird are scheduled to run several more years. In the meantime, many positive steps are being taken to develop viable proposals for new products for this plant.
>
> Again, we appreciate your letter and welcome any additional questions or comments you may have.[11]

The Schaefer letter reflected several aspects of the dialectic between the Campaign and GM. To begin with, the letters were obviously read in Detroit and then sent to Schaefer for the local touch. Second, Schaefer's answers avoided any discussions of social responsibility and repeated GM's perspective that "the market," combined with workers' efforts to be more "competitive," would determine the future of the plant.

But, most important in the exchange of letters, was what was *not* said. For once again the Campaign had seized the initiative, forcing GM to justify its business decisions to a far wider constituency than it was used to. The idea of plant managers engaging in economic and social debates with rabbis was not typical of GM's modus operandi and was not the part of the business at which the corporation was most adept. The letters project was achieving its objective of reminding General Motors that the future of the plant was a subject of intense community concern.

Despite the seemingly endless reservoir of community support, the Campaign organizers continually grappled with the problem of maintaining the interest of the workers themselves. Since the callback of the second shift in May 1983 and the upturn in domestic auto sales, the organizers had to battle a growing sense of complacency among many of the workers and, at times, felt they were grasping at straws to come up with new "angles" to keep their interest. The positive side of this period was that it allowed long-term planning and strategic debate without the day-to-day sense of urgency that characterized the months of the layoff, when many workers had feared that the entire plant was about to be shut down.

Beginning in late 1986, however, events that had been long in the making coalesced into a company counter-attack against the Campaign in the form of demands for a Japanese-style management system called the "team concept," the joint union-management effort "to find solutions to the competitive challenge" that Schaefer referred to. The long and luxurious honeymoon was over. Almost overnight, the Campaign was fighting for its life.

NOTES

1. As was explained in the introduction, all quotations from activists in the Campaign which are not subsequently footnoted are based on discussions or meetings in which I participated. Over the years, in preparation for many articles, the film *Tiger By the Tail,* and this book, I have kept records of important conversations.
2. The remarks by Arzube and Asner are captured in the film, *Tiger By the Tail.*
3. Henry Weinstein, "Factory Becomes Focus of a Cause, *Los Angeles Times*, Metro section, December 5, 1983, p. 1.
4. *Business Week*, November 7, 1983.
5. Conversation with the author, January 22, 1984.
6. Also present at the meeting from the Coalition were Raoul Teilhet, president of the California Federation of Teachers; Jack Koszdin, attorney; Frank Placensia, financial secretary-treasurer of IAM District 727; Al Belmontez, vice-president, Mexican American Political Association; Reverend Richard Gillett and Canon Noble Owings of the Episcopal Church; and Ralph Arriola, executive director of the Latin American Civic Association.
7. All accounts of and quotations from this meeting are based on the author's notes taken during the meeting.
8. *New York Times,* Business section, July 20, 1986, p. 26.
9. Letter dated April 21, 1986.
10. Letter dated October 28, 1986.
11. Letter dated May 16, 1986.

Chapter Ten

GM COUNTERATTACKS: THE TEAM COMES TO VAN NUYS

Shortly after the Coalition's meeting with GM president McDonald, there were signs that the corporation was changing tactics. A new plant manager, Ernest Schaefer, was brought in to quarterback the local situation. Schaefer had formerly been the plant manager in GM's Fiero plant in Pontiac, Michigan, and he had a reputation as a new breed of plant manager who actively intervened in the politics of the local union to advance the company's interests.

Gregarious and outgoing, Schaefer was schooled in the new jargon of nonadversarial labor relations. He walked the assembly lines, shook hands with the workers, and invited himself to lunch in the plant cafeteria: "Hi, I'm Ernie Schaefer; mind if I join you? I want to know your opinions about how we can improve things around here."

His first organized effort was to develop the *Positive Press*, a glossy handout that ostensibly was a publication of both GM and the UAW under the "joint activities" provisions of the 1982 contract, but in actuality was a propaganda organ for management. (After a year of vigorous protest by President Beltran, the company agreed to take the UAW insignia off the masthead).

While not attacking the Campaign by name, Schaefer consistently editorialized against those who spread "negativity." In his early articles, he told the workers that he didn't want to talk about plant closings. If the workers had a positive attitude, they could raise quality, show the Detroit headquarters that Van Nuys was a "world class plant," and avert the unspoken plant closing. Through "joint activities" funds, Schaefer and many of the same committeemen who had been attacking the Campaign began to hold "off-site classes" at local hotels, in which groups of fifty workers at a time (under the rubric of "Quality of Worklife") were taught the virtues of cooperation. As one worker commented: "The first virtue is that we got three paid days off the assembly line."

Mark Masaoka, one of the Campaign organizers observed: "At first, we saw Schaefer's strategy as simply one of co-optation. We felt that he was trying to lull the workers to sleep and make the Campaign appear out in left field. Then, if GM actually moved to close the plant, he could tell the workers, 'We did the best we could,' and move on to his next plant."

COOPERATE OR ELSE!

It turned out, however, that, like the Campaign organizers, Schaefer was an organizer himself. He, too, had developed his campaign in stages. In December 1985, having successfully laid the groundwork, Schaefer began to spread a little negativity of his own. With support from his allies in the local union, he began to put out leaflets warning the workers that the plant was indeed in danger of being closed and that their only chance to save their jobs was to adopt a Japanese-style management system called the *team concept*. While the system claimed to be based on labor-management cooperation, Schaefer emphasized that if the workers did not choose to co-operate, the plant would be closed.

In November 1985, Schaefer began telling the Van Nuys workers that the car they were producing, the Chevrolet Camaro, was going to be manufactured through a new process, with an all plastic body, and was going to be phased out of Van Nuys, probably around 1989. If they wanted a new car--that is, a job after 1989--they would have to agree to many work rule changes, a.k.a. the *team concept.* Whereas in the past the Campaign distributed magazine and newspaper articles warning of future plant closings, while the company denied the stories, this time it was the company reprinting those articles. An *Automotive News* article distributed by management, with the headline, "10 factories may go dark in 4 years," explained:

> William R. Pochiluk Jr., president of *Autofacts* and author of a report on plant capacity, said that based on his analysis the following General Motors plants are the top candidates for closure: *Van Nuys, Calif*; St. Therese, BC; Detroit (Clark Street); Arlington, Texas; one J/N car plant such as Leeds (Mo); and one A-car plant such as Tarrytown (NY).[1]

The threat by itself would not suffice. Schaefer needed a philosophically sympathetic union leader to carry out his plan. He found one in the newly elected shop chairman, Ray Ruiz. Ruiz, who had in the past taken a sympathetic stance toward the Campaign, underwent a transformation shortly after his election in May 1985. He explained that although he previously had been a militant, now he had come to believe that people (such as Pete Beltran) who retained an adversarial stance towards the company were "dinosaurs." He pointed to NUMMI, the GM/Toyota joint venture in Fremont, California, as the cooperative model of the future. Ruiz told the workers that while the Campaign had been a useful tactic to draw attention to the problem, the team concept was the only way to solve it.

Having successfully laid the groundwork, on December 9, 1985, Schaefer and Ruiz organized unprecedented mass meetings on each shift. The goal of the meetings was to ask the membership's permission to "explore" a new contract with the company based on the team concept. Many workers who attended the meetings reacted angrily. "Why are these meetings being held in the plant instead of the union hall?" "Why is the company paying us and stopping production to have these meetings?" "We already have a ratified local agreement that doesn't expire until September 1987. Who gave Ruiz the authority to reopen it?" The meetings broke up in angry debate, with many workers booing Ruiz and accusing him of cutting a deal with the company.

President Beltran explained his opposition in greater detail:

> This reminds me of how GM got the concessions at the national level in 1982. They came to us and said, "We don't want concessions, we just want to "explore" new ways of being efficient. The next thing we knew, GM had $3 billion of our money. The shop committee does not need a membership meeting to "explore" anything. They can explore all they want. But if they want to reopen the contract they have to come to the membership, explain why they want it and get a vote. But why would the company want to reopen the contract, to give us more? The whole thing is a disgrace.[2]

The next day, Ernie Schaefer put out a leaflet of his own explaining his position:

> As you know, plant meetings were held Monday, December 9, on both shifts. Unfortunately, some confusion resulted from the discussions in those meetings. As our future is in jeopardy, I feel it is critical to answer the questions on some items.
>
> At this time we have no product beyond the 1989 model when the present Camaro and Firebird are scheduled to be phased out. Corporate decisions on where to build new products must be made many years in advance of introduction because major changes in the plant facility are required in order to build a new product.

> We prepared a plan which would enable us to build more than one product at the same time. This plan was to be presented to top Corporate officials this Wednesday December 11. However, we had to cancel the meeting due to the decision the people reached on Monday [the unwillingness of the membership to authorize the shop committee to *explore*]. In order for us to take this multimillion dollar plan forward, we must be able to build cars utilizing new approaches like the team concept.[3]

Beltran attacked the "captive audience meetings" as a "deal, negotiated secretly and privately, without the knowledge of the local union president or other members of the shop committee." After raising initial criticisms of the team concept, he indicated a willingness to try it. He focused his criticisms, however, on GM's unwillingness to make a long-term commitment to the plant in return for the workers' acceptance of the team concept:

> Accepting the team concept is not the major stumbling block, instead it is GM's open-ended guarantee....GM's so-called guarantee is meaningless if it rests on consumer demands and if there is no other commitment to retool again, if necessary, to keep GM Van Nuys Open into the 1990s.
>
> For these reasons, a more appropriate exchange for the Team Concept would be a GM guarantee that the GM Van Nuys plant would remain open for at least ten years so that everyone now employed, if the plant should close, would qualify for a guaranteed SUB benefit for a full 52 weeks, followed by a Guaranteed Income Stream Benefits for an additional nine years at 50 percent of their present wages without having to transfer out of state to another GM plant.[4]

Beltran, to the surprise of some of his allies, did not attack the team concept frontally, but instead, as a skilled negotiator, demanded a long-term commitment from the company in return. GM, however, was not proposing the team concept as part of a negotiating posture. Essentially, it was demanding it without conditions. Schaefer argued his case even more strongly:

> We have developed a proposal to build A-cars (Buick and Oldsmobile Cutlass) along with our current Firebirds and Camaros. This plan would cost about $200 million to implement at Van Nuys and would provide products for us to build well beyond 1990.
>
> In discussing our proposal with Detroit we were told that for General Motors to invest $200 million in our plant we would need changes in our local contract that would allow us to implement a team organization. The team organization is needed to allow the flexibility necessary to build two car lines in our plant. *We were told that if we did not have such an agreement, there was no need for us to come to Detroit.* Consequently, the meeting for Wednesday, December 11 to review our plans in Detroit was cancelled.
>
> The bottom line is if the Van Nuys Plant is to be considered for a new product line, we must introduce new and innovative work concepts at our facility.[5]

So, the lines were drawn. Beltran's view was, "Give us a long-term commitment and we'll consider the team concept"; whereas the company's view was, "Give us the team concept or the plant will be closed--but if you do give us the team concept, there is still no guarantee the plant will be kept open."

For those familiar with GM's decision-making structure, the entire plan was based on a deception. While some of Alfred P. Sloan's organizational structures had been modified under Roger Smith, GM's basic staff-and-line management model was very much in place.

Central staff on GM's Executive Committee in Detroit made decisions about long-term capital investment and disinvestment. Plant managers such as Ernie Schaefer, were, in fact, low-level line officers whose responsibility was to implement decisions made in Detroit. Local plant managers had no authority to decide whether plants would be kept open or closed.

Under the new politics of the GM-UAW "joint activities," however, local plant managers and shop chairmen were encouraged to come to Detroit on pilgrimages to present competitive *bids* for their plant. And, as Schaefer had argued, if the workers would not agree to the plan ahead of time, the pilgrimage would be canceled.

But even if the workers agreed to his demand, the very terms of the competition made it impossible for any one plant to ever achieve job security. Since GM had at least four new plants due to come on line, which would add far more productive capacity than market demand warranted, at least four plant closings were assured. As long as it was agreed upon that local concessions would determine who would be kept open and who would be closed, as soon as one local gave concessions and returned home thinking they had saved the plant, another local would appear in Detroit offering more, and the cycle would continue.

THE DEBATE RAGES ON THE SHOP FLOOR

For several months, the workers did nothing but debate the issue. In the first stages, everyone in the plant was asking, "Are you for or against the team concept?" and in the next breath asking, "What the hell is the team concept anyway?" One group that endorsed the concept wholeheartedly was a group of workers with no history of union involvement but a long history of management aspirations. They argued that the "team concept" would give workers more input into the production process and allow autoworkers to use "their head, not just their hands." As it was initially described, groups of seven to ten workers would work cooperatively, be able to repair mistakes "in station" instead of shipping them out to repair stations, and be able to stop the assembly line if mistakes could not be solved in time. According to this view, this would allow workers to handle many problems among themselves rather than refer them to disciplinary, management-dominated procedures. The workers were told they would elect their own team leader, who would serve in a quasi-management, quasi-lead-worker capacity.

At Van Nuys, however, many committeemen and foremen who supported the plan focused on the ability to "weed out the bad workers." They argued that while most of the workers were hard working and dependable, it was the "5 percent," who were not doing their share. These slackers, through poor workmanship and high absenteeism, were threatening the livelihoods of the "95 percent" by making the plant "uncompetitive." This was a clever formulation. In reality, the company (and the company-oriented committeemen) knew that far more than 5 percent of the workers would be cut. But it allowed them to appeal to the votes of the mythical "95 percent" with each person, of course, believing it was "the others" who were among the 5 percent. It also set the stage for attacks on the seniority system, with the argument that "only poor workers have to hide behind seniority." When some of the workers began to say, "I'm going to vote for the team concept so I can get rid of Willie (or Mary, or Jose)," the danger of "the team" turning worker against worker and breaking down even the most minimal union solidarity became apparent.

But the underlying point in every discussion was the company's ultimatum. As Kelley Jenco explained: "With most of the people on my line, a few are gung ho for it, a few are really dead-set against it, and the majority are just resigned to it. They say, 'If GM says give us the team concept or we'll close the plant, why are we pretending we have a choice in the matter?'"

BELTRAN'S STRATEGY

Beltran was portrayed by the opposition as a hardliner who dogmatically opposed any cooperation with the company. In fact, he had a complex and well-thought-out strategy. He was willing to make certain concessions to GM, not out of principle, but out of necessity. Without a strong movement led by the International union or by a coalition of UAW locals to fight plant closings, he believed that some compromises with the largest industrial corporation in the world were in order. What he feared most, however, was the complete disintegration of *collective bargaining* as he knew it:

> No one even knows what the team concept is, and neither Ruiz nor Schaefer want to be very specific. If we can stop all the generalized discussion and get down to specifics, we can bargain over classifications, line speeds, job descriptions, and even manpower levels. But with workers running around the plant asking "what the hell is going on?" and Ruiz and Schaefer saying "trust us," the whole process of collective bargaining is going down the drain. Since when do we reopen contracts every time the company asks? Since when do we package a whole series of company proposals under the name "team concept" and ask the workers if they want it on an all-or-nothing basis?

Beltran's plan had two elements: (1) to make the Campaign more visible, so that the workers would feel they had an alternative to the company's threats, and (2) to engage committeemen and the membership in a discussion of the team concept's *provisions*, so that the mystique of the team concept could be broken down and individual elements could be bargained one at a time.

But, despite Beltran's flexibility and moderation, the faction of the union allied with the company began a systematic campaign to discredit him. The verbal attacks on Beltran followed a consistent theme: "Beltran is a hard-headed egotist who doesn't care about the membership. He wants to stick it to GM and doesn't really care whether they close down the plant." The company advocates were trying to set up Beltran and the Campaign activists as the scapegoats for a future plant closing.

THE CAMPAIGN REGROUPS...AND MISCALCULATES

Opinion in the plant, according to most estimates, was split into three roughly equal camps. One third of the workers were genuinely in favor of the team concept and felt it was in their interest. Another third opposed the team concept but favored voting for it to avoid a possible plant closing. The remaining third was adamantly against the plan, arguing that, while it was risky, the union should call the company's bluff. Thus, in early 1986, most of the seasoned union veterans held a common assessment that the team concept was disliked by the majority of the workers but would pass by a two-to-one margin.

The Campaign activists made two proposals for action. First, acting as individual union members and not in the name of the Campaign, they proposed that the union elect a rank-and-file delegation to visit several plants that already had adopted the team concept and then report back to the membership. They proposed that the delegation visit the GM plant in Wentzville, Missouri, which had been the scene of an eleven-day strike that had led to the company withdrawing some of the team concept plan's most objectionable aspects. The goal was to support Beltran's idea that the workers had to take a hard look at the plan in practice before they decided whether they wanted it.

Second, they proposed another large Campaign rally in opposition to GM's latest round of threats. For over two years, the Campaign had not called any major demonstrations because the company was denying that there was any danger to the plant, and the workers themselves did not see a need for dramatic action. It was hoped that by bringing back the community support and the threat of the boycott the workers who wanted to resist the team concept at all costs, along with those who would agree to it in return for a long-term commitment from GM, would be strengthened.

Many of the Campaign activists, as individual union members, put out a signed leaflet urging that the local send a delegation of ten workers, five from each shift, to investigate the team concept and visit the Wentzville plant. They demanded that Shop Chairman Ruiz stop his efforts to force a vote on the plan before such an investigation.

The idea of the "rank-and-file investigating group" was proposed to counter the plan of the shop committee to investigate "for" the members and to report back. While in general that *was* the shop committee's legal responsibility, their efforts to push through a new contract when a contract already existed provided little doubt as to what their "investigation" would recommend.

After the leaflet, however, the team concept committeemen changed their position from opposing the "rank-and-file" delegation as an intrusion into their bargaining power, to opposing its proposal of five people elected on nights and five on days as "limiting the delegation to a small clique."

In a shrewd tactical maneuver, they proposed voting down the motion to send ten workers and substituted a motion for two workers per department on each shift--a total of thirty-four workers. When Beltran's supporters argued that sending thirty-four workers would cost the local more than $60,000 and was a transparent effort to decimate the funds of the local, the "cooperation faction" was able to turn the debate around: "What are you afraid of? Don't you want the membership to see for themselves as you claim?" The motion for the $60,000 passed with little opposition.

But the vote was won by more than clever argument. The team concept was attracting new supporters from the shop floor and was developing the character of a mass movement. Unfortunately, in the view of many Campaign activists, it was a right-wing movement.

Their activists were aggressive and bold. At union meetings, they would openly argue: "Look around the country. Yesterday's militants are today's flexible thinkers. The days of confrontation are over." "Seniority is important, but it's time that we allowed the best people to rise to the top. My foreman says that I have a lot of potential, but people who don't give a damn are standing in my way just because they have more seniority." Members who had not attended union meetings came into the union hall and demanded to know why the union was spending money on trying to organize immigrants at the nearby Superior Industries. They called for an audit of the Campaign's books. They attacked every line of the monthly financial statement that involved the payment of "lost time" to CAP activists who had been paid by President Beltran, as was standard procedure, to work for the local. Union meetings were taking on the character of an inquisition, and the Campaign activists were very much on the defensive.

APRIL 22, 1986--THE DELEGATE ELECTIONS: BELTRAN SUFFERS A LOSS; SO DOES THE CAMPAIGN

The Campaign organizers, who had in the past been very attentive to changing conditions in the local, were unable to unravel the rapidly unfolding events and resorted to mechanical thinking. In 1983, the Campaign had held a big rally a few days before the UAW convention and had used that initiative to bring the Campaign to Dallas. This time, with the convention planned for nearby Anaheim, California, the organizers resorted to a similar tactic. In early February, the organizers fixed April 26 as the date for a large rally.

The organizers focused almost all of their attention on the upcoming convention, again hoping somehow to impact a broader movement within the union. But they paid scant attention to the fact that the local's elections for convention delegates would be held on April 22. To the degree they thought about the delegate elections at all, they assumed the usual results: both President Beltran and Shop Chairman Ruiz would win, along with a relatively even split between committeemen opposing the team concept and those supporting it. The organizers then went into high gear, preparing leaflets to the membership, speaking to community groups, holding screenings of *Tiger By the Tail,* and holding weekly meetings of more than fifty activists, a significant increase in the core of the Campaign.

The Campaign organizers attempted to separate the upcoming rally from the debate over the team concept, arguing that whether one was for or against the team concept, community pressure was in everyone's interest. This was an evasive and disoriented response. For while a few of the team concept's most active supporters were arguing that the Campaign still played a positive role, the vast majority of the team concept advocates were going on the offensive against the Campaign. As the *Los Angeles Times* reported:

> Other union leaders such as Ray Ruiz, head of Local 645's bargaining committee...don't think much of the boycott threat. If it does come about, and it results in a substantial cut in GM sales, it will mean lay-offs at other GM plants. Those opposed to the Beltran philosophy believe that cooperation offers the best hope for saving the Van Nuys plant and for the revitalization of the labor movement generally.[6]

Ruiz's decision to openly attack the Campaign as leading to the layoff of other UAW members was his right, but it reflected the beginning of an open split in the local, one that some of the Campaign activists were going out of their way to repair with little success.

In retrospect, there were two reasons why the Campaign activists were slow to oppose the team concept directly. On the one hand, through years of organizing, they had become adept at the art of coalition building--the difficult, at times seemingly impossible task, of uniting people with sharp disagreements among themselves in order to confront a common enemy. Because the team concept was new, they didn't want to make the Campaign a partisan issue, and knew from first-hand discussions with many of their co-workers, that many of those who were open to the team concept were also very sympathetic to the Campaign. The subtlety of their outlook and their patience were clearly virtues.

On the other hand, part of the "subtlety" was not very different from old-fashioned fear. The team concept supporters were aggressive, angry, and often physically willing to attack those who did not agree with them. It appeared that there was a landslide of support for the team concept, and while its opponents bravely predicted, "You'll see, people will see through this trick," their statements weren't very convincing, even to themselves. Temporarily, at least, some of the Campaign's organizers were depressed and disoriented, but they pushed ahead with the plans for the rally.

Two weeks before the delegate elections, however, it became clear that the "cooperation team" had put together a very strong slate, called "Responsible Representation," and was running an effective campaign in the plant. With strong backing from the company and the International union, they put out attractive literature and argued that, if the workers wanted to save the plant, they should send a signal to Detroit that they had elected a team that was willing to cooperate with management.

The official leaflets of the team concept slate were indeed "responsible"; but during the delegate election campaign, a series of mysterious leaflets appeared in the plant, attacking President Beltran and leading the workers towards the "Responsible" slate. The leaflets raised a series of unsubstantiated and personal attacks against Beltran, red-baited both Beltran and Eric Mann, and ended with the charge that "Pete wants the plant to close. He has everything to gain (at your expense) and nothing to lose."[7]

The leaflets were signed by "Tom D. Torquemada, the Grand Inquisitor." Mike Gomez researched Torquemada and found the following biography:

> Torquemada, Tomas D. First Grand Inquisitor of Spain....The Inquisition had been established in 1480 at Seville, but Torquemada was the first to give it its organization....During his 18 years in office he burned 10,220 persons and condemned 6,860 to be burned in effigy....His later activities were directed against the Jews and about 1,000,000 of them fled the country to escape his persecution. He was one of the most bloodthirsty fanatics in history.[8]

Nate Brodsky observed: "There have always been dirty election leaflets in the plant, but nothing like this. This was like a combination of the *National Enquirer* and Joe McCarthy."

Under this type of attack, Beltran retreated into a shell. An outgoing and articulate man, in recent elections Beltran had not been an aggressive campaigner. He had moved from committeeman to shop chairman to financial secretary-treasurer to president of the local by doing an excellent job at the positions he was elected to and building powerful coalitions that spanned the union's many factions. But behind a confident public demeanor, he is a shy person and despises back-slapping and glad-handing. He reacted to the slander by completely withdrawing from any campaigning. He argued:

> I have served these people for two terms as president. I have handled people's unemployment claims, fought to get them reinstated when they were fired, stayed up until midnight with the families of injured workers, and worked many seven-day weeks when that was needed. Right now, I'm fighting to save the union from being destroyed. If, after all these years, people can be swayed by this type of garbage, they can have the damn election.

Beltran, as a savvy political operator, knew well that, while virtue may be its own reward, many a virtuous candidate who has campaigned poorly has gone down to defeat. Still, despite increasingly desperate urgings from his closest friends and allies, Beltran did not put together a slate; did not put out one piece of campaign literature--and lost! The Responsible Representation slate, led by Ray Ruiz, won a clean sweep of all seven delegates. It was an impressive organizing victory and gave the cooperation faction just what it needed--a valid mandate for their strategy.

APRIL 26, 1986 – THE CAMPAIGN'S STRENGTHS AND WEAKNESSES EXPOSED

The election results became known on Wednesday, April 23. The rally took place the following Saturday at noon. The crowd was well over a thousand people and reflected many organizing accomplishments. But the most important step forward, from the organizers' perspective, was that, for the first time in the Campaign's history, there was significant participation from the higher seniority workers on the first shift. Traditionally, they had seen the Campaign primarily as a "second-shift" movement, because of its roots in the second-shift layoff of November 1982 and because they had felt more secure about their future--a sense of security the Campaign organizers felt was unfounded but, until now, had been unable to penetrate. But in the growing debate over the team concept many of these workers, with greater ties to earlier and more class-conscious times and a greater knowledge of trade union principles, began to see the Campaign as a necessary tactic in the battle against concessions. John Ochoa, a worker with more than twenty years seniority in the plant, and Willie Guadiana, a worker with over twenty-five years seniority, became leaders of the Campaign and spent many an early morning urging their fellow day-shift workers to attend.

Local 645—UAW

INTERNATIONAL UNION, UNITED AUTOMOBILE, AEROSPACE & AGRICULTURAL IMPLEMENT WORKERS OF AMERICA-UAW

SATURDAY IS THE DAY, PLEASE BRING YOUR FAMILY AND FRIENDS RALLY AND MARCH TO KEEP GM VAN NUYS OPEN

PLEASE SHOW UP BETWEEN 11 AND 12 NOON, UAW #645 HALL
YOUR FELLOW UNION MEMBERS AND COMMUNITY SUPPORTERS HAVE WORKED FOR 3 MONTHS
WE NEED YOUR SUPPORT—THE JOB YOU SAVE MAY BE YOUR OWN!

Our thanks and appreciation to Gary Huck, respected labor cartoonist for the United Electrical, Radio and Machine Workers Union (U.E.) for the contribution of his talents

Many of the second-shift workers who had previously been active in the Campaign but had lapsed into complacent "support" became reinvigorated by the company's constant threats. The nature of the organizing work had changed. It was no longer characterized by, "Why don't you get involved?" but rather, "Which side are you on?"

At the rally, the visible support of striking TWA flight attendants, United Airlines pilots, San Fernando Valley Protestant clergy, and representatives from the Van Nuys and San Fernando Valley Chambers of Commerce reflected some of the new allies the Campaign had made through it organizing work.

Jackson Browne, the singer, opened the program. Before the event he was a little uneasy. "I'm not used to labor rallies; I don't think I know a lot of labor songs," he told the organizers. But they reassured him, "Our movement is interested in more than labor issues, so whatever you sing will be well received; and anyway, people will just be happy to have you there." Browne sang several selections from the album he had just released, including the title song, "Lives in the Balance," about U.S. policy in Central America, and "Lawless Avenue," about barrio warfare. Browne was followed by actor Dorian Harewood, who sang a song he had written and pledged his support to the movement.

The rally had a last-minute addition--the Reverend Jesse Jackson. Jackson had long known about the Campaign, several of whose organizers had worked in his presidential campaign, and had been invited to the rally through another Campaign ally, Los Angeles City Councilman Robert Farrell. Jackson told the workers:

> You are the freedom fighters, battling for economic and social justice against Reagan radicalism and corporate fascism. You are the real freedom fighters, not the contras. They are trying to destroy factories in Nicaragua; you are trying to keep factories open in America. Stand tall, stand proud, keep fighting and you will save your plant.[9]

Jackson's moving words reflected another step forward for the Coalition. Since his 1984 presidential campaign, in which the press attempted to pigeonhole him as "the black candidate," Jackson had utilized his public visibility in support of labor causes throughout the country--marching with the Watsonville, California, cannery strikers, the Hormel strikers in Austin, Minnesota, and the impoverished farmers in Nebraska. And, unlike many presidential candidates who stay away from controversial issues, at that rally he pledged himself and the resources of the Rainbow Coalition to a boycott of GM products if that became necessary.

The rally reflected the strengths and weaknesses of the movement. On the one hand, looking out at that coalition there was no question in anyone's mind that it had the capability to carry out a successful boycott of GM products in Los Angeles. If GM, based on the meeting with the Coalition in January 1984, was inclined towards keeping the Van Nuys plant open, at least for the short run, that rally solidified the decision. It is very unusual for a movement to be able to generate two rallies of over one thousand people three years apart, with the second rally representing an even stronger community base than the first. It is even more unusual for a movement to sustain four years of continuous organizing activity, so that the rallies are the exclamation points of years of lower-key organizing, not isolated, one-shot demonstrations of support.

On the other hand, in the eyes of some allies, the Campaign organizers had compromised their political influence and that of the Campaign because they had virtually ignored the delegate election race, assuming Beltran and several other progressive candidates would be elected, and had severely underestimated the growing strength of the cooperation faction. As one experienced labor leader in the city assessed: "The company and the Ruiz faction are spreading the election results all over the city. While Beltran is still president, they are talking like he's a lame duck. You people had better give top priority to his reelection campaign for president or your movement is as good as dead." For the first time, the labor movement and the broader public were being told that Beltran didn't represent the local, thereby weakening the credibility of the Campaign as well.

The next day's *Los Angeles Times* article placed more emphasis on Beltran's electoral defeat and Ray Ruiz's newfound expertise on preventing plant closings than on the views of the rally organizers:

> Ruiz's stance is gaining favor in the plant according to him and a number of others in the union. They said the growing sentiment for accommodation was manifested last week when a slate of delegates headed by Ruiz defeated Beltran's slate to be the local's representative at the UAW convention in Anaheim this June.
>
> Ruiz opposes the boycott, explaining, "We would be boycotting products built by our brothers and sisters in other GM plants." Ruiz also said he fears that the threat of a boycott would have the opposite effect to what its advocates intend because General Motors, not wanting to appear to be bowing to pressure, would be more likely to close the plant.[10]

Ruiz's public statements sharply contradicted his statements to the Van Nuys workers urging them to adopt the team concept. Contrary to his protestations about his "brothers and sisters" in other plants, Ruiz urged the Van Nuys workers to "look out for number one." As Pete Beltran explained, "In public he claims he is for solidarity, but at every union meeting, when he tries to sell the team concept, he says it's us versus Norwood." Ruiz's supporters echoed those sentiments by putting out leaflets arguing that "we are in a Superbowl competition where there can only be one winner--us or Norwood. The choice is up to you." Ruiz's view that protest would provoke GM to close down the plant had a remarkable similarity to the one advanced by GM management.

Nonetheless, Ruiz and his slate had won the delegate election and Beltran and his allies had not. Until that formulation could be reversed, or at least amended, the

Campaign to Keep GM Van Nuys Open, while still vital, was in a state of decline.

CHANGE OR DIE

If the Campaign wanted to rebound, it could no longer count on the help of the press. Armed with the option of the far more palatable team concept and a union faction advocating it, the press became a combatant in the struggle, placing even more pressure on the workers to accept the company's plan. A Los Angeles *Daily News* editorial, titled "Change or Die," reflected the public pressure that was placed on the workers:

> Auto workers concerned about bread on the table got an earful of baloney from the Rev. Jesse Jackson on Saturday. "You are the freedom fighters" Jackson said at the Van Nuys rally, held to pressure General Motors into keeping its local assembly plant open. "Not the Contras in Central America, the workers in Van Nuys. You are the freedom fighters."
>
> The truth about the Van Nuys plant is less romantic. These people are simply trying to keep their jobs and a number of people, including Jackson, are giving them bad advice about how to do so. The Saturday rally at which Jackson spoke was organized by labor and community activists who threaten to wage economic warfare through a boycott of GM products to keep the automaker from closing the Van Nuys plant.
>
> But the troubles of the Van Nuys plant are more fundamental than anything that might be solved by community action....The Van Nuys plant in its present form lacks a strong economic reason for being. Either it cuts its costs or it closes. Realistic union members

> realize this and they are talking seriously with management about implementing a "team concept" to replace the traditional assembly line and trim the workforce....The more militant workers talk instead about using the threat of a boycott to keep the plant open, with no "team concept" concessions until GM assures them the plant will not close....
>
> The boycott is an empty threat, however....It would turn local against local, national union officials against the Van Nuys militants and GM dealers against the union. For Van Nuys it could well be economic suicide.
>
> Already, just under half of the plant's workforce is due to be laid off on June 9. Rumors abound that the plant will close permanently when GM stops making Camaros and Firebirds in 1989. For the union, the choice is between changing its work rules and meeting management halfway, or dying. It's not a choice that can be scared away with a rally.[11]

The rally left General Motors with two clear, if somewhat contradictory, messages. On the one hand, the corporation saw that after four years, the Campaign was alive and well and, in many ways, even more of a threat than ever. The April 26 rally was objectively the strongest reflection of the coalition's support. Several foremen, whose jobs would also be lost in a plant closing, told Campaign organizers on the line that "Detroit was very impressed with the rally"; and only half-jokingly added, "Maybe you troublemakers will save our jobs after all."

On the other hand, the corporation intensified its efforts to defeat the Campaign within the local. If the public could be convinced that the workers had *voluntarily* rejected the Campaign and accepted the team concept, over time the Campaign could be stripped of its legitimacy and the boycott threat disarmed. Then, a plant closing, if necessary, could take place unchallenged.

THE COOPERATION FACTION ABUSES ITS MANDATE: WORKERS DEMAND A "HINGED ACCEPTANCE"

In every political battle, as long as the issues are not resolved, there is the possibility of reversal. As the UAW convention approached, the "cooperation team" leaders felt it would boost their standing with the International if they could get the membership to ratify a team concept agreement and deliver that package to the convention. There were two problems with that plan: first, the thirty-four workers who had recently returned from their investigation of the team concept had not finished their reports to the membership; and second, there was no logical reason, except for the "deadline" of the UAW convention, to push through a vote. In examining this process further, the decline of the cooperation faction can be better understood.

The thirty-four workers who had been elected to investigate the team concept were rerouted away from the Wentzville plant where, GM management told them, some "labor difficulties" made a visit impossible. Instead, they were sent to investigate the Pontiac Fiero plant, which coincidentally had been the former plant of Van Nuys plant manager Ernie Schaefer. The majority of the workers elected had been sympathetic to the team concept to begin with, but, except for a few overtly procompany workers, most of them tried to develop an analytical and open-minded approach, and took their job of representing the people in their department very seriously. They took copious notes on their trip and worked very hard to prepare their reports when they returned.

In that the union had spent $60,000 for their trip (including a week's compensation for lost wages), some very strict ground rules had been set up: upon returning, every observer would write a report expressing the pros and cons of the plan; the union would print a special edition of its newspaper, the *Fender Bender*, that would include all the reports; and those reports would form the basis for an informed vote by the membership on whether to adopt, modify, or reject the team concept.

Before this process could be completed, however, Shop Chairman Ruiz distributed a leaflet to the workers in the plant announcing that a ratification meeting was to be held on Wednesday, May 28, at which they would receive the shop committee's report, to be followed by an immediate vote. Many of the elected observers, who were still in the process of finishing their reports, explained to Ruiz that his planned ratification meeting was before the agreed-upon deadline for the *Fender Bender* and thus, the vote would take place without any input from the thirty-four elected observers. They asked Ruiz to postpone the vote until one week after the union newspaper was distributed to the workers. Ruiz overruled their objections.

In a surprise development, more than twenty of the elected observers, many of whom had supported both Ruiz and the idea of the team concept, signed a leaflet criticizing him for preventing a democratic ratification process by the members. Others on the shop floor went further, angrily criticizing Ruiz for squandering $60,000 of the local's money for reports he had no intention of listening to. The uproar grew louder. Workers demanded that the vote be postponed at least until the day after they had heard the shop committee's proposal for a new contract, so that they could have time to digest the information and talk among themselves. Ruiz backed down on that issue and agreed to a one-day hiatus between the report and the vote.

At the mass meetings at which the proposed contract changes were presented, there was an effort made to prevent President Beltran from speaking, which ended when Beltran fought his way to the microphone. He spoke against the team concept and urged a "no" vote, pointing out that behind all the talk of democratic cooperation in the workplace was a heavy-handed effort to impose a contract on the workers. He taunted Ray Ruiz, asking "what is the hurry for this vote?" The workers already had a local contract in place and there was no "deadline" in Detroit except one that Ruiz and Schaefer were artificially creating. In a prophetic observation, he pointed out that if Ruiz and Schaefer could dictate the reopening of the contract any time they wanted, there was no guarantee that they wouldn't try it again. Finally, while expressing his strong opposition to the plan, he took up the Campaign's demand for a ten-year commitment to the plant, and challenged Ray Ruiz and Ernie Schaefer to come back with such a commitment.

Beltran's challenge went a long way toward shaping the debate that followed. Beltran repeated that even those who wanted the team concept should demand a long-term commitment in return for their vote. Schaefer and Ruiz, sensing that the pendulum was swinging away from them and frightened that the team concept might not pass at all, promised the workers that they could vote what was called a "hinged acceptance"--that is, the new team concept agreement, if ratified, would not go into effect unless and until GM made a clear commitment to bring in a new model. The exact wording of the proposed contract was, "If ratified, this agreement will become effective only when a new product is announced for the Van Nuys Plant."[12]

While this helped GM get more votes for the team concept, it was a far cry from its original demand, "Vote for the team concept or we will close the plant." It reflected a significant modification of their position because of Beltran's, and the Campaign's, pressure.

Several months before the vote, most observers predicted the team concept would pass by a margin of two to one, and those estimates were even higher after the Responsible Representation slate's delegate election victory. But in just one short month, the undemocratic measures against the membership had taken enough of a toll that the team concept contract passed by a narrow margin of 53 percent "yes" to 47 percent "no."

One night-shift worker who had originally planned to vote "yes" explained why she changed her mind:

> I have always been active in the Campaign and you always tell us how GM may close the plant, and I agree. So when they told us to vote for the team concept or they would close the plant, I figured that I would give it a try. If it was very good, which I don't

expect, then that would be a plus. If it is a little bad, well, life is sometimes a little bad and I can live with that. And if it turns out terrible, then we can vote it out and tell them, "OK, close down the plant; I'm tired of being threatened."

But when I got to the meeting I could tell they weren't being honest. Every question we asked they said, "That hasn't been decided yet" or "The team will decide that." All they told us is that *we will eat in the cafeteria with our foremen.* But I don't want to eat with my foreman; I like it better when they eat in their cafeteria and we eat in ours.

And you know they aren't making such a big fuss to get us to vote for this thing just so we can all eat together or use the same parking lot. I want my job, but when I left there I didn't think that Ray Ruiz was telling me the truth. I think the company knows exactly what the team concept will be like but they don't want to tell us everything. So I voted "no."

The worker next to her on the line expressed his view as to why he voted "yes."

To me, "team concept" means "speed-up." But I still voted for it. When GM says they may close this place they aren't kidding. I was at Southgate for twenty years and I saw what it was like when they closed that place. It may be when they finally get the system organized, the jobs will be so hard that I won't be able to do them. But that won't be for a few years, and by that time I'll be close to retirement.

As far as Beltran is concerned, that was the first time I had heard him speak. They say he's hard-headed, but he was the only one up there who seemed to believe in what he was saying. I voted "yes" on the team concept, but I'll vote for Beltran when he runs again for president.

At the UAW convention the next week, another incident took place that weakened the mandate of the cooperation faction. Throughout the election campaign, they had pursued a strategy of simultaneously benefiting from the anonymous leaflets slandering President Beltran and disassociating themselves from them. But at the convention, several of the "Responsible Representation" delegates were seen openly distributing Tom D. Torquemada leaflets to other UAW delegates. Delegates from other locals, disgusted by both the "responsible" delegates and their leaflet, brought the practice to the attention of Joe Henderson, a long-time Beltran ally, and the editor of the *Fender Bender*. Henderson said, "It's a sad reflection of how much these guys are in with the company that they would choose some right-wing mass murderer as their symbol. I'm going to write an editorial, 'Will the real Tom D. Torquemada please stand up.'"[13] Tragically, Joe Henderson was killed in an auto accident the next day. He could not carry out his plan.

During the summer of 1986, both sides maneuvered for position. On July 3, 1986, five weeks after the vote, GM laid off the second shift at Van Nuys in response to the more generalized problem of poor sales throughout the GM system. The team concept advocates argued that because of their better working relationship with the company the second shift would be brought back as soon as possible. The team concept opponents argued that the second-shift workers had been used, in that the company had pushed through the vote, taken advantage of the lower seniority workers' insecurity to pass the team concept by a narrow margin, and then laid them off.

RAY RUIZ'S RAPID ASCENT... AND EQUALLY RAPID DECLINE

In October 1986, a series of events took place that once again changed the balance of power in the local.

In May, the team concept had narrowly passed because of the guarantees of a "hinged acceptance"--that the agreement would become effective only when a new product was announced for the plant.

But in October 1986, Chairman Ruiz, arguing that conditions had changed dramatically, urged the workers to allow him to implement the team concept immediately, without the guarantee of a new model. In a leaflet to the membership, Ruiz raised the following arguments:

> We are in a drastically different position today than that of four or five months ago during negotiations. First of all, we were running with two shifts of production....There is also a major concern that when the 2.9 percent interest rate is discontinued...the sales projections seem even worse than originally anticipated.
>
> Further, while in May when our contract was ratified we were on the leading edge of innovative contracts and were viewed in a very positive light, since then...the St. Therese plant in Canada recently ratified a new agreement, as have Janesville and Fairfax. On October 8 the Arlington plant will take a ratification vote on the issue of the team concept. So you see that we are the plant that has been leading the way instead of following the others....
>
> I have been exploring ways of bringing a significant number of our members back to work through a training program designed for the team leaders and group leaders....Thus, I will propose team concept implementation at today's meeting.[14]

Ruiz's plan produced an uproar in the plant. Many of the workers who had voted for the team concept had done so only after the promise of a new model. Now Ruiz essentially had negotiated another new agreement with the company that superseded the "hinged acceptance" team concept agreement that had superseded the regular local contract. Beltran's warning that the practice of acceding to company demands for reopeners would lead to the disintegration of even minimal contractual protections had proven accurate.

On Thursday, October 3, almost four hundred workers stormed across the street to the UAW hall and voted unanimously to remove Ray Ruiz from office for improperly using his office of shop chairman to deny them their right under the UAW constitution to ratify their contracts. Ruiz and his supporters boycotted the meeting.

The following day, the International union ruled that Ruiz had been removed through a "procedural error" and that a trial had to be held to remove him from office. Some angry workers felt this was an effort by the International to protect Ruiz on a technicality, but they were mistaken. Without orderly rules, groups of three hundred or four hundred workers could come across the street any time they wanted to and take turns removing Beltran and Ruiz.

A recall movement was organized to carry out Ruiz's removal according to the local's bylaws. "Let's do it right this time," his opponents said. The odds-makers in the plant gave the recall an excellent chance to succeed. The theme of Ruiz's broken promise was reported in the *Los Angeles Times*:

> The local's vote came at a meeting called by Beltran. The local president charged that Ruiz broke a promise to block introduction of Japanese-style labor practices at General Motors' Van Nuys plant until the company made a long-term commitment to keep the factory operating. Supporters of Ruiz deny that any such promise was made.[15]

As the team concept movement barely took its first steps, it became apparent that the perpetual breaking of the contract and its eventual replacement with "informal understandings" between union and management had become tantamount to policy. Many of the workers on the first shift took the contract and its provisions very seriously. They carried their contracts in their overall pockets and could quote chapter and verse to any foreman. But as one worker who voted for Ruiz's recall explained:

> Hell, in recent years we've had some sell-out contracts, but they've still been contracts. This team-concept movement tears up contracts as quick as we can vote them in. Under the new system, any time the shop chairman and the plant manager cut a deal, they tell us the conditions have changed and the deal becomes legal.

Moreover, when the Ruiz faction tried to deny that they had agreed not to implement the plan without a long-term commitment from GM, they were contradicting one of the few written safeguards the team concept agreement gave the workers. Ruiz's credibility had reached an all-time low.

On October 30, after qualifying petitions had been circulated in the plant, a mass meeting was held in the UAW Local 645 parking lot to vote on a recall of Ray Ruiz. This time it was not a spontaneous movement of four hundred workers, but an official meeting of the GM Unit attended by more than one thousand workers. President Beltran charged Ruiz with violating his duties as shop chairman and abrogating the membership's right to ratify all local contracts. Ruiz sarcastically thanked the members for showing up for his "party" and dismissed the meeting as illegal. UAW Unit Chairman Nate Brodsky called for a "division of the house," in which members supporting the recall would walk to one side of the parking lot, and members wanting to retain Ruiz in office would walk to the opposite side. Approximately eight hundred workers voted to remove Ruiz; approximately two hundred voted to retain him. The political message was clear: Ray Ruiz had lost the confidence of the membership less than six months after he had been elected delegate with the highest vote total.

While those voting for recall had more than the necessary two-thirds margin, there were legitimate questions about whether the total votes cast were sufficient for a legal quorum. But this time the International union chose not to overturn the election on a procedural issue. Ruiz's influence having waned, he was given a job with the International union in Detroit.

NOTES

1. Reprint distributed to GM workers, December 1985.
2. Discussion with the author, December 1985. All subsequent statements without footnotes represent conversations with the author or remarks made at union meetings or on the assembly line.
3. Letter to the workers from plant manager Schaefer, December 10, 1985.
4. Pete Beltran, "GM Van Nuys Report," leaflet distributed to the membership, December 17, 1985.
5. "Positive Press Newsletter," December 16, 1985.
6. "UAW Divided Over Way to Save Plant," *Los Angeles Times*, Business section, April 9, 1986, p. 1.
7. Leaflet signed "Tom D. Torquemada, the Grand Inquisitor," distributed anonymously in the plant.
8. *Encyclopedia Americana*, Volume 26, 1966, p. 78.
9. "Autoworkers Rally to Keep GM's Van Nuys Plant Open," *Herald Examiner*, April 27, 1986, p. 3. The front page had a picture of Jackson with the headlines, "Jesse in Van Nuys," and "Jesse Jackson, actor Ed Asner and singer Jackson Browne join autoworkers rally to demand that GM keep Van Nuys plant open."
10. "Coalition Supports Bid to Keep GM Plant Open," *Los Angeles Times*, Metro section, April 27, 1986, p. 5.
11. "Change or Die," Editorial, *Los Angeles Daily News*, April 29, 1986, p. 12
12. "Summary of Proposed Agreement," May 1966.
13. Conversation with the author, June 3, 1986.
14. Ray Ruiz, "Shop Chairman's Report," September 29, 1986.
15. *Los Angeles Times*, Valley edition, Business section, October 6, 1986, p. 1.

Chapter Eleven

WHO "SAVED" THE VAN NUYS PLANT?

After the dramatic downturn in GM sales in the summer of 1986 and the shutting down of the second shift at Van Nuys in July of that year, rumors began to surface, stronger than usual, that another wave of plant closings--predicted for 1988 and 1989--might be coming sooner than expected. As was always the case, GM Van Nuys was mentioned as a likely candidate. The tension within the plant began to mount as the newspapers indicated that shortly after the November 1986 congressional elections GM would announce the closing of several plants. On Friday, November 7, the *New York Times* ran the front-page headline: "General Motors to Shut 11 Plants; 29,000 Workers Will Be Affected." In the predictable rhetoric of these occasions, GM President McDonald argued: "These actions will benefit all who have a stake in the continued well-being of General Motors."[1]

Included on the list of the eleven plants to be closed was the Chevrolet-Pontiac plant in Norwood, Ohio, the sister plant to Van Nuys that also produced the Chevrolet Camaro and Pontiac Firebird. After four years of a GM-choreographed interplant competition, which the Campaign had done everything in its power to oppose, Van Nuys--assumed to be most vulnerable because of its West Coast location--was kept open, while Norwood--assumed to be safe because of its Midwest location--was closed.

GM'S EXPLANATIONS

Some of the Van Nuys organizers had, naively perhaps, expected Roger Smith and F. James McDonald to acknowledge the Campaign as their reason for keeping Van Nuys open. Nate Brodsky ridiculed this idea, and in an imitation of company rhetoric, he mocked: "We would like to admit that the Campaign to Keep GM Van Nuys Open brought us to our knees. Without the Campaign, Van Nuys would have been dead meat. We are certainly glad other UAW locals are not paying attention to those Van Nuys troublemakers, because we sure hate boycotts." Other activists searched the press for recognition of the Campaign's achievement, but the previously highly publicized Campaign had somehow been omitted from every news story about the survival of the plant. What was more objectionable, the press presented a wide variety of highly speculative and contradictory "theories" to the public as to why the plant had been spared; but the theory of the preemptive boycott protecting the plant was systematically excluded from the free marketplace of ideas.

In fact, it is difficult to assess how GM made its decision. GM had, over the years, created a web of disinformation and mystification in order to convince workers in more than a dozen plants that they were simultaneously on and off the "danger list." A June 1986 *Automotive News* story, titled "McDonald Tells How GM Targets Plant Closings," gave Detroit's official version:

> McDonald said that plant age and design aren't the only factors GM considers when closing plants....He said he tells them, "If you have an organization that's producing the highest quality at the lowest cost, we're going to continue to invest in that operation.

> *If you have one that's continually fighting* and the quality is not good, we aren't going to put a nickel into it."[2] (Italics added)

So, by McDonald's criteria, could it be said that GM Van Nuys was a well-behaved plant? Hardly. Four years of marches, demonstrations, and hundreds of letters from GM Van Nuys workers threatening a boycott hardly endeared the local to GM management. Only six months before its plant-closings announcement, 47 percent of the Van Nuys membership voted against the team concept amidst stormy union meetings at which union leaders on both sides of the argument, as well as local managers, were booed by angry workers. If there was one plant that *was* continually fighting, albeit over GM's threats, it was Van Nuys. So, clearly, labor peace was not the reason Van Nuys was kept open.

Perhaps it was because GM Van Nuys produced "the highest quality at the lowest cost." Again, this is untrue. Both the Campaign organizers and local plant management agreed that while quality at Van Nuys was high, there were additional shipping costs involved because of the plant's West Coast location. On the other hand, the other GM plant producing Camaros and Firebirds, in Norwood, Ohio, had other cost problems: it was an older, multitiered plant with, according to GM officials, a less up-to-date infrastructure.

The issue of "which plant made the car cheaper" was one that GM manipulated to its advantage. As late as a day before GM's November announcements, a *Los Angeles Times* article repeated the GM story that "it costs an estimated 70 million a year more to produce Firebirds and Camaros in Van Nuys than in Norwood. This differential comes out to about $400 a car."[3]

This story was based on repeating GM's claims, since independent industry analysts (quoted above in Chapter 8) took strong issue with GM's estimates. But even assuming that the shipping cost differential was well under $200 per unit, and other production costs at Norwood reduced the overall differences to less than $100 per unit, few at Van Nuys attempted to argue that the plant was saved because the workers produced the car more cheaply than at Norwood--and the Campaign explicitly rejected entering into those types of comparisons. Ironically, as will be shown, the explanations advanced by GM management in Detroit, local GM management in Van Nuys, and the Campaign's leadership all concurred that it was *not* lower unit costs that kept the plant open.

In developing a "Campaign-free" analysis of the situation, GM officials in Detroit came up with a new theory to explain the closing of Norwood and the keeping open of Van Nuys--"the landlocked theory":

> GM President F. James McDonald said the Norwood plant was closed mainly because it is aging and multi-storied, like many of the others targeted for closing.
>
> He said the Ohio facility, situated in a congested urban setting, would be difficult to renovate. Newer auto plants tend to be sprawling, single-story buildings with lots of room for expansion or modification of production systems. "Norwood is certainly a land-locked plant, and it just doesn't look like it has a future." McDonald said. "We hope that Van Nuys will. But we will have to keep looking at that."[4]

It was difficult to fathom what it was that McDonald would have to keep looking at. Van Nuys, like Norwood, was also a multi-story plant, although with a better overall design. Also, GM Van Nuys, like Norwood, was located in a congested urban setting and, while having some room to expand, was hardly the "vacant lot" area it had been in 1947.

But what is most ironic about McDonald's after-the-fact rationale is that the subject of multi-story versus one-story plants, and the problems of "landlocked" plants had *never* been discussed before the closing of the eleven plants. With contradictory logic, the company had argued for four years that the future of a plant is in the workers' hands (citing "labor climate," good working relationships, "teamwork") in an effort to extract concessions. Then, when announcing the closings, the corporation told the workers that in the final analysis they were victims of geography or architecture ("located on the West Coast"; "landlocked in the Midwest"). Did it take GM four years to realize that Norwood was a multi-story plant or that GM Van Nuys was on the West Coast? And what happened to the shipping cost argument? After years of being used as a threat against the Van Nuys workers, that argument was not even mentioned in McDonald's analysis, making Detroit's writing of history highly suspect.

DID THE TEAM CONCEPT "SAVE" THE PLANT?

While a compliant press dutifully reported McDonald's theories without critical comment, even local plant manager Ernie Schaefer did not agree with Detroit's analysis. He articulated the view that it was the workers' acceptance of the team concept (and his own role in selling it to them) that saved the plant. Another article in the *Los Angeles Times* on November 7 explained:

> At a news conference in Van Nuys, company and union officials said the local plant was saved mainly because UAW Local 645, which represents the workers, narrowly approved GM-backed Japanese-style management techniques in May....The Van Nuys plant manager, Ernest D. Schaefer, said that the plant's future depends on its ability to execute the team concept. "If we're successful...then this plant has nothing to worry about," he said. "On the other hand, if we don't do a good job, then we, like all the other plants in the General Motors system, will appear on the endangered species list."[5]

Despite Schaefer's assertion that the plant had been saved because the workers had voted for the team concept, a close scrutiny shows the problems with that analysis.

To begin with, to claim that the narrow voting margin for the team concept in late May 1986 impacted GM's *announced* decision in November of 1986 contradicts everything that GM and industry analysts say about the lead time necessary for plant closing decisions.

At the meeting with the Coalition in January 1984, GM president McDonald told its leaders that GM would have to make some critical decisions in 1986 about plant closings it anticipated in 1989. McDonald explained that he could assure Van Nuys two more years but no more because the corporation schedules plant closings at least two years ahead. Thus, while it may change its mind about *when* to close a plant (as market conditions change), the corporation usually knows *which* plant it plans to close years before the workers find out.

In his own letter to the GM workers urging them to adopt the team concept in 1986 in order to qualify for a new model in 1989 or 1990, Schaefer argued that "Corporate decisions on where to build new products must be made *many years in advance*."[6] For Schaefer then to turn around and argue that as late as May 28, 1986 GM was waiting to see whether the Van Nuys workers voted for the team concept before deciding whether to close the plant five months later completely contradicts both his earlier statement and GM's modus operandi on plant closings.

The question of how much time in advance GM needs to plan plant closings is complex. The scenario of the 1984 meeting with GM President McDonald, and even the Ernie Schaefer scenario of a decision in 1986 to insure future car production in 1989, was based on GM's predominant control of the market and an "orderly" process of closing down some plants and opening up others. These scenarios assumed that *demand* for GM cars would remain relatively constant, and as *supply* increased through the opening of new plants, other plants would have to be closed to balance the relationship.

But as GM sales and market share began to decline again in 1986, it is conceivable that GM was pushed into a decision to close plants more rapidly than it had expected. Moving up the timetable, however, would not change *which* plants GM would close, but rather, *when* the already doomed plants would be closed.

For the sake of argument, however, let's pursue Schaefer's statements further, particularly his claims that as late as June 1, 1986, GM had not yet decided which plants to close and that the team concept vote was the decisive factor in protecting the plant.

Since it has been argued that the team concept is, in actuality, a plan to eliminate jobs and dramatically reduce labor costs, it is possible that GM would see both short-term political, and long-term economic, benefits in imposing such a system at Van Nuys. Had the Van Nuys workers voted overwhelmingly for the team concept it is conceivable that GM would have wanted to keep the plant open for "showcasing" reasons: "Formerly Militant Local Sees the Light and Adopts Cooperative Labor Relations."

There are three fallacies in that argument. First, the 47 percent "no" vote, even in the face of overt company threats to close the plant was a harbinger of long-term opposition. Second, since the company realized it would be laying off the second shift, where it had received the greatest support for the team concept, shortly after the vote, and would be retaining the higher-seniority first-shift workers, management well understood that there was the likelihood of *escalated* opposition to the team concept. Third, contrary to its original plan, the company was not able to get a no-strings-attached vote. In order to win even a 53 percent "yes" vote, it had to accede to a demand for a "hinged acceptance," in which the team concept would go into effect only if the company delivered a new model that would take production into the 1990s. This was hardly the model of "cooperation" that GM wanted to market to other GM locals. From the perspective of company objectives, the team concept vote was both a political victory and a political setback. Thus, the decision to try to implement the team concept over substantial worker opposition would only make sense if the company was *already* committed to keeping the plant open.

So, even on the unlikely premise that GM held up its final decision on the Van Nuys plant until immediately after the vote, even as late as June 1986 there was no overriding company objective served by the team concept vote. To carry the argument one step further, however, some would argue that GM might have been willing to suffer an initial period of short-lived opposition, with the hope that after a brief period of resistance, support for the team concept would grow, opponents like President Beltran would become isolated, and a new hero, Ray Ruiz, would emerge as the model of the cooperative local leader who saved his plant. If this was GM's plan, then again their hopes were thwarted. Four months later, as angry workers voted twice to remove Ruiz from office and the tensions in the local over the team concept had become a continuing news item, "the Van Nuys model" was hardly something that GM would want to package. If anything, according to McDonald's official story, GM Van Nuys would be closed down as a plant that was "continually fighting."

A *Los Angeles Times* story, titled "The Rift: A Battle Between Two UAW Factions is Escalating Along with Emotions at Endangered GM Assembly Plant," captured the flavor of the labor climate:

> With General Motors due to announce shortly what factories will close late next year, tensions are running high at the company's long-threatened Van Nuys Assembly plant....Ruiz's star appeared to be rising at Beltran's expense since the spring, but amid fresh concern over the future of the Van Nuys plant, Beltran is trying to mobilize support to oust his younger rival....The issue has divided workers, helping to set the stage for a heated confrontation last Thursday in the parking lot behind union headquarters. It was the second anti-Ruiz rally orchestrated by Beltran in a month. During the first, on October 2, an estimated 300 to 400 union members voted unanimously to suspend Ruiz indefinitely. The UAW overturned the vote, saying it did not follow proper procedures.

> Last week's session attracted a total of nearly 1,000 workers from both sides who came...ready for a shouting match. Some challenged the authority of speakers, jeering at them and calling them names. Fear of a plant closure does not give Ruiz "the right to waive our...rights to self-government" Beltran told the crowd from the bed of a flatbed truck.[7]

The battle within the local was certainly of GM's making, but it was not reflective of the type of compliant labor climate that GM has been dreaming of, or the exemplary plant that GM would want to keep open--unless other factors were compelling it to. Whatever the reasons for keeping the Van Nuys plant open, the two advanced by GM--that Norwood, despite making cars at least $100 cheaper than Van Nuys, was "landlocked"; or that Van Nuys had adopted a team concept plan a few months before the closing--were certainly not the reasons.

THE CAMPAIGN'S SIDE OF THE STORY

Despite the unconvincing nature of GM's arguments, on what basis can the Campaign organizers claim that *their* efforts were the decisive factor in GM's decision? Why is it reasonable to assume that the *threat* of a boycott by a single UAW local and a community-based coalition would be sufficient to convince the number one corporation in the Fortune 500 to keep a plant open against its will? The reasons can be found in both GM's history and the specific history of the Campaign.

Despite GM's colossal size, since Alfred P. Sloan's ill-fated crusade against President Roosevelt in 1936 the corporation's leaders have shied away from the political limelight and tried to avoid open confrontations. Throughout GM's history--in the battle of Flint, in many of its confrontations with Walter Reuther, and in its bungled efforts to silence Ralph Nader--one trend remains constant: GM does best when it can resist social movements by the weight of its economic power; GM does worst when it is required to justify its actions in the public arena in terms of larger social objectives.

In the early days, things were simpler. Alfred P. Sloan could honestly, if ruthlessly, declare: "You can say perhaps that I am selfish, but business is selfish. We are not a charitable institution; we are trying to make a profit for our stockholders."[8] But when later generations of GM executives tried to rationalize that selfishness as being in the "public interest," the result was usually a public relations disaster. Three factors, based on other events of that period in which GM made its decision, reinforce the view that GM chose to avoid a test of the Los Angeles-based boycott.

First, GM's declining credibility with the business press. In April 1986, six months before it was to resort to a 2.9 percent financing scheme to unload its massive inventories, GM first tried a 2.9 percent price increase to generate greater profits per car from the consumer. The industry journal, *Automotive News*, lambasted GM's decision. It criticized "GM's profit preeminence" in setting the goal of more profit per car instead of maintaining higher sales at lower profits. It argued that, because of GM's greed, "more production cuts, layoffs and even plant closings could follow. And en route to those profits, GM seems to be talking out of both sides of its mouth."[9]

Automotive News has never been known as a critic of auto company behavior, but its sarcasm and even disdain towards GM's public statements reflect GM's declining credibility. If GM closed down the plant, the response of the business press towards a subsequent GM boycott would depend largely upon its success or failure. If the boycott fizzled, there would be editorials praising GM's "cost-cutting in the face of union bravado." But if the boycott showed early signs of success, business reporters would begin inquiring: "Could GM have headed off this confrontation?" From a purely business perspective they would ridicule GM for provoking a boycott in the largest new-car market in the United States. GM's perception of its vulnerability in the media was one factor in its decision not to risk calling the Coalition's bluff.

Second, GM's efforts to avoid public confrontations even at the expense of greater short-run costs--as evidenced by their handling of the H. Ross Perot affair. Shortly after the closing of the eleven GM plants in November 1986, Perot, GM board member and founder of GM subsidiary Electronic Data Systems, sharply criticized GM management, and Roger Smith in particular, for a bloated middle-management structure that drove up cost per unit and inhibited corporate decisiveness. Smith responded by removing Perot from the board and paying him $700 million for his GM securities, an amount that was far above their actual value. According to the *New York Times*, "a dozen pending shareholder suits contend that Mr. Perot was paid more than market value for his shares....California State Treasurer Jesse M. Unruh said he still believed 'there is a tinge of greenmail about what is being done here.'"[10]

But why did GM resort to "greenmail"? Didn't GM believe in maximizing profits? The reason is that the corporation was having so many production and sales problems that it could not also afford highly visible public controversies. It was willing to pay an additional premium to Perot to avoid a lengthy battle that might hurt its long-term profit picture even more. In a similar vein, the Campaign organizers believed that GM used this reasoning in response to the boycott strategy.

Third, GM's growing, and potentially spiraling, market vulnerability. The 1987 advertising campaign for Oldsmobile--"Isn't it time you put Oldsmobile on your list?"--vividly reflects GM's declining industry position. In past decades, GM could assume that one out of two Americans would buy a GM car, and that virtually everyone had GM on their list. In the 1980s, the changing tastes of new car buyers, combined with the virtual disintegration of "brand loyalty," are reflected in an ad campaign that attempts to convince consumers at least to put Oldsmobile on the *list* of cars to look at, let alone buy. In past years, GM could more easily dismiss the claims of boycott organizers, trusting that an army of "loyal" GM consumers would withstand even the best-organized efforts. But, under the changing market conditions, GM was very aware of its market vulnerability, especially with the rise in popularity not just of the imports but of Ford and Chrysler as well. Because of those three factors--GM's declining credibility with the media, its inclination to avoid public controversy, and its eroding consumer loyalty--the organizers believed that the threat of the boycott was the decisive factor in GM's decision.

Those arguments, however, while setting out the general circumstances underlying specific decisions, do not fully or satisfactorily explain them. The Campaign activists trace a more direct relationship between their actions and those of General Motors to keep the plant open.

Their version begins in January 1984, as the meeting between the Community Coalition to Keep GM Van Nuys Open and GM president McDonald was breaking up. Assemblywoman Maxine Waters asked GM president McDonald: "Do I have your commitment to take a full report of this meeting back to the GM board of directors?" McDonald indicated that he would. Waters pressed on: "Will you explain to them the extent of our commitment to this boycott and our ability to carry it out?" Again, McDonald agreed. Reverend Ignacio Castuera, at the time the director of the Los Angeles District of the United Methodist Church, continued: "Please convey to the board that I have just concluded several years of activity on the Nestle boycott, which ended with a settlement with the corporation. I don't see why you would want to risk the same thing that happened to Nestle."

When McDonald went outside to face the press, he was asked by Henry Alfaro of ABC news: "Did the threat of the boycott in any way make you more agreeable to this meeting?" McDonald replied:

> Well, you know, I don't think threats solve anything, threats on our part or threats on anybody else's part. We don't ignore people talking about boycotts; we simply don't think

> they're good for business. They would hurt business. So if somebody says that we don't pay attention to it--we do pay attention to things like that; but that's not the way to solve problems today.[11]

From that day on, the objective of the Coalition was to convince GM management that it had the sustained capacity to keep the pressure on the corporation--and to be far more troublesome than a critical article in *Automotive News* or a short-term blowup with an outspoken board member that would grab the headlines one day and be forgotten the next. The costs of that boycott would be far greater than simply unsold cars; although that alone would be substantial. They would be picket lines, press conferences, dealer complaints, demands for more meetings by church and political leaders, endless calls by the press, and lots of bad publicity--not over a week, or even a month, but at least a year--publicity that might spark other labor and community-based initiatives against GM in other parts of the country as well.

The Coalition members believe that on January 23, 1984, McDonald made the assessment that closing down Van Nuys, at least in the foreseeable future, was too great a risk. In an effort to reinforce that decision, over the next two years, the Coalition was able to show GM that it had a capacity for *sustained activity.*

The Coalition generated boycott letters from dozens of community groups and community leaders over a two-year period, indicating to GM officials in Detroit that the meeting with the Coalition was not a one-shot affair. The Campaign organizers consciously tried to show GM that the movement was growing and that it was reaching out to new constituencies and new areas of the city, with the hope that someone in GM's Detroit office was tracking the progress of the followup organizing work. It must be remembered that over that two-year period GM received over one thousand individually signed boycott letters.

The public and critical acclaim for *Tiger By the Tail*, and the fresh organizing opportunities that the film presented, gave GM a sense that the Campaign was tactically resilient and relentless. While several television stations explained that they did not want to run the film for fear of antagonizing GM as a potential sponsor, GM management became well aware of the film's existence.

The April 26, 1986, rally demonstrated the Campaign's ability to mobilize over one thousand community leaders and other supporters at the first word that the plant was once again in danger. Also, the visible role of Reverend Jesse Jackson should not be underestimated. GM was well aware of Jackson's impressive track record in confronting some of America's largest corporations. This influence was magnified by Jackson's growing influence as a major Democratic Party presidential contender. In the view of many observers, if there had been any doubt in GM's mind before that rally as to whether the Campaign was alive and well, the Campaign's mobilizing capability, combined with the visibility of Jackson, Ed Asner, Jackson Browne, and other allies, reinforced GM's inclination not to risk a closing at Van Nuys.

Based on a reading of GM's history, it seems fair to conclude that the Campaign--expanding its base both to the Chamber of Commerce and the Rainbow Coalition and sustaining four years of organizing activity--had a far greater impact on GM's final decision than a narrow and bitterly contested team concept vote.

This analysis allows the team concept movement to be seen in a different light. Rather than having *saved the plant*, as its proponents argue, the team concept allowed GM to *save face*. It gave the company a chance to turn a political defeat into a potential political victory.

It seems most plausible that General Motors, feeling temporarily out-maneuvered by the Campaign, chose to keep the plant open in contradiction to its original plan--if only for awhile. On the other hand, GM was powerful enough and resilient enough to realize that if it could use the constant danger of the plant closing to impose a system of labor relations on the workers that advanced corporate objectives and weakened the union, then, although the Campaign might have saved the plant, GM would ultimately reap even greater benefits. In 1986, at the time of its announcement, it is this author's view that GM turned its attention from asserting its "management rights" on the issue of plant closings to the issue of making GM Van Nuys a "model" of compliant labor relations.

This decision was made even more palatable to GM by a compliant media. For, if GM agreed to keep the plant open and focused its attention on the imposition and refinement of the team concept, there was a bonanza of praise for "GM's cooperative labor relations."

With the Coalition temporarily at arm's length with the announcement that the plant had been kept open, and with the press applauding GM for its statesmanship, the corporation assessed that maybe "Keep GM Van Nuys Open" wasn't such a bad slogan after all. Now, it could turn its attention to controlling the conditions on the shop floor and rewriting history to serve its own objectives.

NOTES

1. New York Times, November 7, 1986, p. 1.
2. *Automotive News*, June 30, 1986, p. 50.
3. "Plan Could Save GM's Plant at Van Nuys," *Los Angeles Times*, Business section, November 5, 1986, p. 1.
4. "GM To Close 11 Midwest Plants," *Los Angeles Times*, November 7, 1986, p. 1.
5. "Reprieve for GM Plant Has No Guarantee," *Los Angeles Times*, Business section, November 7, 1986, p. 1.
6. Letter to GM Employees from Plant Manager E.D. Schaefer, December 10, 1985.
7. *Los Angeles Times*, Valley edition, Business section, November 4, 1986, p. 5A.
8. Ed Cray, *Chrome Colossus* (New York: McGraw Hill, 1980), p. 271.
9. "Both Sides of GM's Mouth," *Automotive News*, April 7, 1986, p. 10.
10. "Head of GM Sees End to Perot Controversy," *New York Times*, February 29, 1987, p. 28.
11. McDonald's statements recorded in the film, *Tiger By the Tail*, by Michal Goldman.

Chapter Twelve

THE CAMPAIGN OR THE TEAM CONCEPT? JUNE 1987 LOCAL ELECTIONS

No sooner had Van Nuys been saved than GM renewed the threat of its closing. The *New York Times* predicted, "Further Closings Seen in Cost Cutting Move," and the *Los Angeles Times* emphasized, even on the day of the announcement, "Reprieve for GM Plant Has No Guarantee." If two words had become profanities in GM's labor relations vocabulary they were "job security." GM had come to believe that keeping the workers in a permanent state of job insecurity served its interests. For almost 350,000 GM workers, life had become a virtually endless cycle of plant closing threats and demands for concessions. And even for those who acceded to the threats and granted the concessions, the cycle was just repeated again. Plant manager Schaefer warned that the Van Nuys plant's future would hinge on the worker's obedience:

> If we're successful...then this plant has nothing to worry about. On the other hand, if we don't do a good job, then we, like *all the other plants* in the General Motors system, will appear on the endangered species list.[1]

Unwittingly, perhaps, Schaefer had captured the essence of the master plan, one in which "all the other plants" had become candidates for the endangered species list.

The growing sense of desperation throughout the GM system was most vividly reflected in the whipsawing of individual UAW locals. Shortly after GM's announcement that Van Nuys would be kept open and its sister plant, Norwood, would be closed, a headline in the Los Angeles *Herald Examiner* proclaimed, "Shut Van Nuys, Say GM's Ohio Workers":

> In an 11th hour attempt to save jobs, the union local in [Norwood] Ohio argued that its workers can make cars cheaper than their fellow UAW counterparts in Van Nuys. The argument saddened Van Nuys union officials, made national union officials uneasy and raised charges that GM pitted one union local against the other. Yesterday, officials at United Auto Workers Local 674 in Ohio told the *Herald* that the local's task force had figured the Norwood plant could make cars for $112 million less a year than Van Nuys....Cleon Montgomery, a committeeman-at-large...said the Norwood plant would save GM $70 million alone in the costs of shipping parts to California for assembly and shipping cars to markets in the East and Midwest....[2]

At first, many Van Nuys workers, and even many of the Campaign's organizers, viewed the news story uncritically, and took it at face value. They believed that the Norwood workers, out of desperation, had played the only card they had left--an effort to reverse the verdict by substituting victims. While to some degree this was true, it was, at least in part, a reaction to what the Norwood workers believed had been a betrayal by the team concept advocates at Van Nuys.

At the UAW convention in June 1986, speaker after speaker from the anti-concessions wing of the union denounced NUMMI, Saturn, and Van Nuys as the Trojan horses in the union's midst. Many of the Campaign's advocates felt this was unfair. Didn't these delegates know that Van Nuys was where one of the most advanced movements against plant closings had been initiated?

Didn't they know that 47 percent of the membership had voted *against* the team concept?

While the Van Nuys activists were right in seeing that some subtlety may have been lost, they were not taking responsibility for the political truth: at the June 1986 UAW convention not one anti-team concept delegate had been elected, and in June 1986 a signed and ratified team concept agreement existed at Van Nuys which was then being used against the Norwood workers and other workers in the GM system.

While the Local 645 members identified with the Beltran camp were still respected members of the insurgent forces in the national UAW, it was hard for them to grasp that in a few short months Van Nuys had dramatically shifted from a symbol of resistance to a symbol of compliance. In that context, the response of the Norwood workers needed further clarification. Cleon Montgomery, the committeeman who was quoted in the *Herald* article, gave his own version of events to this author:

> When we heard what the Los Angeles newspapers had reported, we were very upset. It sounded like we were telling GM to close you all down and keep us open, and that is not true. Let me give some background.
>
> Several years ago, the company came to us and said that the plant was in danger and we had to become more competitive. We considered ourselves a pretty militant local. We tried to develop a five-year business plan to make the plant more competitive. But we never agreed to a big Quality of Worklife push; in fact, it never went over very big around here. In fact, our goal was to figure out how to make the plant more competitive *without* modifying our local agreement: things like cutting down on absenteeism and organizing the work more efficiently.
>
> We had heard that all of you at Van Nuys were doing a good job in keeping your plant open. We had seen *Tiger By the Tail*

> and we liked the part where you said you wanted to keep your plant open without cutting Norwood's throat.
>
> But then, out of the blue, we heard that you had signed a team concept agreement; that you said you could make the cars cheaper than us; that you had torn up your local agreement--and we wondered what had happened to the so-called militant Van Nuys local.
>
> I have to be honest. The workers here felt that you guys at Van Nuys *did* cut our throats; that you signed an agreement to save your plant that jeopardized all of us. The guys here didn't understand that the vote was 53 to 47 percent and that a lot of people were fighting against it. We hadn't heard that you had voted out Ray Ruiz until after our plant was closed--and by that time we didn't much care.
>
> After our plant was closed, a lot of newspapers called us and asked, "How come you guys can't produce the car as cheaply as Van Nuys? How come you aren't efficient like they are?" We got damn angry, and in our efforts to explain that we had certain efficiencies that you guys didn't have and the way we talked about your higher shipping costs, it sounded like we were saying to close you down instead of us. After they hung up I realized I shouldn't have talked to those reporters and that whatever I said would only be used to create divisions among us.
>
> I think the saddest thing is that we didn't communicate more. You never really called us and we never called you. We never worked together. I think that was the greatest tragedy.[3]

The failure of the Campaign activists to reach out to the Norwood workers during that period was partially because the team concept agreement was a function of the shop committee, where they had little power. But additionally, it was a result of the disorientation and regrouping brought about by the team concept itself. At the UAW convention, nonvoting observers from the Campaign had to watch the team concept delegates talking to other delegates and the press about the victory of the "new" labor relations over the "old." It became clear that the June 1987 local elections would be a critical battleground.

Encouraged by their delegate victories, the team concept advocates made it clear they would challenge President Beltran for the presidency in June 1987. Thus, the upcoming presidential race would become the test case of the Campaign's strength and its continued ability to speak for the local. That election would become a plebiscite on three issues--the team concept, the Campaign, and whether the Van Nuys local would be a symbol of union solidarity or one of whipsawing.

JANUARY 1987, SIX MONTHS BEFORE THE ELECTION: CLEAR QUESTIONS AND UNCLEAR ANSWERS

At the April 1986 rally, George Cole of the Steelworkers, Phil Giurizzo of the Service Employees, and Eloy Salazar of the Machinists, all strong allies of the Campaign, had warned that in the labor movement in Los Angeles, all eyes would be on Beltran's reelection bid. The model of a local union challenging the strategy of its international union was understandable, and many local unions would still support a boycott if called by an individual UAW-based coalition. But, if Beltran lost control of the presidency, the legitimacy of the Campaign would be severely undermined. In theory, community organizations could still call their own boycott. But, in practice, if the workers themselves were to vote out a progressive president, no matter how much pressure there had been from the company to do so, the future of both the Campaign and the plant it was trying to protect was grim.

By January 1987, after the rapid rise and fall of Ray Ruiz, many Campaign leaders felt the political winds had shifted. Wanting to avoid the errors of the past, they discussed a plan to reelect Beltran and elect a full slate of progressive candidates to the local's executive board. Those discussions were based on the following premises.

First, the reelection of Beltran was the key objective. If Beltran was defeated by a candidate hostile to the Campaign and a team concept oriented shop chairman was elected as well, the Campaign's only tactical option would be to mobilize the general membership in spite of the opposition of the two most powerful officers in the local--a theoretical possibility but a practical impossibility.

Second, the effort to run a candidate for shop chairman opposed to the team concept was of increasing importance. In the early stages of the team concept discussions, when the company and shop chairman proposed "exploring" new methods of work, many of the Campaign's supporters and even some of its activists were open to some form of team concept agreement. As a result, the Campaign leadership attempted to keep the issues of the Campaign and the team concept almost entirely separated, in order to preserve the Campaign's broad-based coalition in the plant. Accordingly, Campaign members who openly opposed the team concept did so with leaflets written and paid for by individual union members with a clear disclaimer that they were expressing their own views, not those of the Campaign.

The team concept advocates, however, now that they had an "alternative" to the Campaign, felt free to openly oppose it. At every union meeting, team concept advocates attacked the Campaign. Some of its more ideological advocates put out leaflets arguing that corporate social responsibility bordered on socialism, whereas the team concept was based on the corporation's right to accumulate maximum profits.

The entire ideological framework of the team concept--based on worker obedience and class cooperation--was in direct conflict with the ideology of the Campaign--based on worker assertiveness and class confrontation. It soon became apparent that the team concept was taking the offensive and sapping the lifeblood of the Campaign. If the team concept was not reversed, the Campaign would become a hollow shell. Thus, greater attention had to be given to running a strong candidate for the shop chairmanship who would openly oppose the team concept.

Third, the Campaign activists assessed that an election victory by a candidate for shop chairman opposed to the team concept was not in the cards for 1987. The team concept itself would not be implemented at full speed until after the election. Thus, based on the experience of the NUMMI workers in Northern California, the Van Nuys workers anticipated a "honeymoon period" of at least a year, followed by greater resistance as the team concept became fully operational. They felt it was unrealistic to expect the majority of workers to vote for a shop chairman opposed to the team concept so soon after management claimed that it had saved the plant.

The best-case scenario was that Beltran would win reelection as president, while his running mate for shop chairman would make a strong, but unsuccessful, showing. Then they would spend the next two years rebuilding the Campaign and becoming an opposition caucus on the issue of the team concept. After two years of the workers experiencing the team concept in practice, and two years of active organizing, it would be possible to elect a shop chairman opposed to the team concept in 1989.

Even this plan, however, would depend upon the effective organizing of the plant's second shift. The first-shift opposition to the team concept was substantial, while the lower-seniority second-shift workers, if not in favor of it in principle, were far more sympathetic to giving it a try. While company spokespeople said that the second shift, laid off in July 1986, might not be called back before the summer of 1987, and always acted as if they were unaware that there would be local elections in early June, opponents of the team concept said they would bet their life savings that the company would bring back the second shift before the elections.

Without such a callback, the elections would be held almost exclusively on the higher-seniority first shift, in which case Beltran's reelection would be virtually assured and the election of a shop chairman *opposed* to the team concept would be a substantial possibility. (While the 2,200 second-shift workers would still be eligible to vote even if they were not called back to work before the election, no more than 200 of them could be expected to vote.)

Thus, with the return of the second shift prior to the election virtually assured, the Campaign activists felt that two major adjustments had to be made if Beltran was to pick up enough second-shift votes to win.

First, the fears of many second-shift workers had to be allayed. The workers on the second shift had ambivalent feelings toward Beltran. When they were feeling safe and secure, or believed company promises, they tended to see Beltran as "too militant" and one whose militancy might lead to the plant being closed. But when they felt abused by the company, or by those in the union who were most cooperative with the company, they ran across the street to seek out Beltran's help.

Beltran's supporters would argue that the team concept advocates, in their efforts to reach agreements with the company, had a long history of violating the workers' rights. If the workers did not want continued violations of their rights in the future, they had to elect Beltran to one of the top two positions in the local. The strategy was called "Vote for Beltran, Keep Your Options Open."

Under this plan, it was assumed that, while there was strong opposition to the team concept already, there was not an electoral majority against it. Many workers, it was assumed, would be afraid to elect a shop chairman directly opposed to the team concept for fear the company would close the plant in retaliation. On the other hand, since they also feared company abuse of the team concept and a possible doublecross on its promise that the team concept would keep the plant open, they would elect Beltran as president to preserve the option of fighting against it at a later date. The plan was to convince second-shift workers that it was in their interest to keep Beltran in the presidency and the Campaign in the forefront of the local's activities.

Second, the bulk of the campaigning on the second shift for Beltran would have to be done by the second-shift-workers themselves. Beltran's past practice of not getting out on the shop floor with the second shift workers was not necessarily something that his allies could change. While Beltran had a reputation as an excellent campaigner early in his career, he had spent many years in the president's office across the street and had developed a certain isolation from the essential political process of "walking the line."

This was reinforced, structurally, by the plant's two-shift operation. In many ways, the two shifts were like two different plants, living different lives, barely seeing each other. The union hall was open during the day and closed at night. While only the most active second-shift unionists came to work early and hung around the union hall, the vast majority of first-shift workers, over a year's time, would come to the hall during their lunch break or after work for meetings, services, or activities--times when the president was in his office and easily accessible. This difference was reinforced by Beltran's far stronger personal ties to the first-shift workers based on his twenty-eight years of seniority and years as committeeman and shop chairman. Thus, on the first shift where his strength was greatest, his weaknesses as a campaigner would not hurt him significantly. It was the second shift, where his personal ties and political support were weakest, where Beltran's presence was needed most.

Beltran's closest second-shift allies decided, however, that rather than be frustrated in an unsuccessful attempt to get Beltran to campaign aggressively on the second shift, they would have to do it for him. They would put together a strong slate of candidates for second-shift committeeman positions, run well-known second-shift workers for executive board positions, and put out many leaflets to the second shift explaining Beltran's positions. While this was not at all an ideal tactical plan, it was an effort to adjust to reality and do the best they could.

The Formation of the "Fighting Back" Caucus

These initial formulations, however, were made in relative isolation from many other forces in the plant that were also in motion. While initially many Campaign activists had seen the election primarily from the vantage point of the movement to keep the plant open, it soon became evident that the central question facing every political aspirant was: "Are you for or against the team concept?" Traditional lines of political demarcation in the local were breaking down as many different factions and caucuses coalesced into two large caucuses reflecting this strategic conflict--Responsible Representation (composed of the team concept advocates) and Fighting Back (composed of its opponents).

The formation of the Fighting Back caucus was a response to past errors by opponents of the team concept as well as to the electoral success of the Responsible Representation slate in the 1986 delegate elections. When President Beltran, Financial Secretary Joe B. Garcia, and Committeemen Mike Velasquez and Pete Lopez all lost in the delegate elections, many of their closest supporters on the shop floor, who were not afraid to express their views, raised the following criticisms:

"Stop fighting among yourselves." Many of the Chicano committeemen who had no real political disagreements on the issues had refused to form a unified caucus because of historical and personal conflicts. The workers argued that they could no longer afford the luxury of both a "green ticket" (Velasquez, Lopez, Garcia) and a Beltran ticket. There was a need to run one unified slate against the team concept.

"You guys were out-campaigned." The Responsible Representation slate ran a better campaign. Their leaflets were better, their posters were better, and they gave the appearance of being unified and well-organized. The team concept opponents were told: "If you want to win the election you had better start early and run a professional campaign."

"Stop pulling your punches on the team concept." Beltran, to his credit, was the only one who had spoken out forcefully against the team concept. Other committee-

men who attacked it in private felt that the workers on the shop floor were not yet against it, so they tried to straddle the fence. The Responsible slate accused them of hiding their real views--and they were right. Those committeemen who said privately that they opposed the team concept but publicly said "they had a lot of questions" were all defeated in the delegate election. Shop floor workers warned them: "If you want to win this time, you have to stop playing it cute and start offering a clear alternative."

Out of these criticisms came a unified and outspoken Fighting Back slate. The plan was to run Beltran for president and Joe B. Garcia for financial secretary-treasurer--both as incumbents seeking reelection--and Paul Goldener, a former president of the local whom Beltran had defeated in 1978, for shop chairman. Goldener, who had not been active in the local for almost a decade, was still respected by many of the first-shift workers, but his base on the second shift was very weak. It was felt that Goldener's candidacy would bring a third grouping to the caucus, would guarantee that he would not run an independent candidacy for president against both Beltran and the Responsible candidate, and that, while he was a long-shot to defeat the Responsible candidate for shop chairman, he would deliver additional first-shift votes to the entire slate.

March 1987--Beltran's All Or Nothing Gamble

As the June elections approached, in March, the Fighting Back caucus held a large meeting to reach final agreement on its candidates for each position. While it was assumed that only a few minor decisions remained, almost out of the blue came a major one: Beltran changed his mind and decided to give up the presidency to run for shop chairman.

Beltran had given his decision considerable thought. He explained that many of the first-shift workers had been asking him--essentially drafting him--to run for shop chairman. They argued that he could not continue to act as an outside critic. If the team concept was as bad as he claimed, he had the responsibility to come back into the plant and lead the fight against it. With a strong shop chairman there were many committeemen who would be willing to stand up against the company. Every movement needed a leader, a point person.

Beltran was aware of the risk, but it was time to go right to the heart of the problem. He argued that while there would be spontaneous acts of resistance, such as the movement to remove Ray Ruiz from office, over time the team concept would develop a permanency and legitimacy that would be hard to reverse. While some might argue that the company's excesses would eventually spark resistance, there had also been many instances when company domination wore people down and produced cynicism and resignation. If he stayed in the president's office while the company implemented the team concept with the full support of a compliant shop chairman, he would become increasingly isolated and peripheral to the politics of the local. Eventually, rather than having two years of organizing to get rid of the team concept, two years of the team concept would get rid of the Campaign, the progressive executive board, and the Beltran presidency itself.

Finally, Beltran argued that the eight hundred to two hundred vote against Ray Ruiz was a forerunner of electoral opposition to the team concept. The first-shift workers told him that they had voted Ruiz out, only to have him replaced by an appointed successor, Richard Ruppert, also a supporter of the team concept. Since Beltran had been active in Ruiz's recall, he had to take the responsibility for coming up with an alternative.

Beltran felt his arguments were persuasive, but it went beyond argumentation. There were gut feelings involved as well:

> When I got involved with the UAW, I looked up to people like Walter Reuther and Emil Mazey and was so proud to be in this union. Now I see the union going downhill. I see virtually everything we fought for being wiped out, and I don't want to sit in my

> office watching it. I was elected president after years on the shop floor. The Campaign was one of the high points of my work for the union. But now the guys I have spent twenty-eight years with are asking me to come back into the plant to lead a fight. What am I supposed to say--that I can't run because I might lose?[4]

The activists most closely identified with the Campaign, many of whom worked on the second shift, strongly disagreed with Beltran's decision. For several reasons, they were worried, if not panicked, about the consequences of a Beltran defeat:

First, they felt that Beltran was basing his decision almost exclusively on the opinion of the first-shift workers. In March, the company still had not announced a decision as to whether to recall the second shift. The first shift had been working alone since July and, in many ways, the political reality of the plant had become a one-shift operation. Based on public opinion and voter projections of the first shift, the decision to give up the presidency and run for shop chairman was a sound one. But when the second shift came back, all that would change.

Beltran's support on the second shift was weak at best, but he had far more support on the second shift for president than for shop chairman. Even before the layoff, his supporters had been pushing the idea of re-electing Beltran as a counterweight to the team concept, with some success. The idea of electing Beltran to dismantle the team concept, however, was not one that would win much support among second-shift workers, especially since the Responsible Representation candidate for shop chairman, Richard Ruppert, was extremely popular on the second shift.

Second, they felt that Beltran was underestimating the disastrous consequences of a possible defeat. Both the Campaign and the fight against the team concept depended upon Beltran's control of one of the two top offices, either the presidency or the shop chairmanship. As shop chairman, he would relinquish direct responsibility for the Campaign but, as an extremely powerful figure and a member of the executive board, he would still provide the mandate for it. Conversely, as president he would have little institutional power in the bargaining process but, along with Fighting Back committeemen, he could still play a very active role. (In fact, as president, Beltran had been criticized for playing a less active role than he was legally allowed to in the team concept negotiations. Beltran countered that when he walked into the team concept discussions he felt it was "a giveaway, not a negotiation" and chose to disassociate himself from the "fiasco" so he could better lead the opposition. Still, if reelected president, he would have the right to play a significant role in the actual shop floor process.)

This is not to say that any of the Fighting Back caucus members felt that these positions were of equal strategic importance. Everyone agreed that the most central fight was on the shop floor and that the possibility of Beltran's election as shop chairman would place him at the heart of the historical process. But if Beltran gave up the presidency, to which he was heavily favored to win reelection, in order to attempt a long-shot battle for the shop chairmanship and lost, even by the most narrow of margins, the consequences would be almost unimaginable. An electoral sweep by a president hostile to the Campaign and a shop chairman supportive of the team concept would provide a field day for the Responsible Representation slate, the company, and the media. A movement that had taken five years to build would be flat on its back and would have to begin its recovery not from the president's office, but from the intensive care unit.

After all the arguments had been presented and Beltran had argued strongly for his position, he agreed that he would be bound by the vote of the caucus. After a lengthy and democratic debate, the caucus members voted overwhelmingly (approximately fifty to twenty) to support Beltran's bid for the shop chairmanship. The debate was over and a decision had been made. As Mike Gomez, who had argued against the decision, explained: "We can sum the whole thing up later. Right now our job is to win the damn thing."

MARCH-JUNE 1987: UNION DEMOCRACY AT WORK

Pete Beltran began his election campaign in March, whereas his opponent, Richard Ruppert, had begun his months earlier. When Ray Ruiz took a position with the International union in November 1986, Beltran and his supporters had called for an immediate election to fill the vacancy. But the International disallowed their protest and appointed Ruppert to fill Ruiz's position. Upon assuming the shop chairmanship in November 1986, Ruppert set his sights on the June 1987 elections. In many ways, the Beltran-Ruppert contest was a perfect match, because both candidates were the best possible representatives of their points of view.

Richard Ruppert was a relative newcomer to the plant, having begun working at Van Nuys in 1976. (Some of the "old-timers" viewed Ruppert, with "only" ten years seniority, as making his move too soon for the top shop-floor office.) Ruppert had risen through the elected ranks quite rapidly. He began as a committeeman in the night-shift paint department, where he quickly developed a reputation as an unusually dedicated representative. Unlike some committeemen, he did not hide behind the contract's limitations to excuse inaction. As a hard bargainer and an articulate debater, he was frequently able to win settlements that other committeeman could not.

Based on his good work, Ruppert was elected "committeeman-at-large" on the second shift. Since the shop chairman, while legally on both shifts, in practice spends most of his time on the first shift, Ruppert was virtually the shop chairman on nights. When workers were dissatisfied with the representation from their district committeeman, they would go to Ruppert--and usually get results.

Ruppert was also one of the few pro-team concept committeemen who was sympathetic to the Campaign. When other committeemen tried to red-bait the Campaign, Ruppert opposed their actions. He argued: "I see the Campaign as an insurance policy. When I go in to negotiate with the company, it's good to know that the community is behind me."

One of Ruppert's main tactics was to present himself as the candidate who was above politics. In virtually every speech at union membership meetings, Ruppert would preface his remarks by saying, "I'm tired of all the politics and maneuvering going on around here...." This brought cheers from the uninitiated and smiles from the regulars, since Ruppert was one of the most astute politicians in the local and could wheel and deal with the best of them.

As the team concept movement developed, however, it was Ruppert's strategy, not his personal qualities, that many workers took issue with. On the one hand, his personal integrity was still unquestioned. At a time when some committeemen were learning that supporting the team concept could be lucrative--junkets to New Orleans and New York with "joint activities funds" to "study" cooperation; a growing number of "easy money," full-time "joint activities" positions--an opponent of the team concept said, "I think that Ruppert is the only one of those guys who actually believes in the thing." On the other hand, as the team concept's implementation began to be characterized by wholesale violations of contractual rights, many workers began to reevaluate his role.

Thus, as the boxing promoters would argue, this was a "dream fight": two highly respected and articulate advocates of two diametrically opposed strategies, each one the best possible representative of his cause.

Ruppert began his campaign with a strong appeal to the laid-off second-shift workers, and with a considerable boost from the company. On December 15, 1986, Ruppert wrote a letter to the laid-off workers announcing his appointment as shop chairman and describing his efforts to convince the company to bring back the second shift:

> As many of you know, Ray Ruiz has accepted a position with the International union....In his absence I have been appointed Shop Chairman. We have recalled a total of 120 people to replace the hourly folks who will be trainers for the Team Concept. Approximately 250 laid-off brothers and sisters will be called back to work in February to replace team leaders in training for the first shift.
>
> The training is going very well. On December 11th, Manny Granillo and I met with Dave Campbell, CPC Vice-President, and members of his staff in Detroit. Ernie Schaefer, Marlin Hess, Jim Gaunt and Joe Ponce represented CPC management at this meeting. We again reviewed our training program and requested needed support. Once more our plans were praised and our support was promised. Over and over again the future of the second shift has been addressed with all levels of management. While the rising field supply [of Camaros and Firebirds] is a concern, our goal remains to have the second shift return before their benefits expire. We are doing everything possible to make this happen.[5]

To many, Ruppert's plan seemed reasonable, if not commendable: working with the company to develop a training program, flying to Detroit to negotiate with top GM officials, bringing back some second-shift workers as trainers, and attempting to bring back the entire second shift. But how would GM bring back a shift if sales were down? Why would GM bring back a shift even though a "rising field supply" created no need for more production? And how would discussions about "training" convince GM to bring back 2,000 workers? Those questions were not answered.

Then, in November, when GM announced the closing of eleven plants and Van Nuys was kept open, a joint letter from plant manager Schaefer, outgoing shop chairman Ruiz, and committeeman Ruppert was mailed to "all laid-off employees":

> Although you have probably seen or read various news media reports regarding the closing of eleven GM plants, we wanted to also communicate to you in a timely manner that the Van Nuys Plant is not one of the plants scheduled for closure. This is truly welcome news for all our employees....
>
> Many factors are considered in the decision of which plants will close. There is no doubt that our innovative new labor agreement and implementation of Team Concept were the strong points in our favor. We must now move forward to make real progress to demonstrate to the people in Detroit that they made the right decision....We accept this opportunity and will do all that we can to keep the plant operating and to *bring the second shift back as quickly as possible.*[6] [Italics added]

Again, there was no explanation provided as to *how* the second shift was to be called back, except by doing "all that we can." Moreover, the view that somehow union officials and local management could work together to convince Detroit to bring back a shift even though sales were poor contradicted the most elementary understanding of the auto industry.

When the Campaign first began its organizing work, both its union and management opponents argued that decisions as to whether plants were kept open or closed were based solely on market factors: "Look, if the car isn't selling, what is GM supposed to do, hire people out of charity?" The Campaign advocates responded that of course they didn't expect GM to keep people working if sales were down. Management's decisions to hire or lay off a shift of workers were based almost exclusively on market demand and field supply--on solely economic grounds. That was why the UAW had fought for and won supplemental unemployment benefits--to protect workers from the ravages of the boom-and-bust cycle in the auto industry.

In contrast, the decision whether to close down the Van Nuys plant after GM had already closed its other Los Angeles auto plant was a political as well as an economic decision, since market demand obviously existed for GM products in Los Angeles. That decision *was* subject to political intervention, which was the underlying assumption of the Campaign.

Thus, the promise to the second-shift workers that somehow "cooperation" could bring back their shift was an outright deception. Many workers commented that the promises made to the second-shift workers had at the very least a strong overtone of the politics that Ruppert claimed he was above.

In April, when GM officially announced the callback of the second shift, the laid-off workers received still another letter:

> We are most pleased to announce the return to full, two-shift operations effective May 20, 1987. The Plant will operate under the team concept. All Van Nuys employees will participate in seven days of orientation and awareness training prior to resumption of full, two-shift production....We plan to recall all our laid-off, second-shift employees to attend the training sessions from May 11 through May 19, 1987, with both shifts operating start of shift May 20, 1987....
>
> The return of the second shift is a result of the proactive efforts of the Plant Union Leadership and Management. As you are aware, since January 1987 we have followed a communications and training plan to be fully prepared to quickly implement a return of full, two-shift production....This progressive action was most appropriate and critical to the decision to return the second shift.[7]

The letter was signed by "Richard A. Ruppert, Shop Chairman and Ernest D. Schaefer, Plant Manager."

Before a single "official" campaign leaflet had been distributed by either candidate, Ruppert, through a series of letters co-written with plant manager Schaefer, had promised the second shift he would do everything in his power to bring them back, and then, according to his own assessment, had delivered the goods. How had he done it? Through "proactive efforts." What were "proactive efforts?" No one knew, but it hardly mattered. More than two thousand workers, and their votes, were coming back just in time for the election. Perhaps coincidentally, the Ruppert/Schaefer team would be training the workers in "awareness" just three weeks before the election, and then sending them back to the shop floor, where the Fighting Back slate would have only two weeks to make its case. From the perspective of Beltran and his supporters, the prospects looked bleak.

Several of his supporters had asked, if not pleaded with, Beltran to send at least one letter to the laid-off workers, explaining some of the developments in the plant from his perspective and criticizing the blatantly political efforts to take credit for a callback that was based on market conditions. But Beltran did not feel such a tactic was important. He was looking for a more dramatic one.

Beltran Goes to Court to Block the Team Concept

On April 9, 1987, a week after the announced callback, Beltran went to court to block the implementation of the team concept agreement, asking for injunctive relief. He made clear that he was *not* trying to prevent the second shift from coming back, but rather protesting the conditions under which they would be asked to work. Beltran, former president Paul Goldener, and committeeman-at-large Mike Velasquez filed a court action that Beltran explained in his column in the local union newspaper, *Fender Bender*. The charges can be summarized as follows:

- The company used the promise of a "hinged acceptance" and a new car model to induce workers to vote for a team concept agreement, and then reneged on its promise.

- The company had been hand-picking *which* union officials it wanted to negotiate with, bypassing certain duly elected members of the local bargaining committee.

- The company had been signing "side letters and agreements" with local union officials that violated both the contract and the rights of union members--the so-called "living agreement." In the past, after a contract had been signed, there were opportunities for the union and management to make *slight modifications* consistent with its provisions through "memoranda of understanding" or "side letters." But in the practice at Van Nuys, according to Beltran, any time local management wanted to change the conditions of work, they would simply draw up a "side letter" and, with the help of certain local union officials, supersede the signed agreement.

This legal brief and the charges it contained were the opening volley in Beltran's campaign, an effort to present his concerns in a systematic and comprehensible manner. While many of Beltran's supporters on the first shift felt the court suit was long overdue, his supporters on the second shift felt its timing was an electoral mistake. While Beltran explicitly argued that he was not trying to block the second shift from coming back, GM management and their local supporters, who had argued that the team concept was the only reason for the second-shift recall, charged Beltran with jeopardizing the livelihoods of the second-shift workers.

On Monday, April 14, Beltran, Velasquez, and Goldener held a press conference at the local union hall to explain their law suit. While the first shift was held over to work overtime, more than seventy-five team concept trainees marched over from "training class" to challenge Beltran. As Beltran tried to explain his position, angry team leaders challenged him at every point, engaged in a shouting match, and, essentially, disrupted the press conference. The *Los Angeles Times* reported:

> Three United Auto Workers officials have filed suit against General Motors, seeking to halt vast Japanese-style work-rule changes scheduled to be put in place at the company's Van Nuys assembly plant next month.

> The suit was filed with the National Labor Relations Board on Friday by members of the so-called "militant" faction of Local 645 in Van Nuys, who seek to keep in place GM's existing manufacturing techniques.
>
> The suit charges that GM reneged on a promise to make a long-term commitment to keep the Van Nuys plant open in exchange for gaining worker support for the "team concept" agreement which was narrowly passed by 4,500 rank-and-file workers last May....Team concept has repeatedly been cited by Van Nuys plant manager Ernest D. Schaefer, as well as some union officials, as the reason that the San Fernando Valley plant was spared from a sweeping round of GM plant closings last November.
>
> The militants, however, say team concept is merely an excuse for speeding up the assembly line. The suit claims that GM inappropriately dealt with local UAW members in negotiating the labor agreement. It also alleges that the local's bargaining committee was unfairly excluded from the process. Beltran said the suit is not intended to prevent GM from calling back to work the plant's laid-off second shift.[8]

While Beltran tried to give assurances that his court suit would not jeopardize the callback, the timing of the court suit was another setback to the work on the second shift. The court case was a valid tactic, but why not wait until after the election before filing such charges; or at least until after the second shift had returned to work? In that way, company claims that the litigation jeopardized the jobs of second shift workers could be rebutted. And why not call a general membership meeting to explain the strategy to workers on both shifts, so that even those who disagreed with the tactic could understand its rationale? Those questions were asked, but for many second-shift Fighting Back members, no satisfactory answers were provided.

Angry second-shift allies told Beltran that things were getting out of hand. It was almost as if the first shift was getting so defiant that they didn't care what the people on the second shift thought and were ignoring even the advice of the slate's second-shift candidates.

Several second-shift people had argued against the press conference, predicting that it would become a target for the team concept advocates. And they had opposed the initiation of the court case before the elections, arguing that the Responsible Representation slate would gain even more ground on the second shift through misrepresenting its intentions. Since the court case was simply a tactic, what good would it be to "win" a long-shot legal decision if, by the time it was decided, all of the plaintiffs had been defeated in the elections?

Also, many of Beltran's closest second-shift supporters strongly disagreed with the characterization that the first shift was union-oriented and militant, whereas the second shift was company-oriented and frightened. Some of what appeared to be greater militancy on the first shift was simply a reflection of far greater job security. If the plant closed in a few years, many of them had enough years to retire, or take early retirement. Others, with more than ten years seniority, while not eligible for retirement, had relatively small house payments on homes they had purchased over a decade ago, plus a Guaranteed Income Stream payment to protect them in the event the plant closed. This gave them a greater sense of security and a greater willingness to stand up against company threats. But, if those same workers were to switch places with the second-shift workers and inherit their seniority and life situations, they too would be more cautious before taking a hard line with the company.

Thus, what was needed was a comprehensible and reasoned militancy, one that could reassure workers on both shifts that, while risks would be necessary, they would be taken in order to achieve greater job security. Unless the Fighting Back slate could convince the workers that they were fighting for job security, not just fighting back, the prospects for victory were remote. While those disagreements were not resolved fully, through up-front debate and the trial and error of the press conference at the union hall, a greater strategic agreement was reached.

The Team Concept Classes:
What Exactly Was the Subject Matter?

The theory of the team concept is to involve workers in the productive process, to use "their heads as well as their hands," and to develop worker initiative in correcting both poor labor relations practices and technical roadblocks to productivity.

Workers were told that "in managing conflict in a constructive way, it is important that members of the group...seek an answer to the agenda issue that provides a 'win-win' or 'consensus' solution."[9]

Kelley Jenco, an outspoken critic of GM's application of the team concept, expressed her reservations:

> It isn't so much the content, it's the company's motives that are so dangerous. As long as I have worked for GM they have dumped on the workers; and many workers have low self-esteem. Now, all of a sudden, the company says, "We have been wrong. We want to be your friend"; and the workers get a chance to get dressed up and have long lunches and sit around talking about cooperation, far from the assembly line.
>
> The classes talk about improving your family life and resolving problems without fighting; and when it comes to the family I completely agree. But then the people will come back to the assembly line, and their foreman is going to give them more work, and they are gonna get mad, and their group leader will say, "Now remember what we learned in class. There's no need to have a big conflict." I'm afraid they will become brainwashed, at least for awhile.

> Now, when they get back on the line and work for a few months and the company starts adding work onto their jobs and they can hardly keep up and the line gets speeded up I think a lot of them will change their mind. But we only have two weeks before the election and I think these classes are a big campaign trick. The problem is, I'm afraid the trick is going to work.[10]

Two weeks before the election, many of the Fighting Back candidates were worried. Ballpark estimates were that the first shift looked 60 to 40 percent in favor of Beltran, while the second shift appeared to be 80 to 20 percent in favor of Ruppert. Mark Masaoka, Kelley Jenco, Manuel Hurtado, and other second-shift Beltran supporters began to discuss what would be required to turn the situation around.

They began with the assumption, based on past practice, that there would be at least one hundred more voters on the first shift than the second because of the more advantageous voting conditions for the first shift. While the polls were open all day, when the first shift workers came out of work at 3 o'clock in the afternoon, it was a more "normal" time to go to a polling place; whereas, when the second shift got off work at 1 o'clock in the morning, it was pitch dark. Many workers would get in their cars, and drive right past the polls. While that difference had often led to as many as three hundred more votes cast on the first shift than the second, because of the highly charged nature of the election and the stake most workers felt in it, it was assumed that difference would be far less than usual--thus, the one hundred vote estimate.

It also was assumed there would be a very high voter turnout. With approximately 2,200 workers per shift, and over 200 on the third shift, they estimated that 1,500 workers would vote on the first shift, 1,400 on the second, and 100 on third shift (graveyard).

Based on those estimates, if Beltran could carry the first shift by a 60 to 40 percent margin, break even on the third shift, and get at least 40 percent of the second-shift votes, he could win a narrow victory. The projected vote totals, based on this strategy, were as follows: If 1,500 workers voted on the first shift and Beltran got 60 percent of the vote, he would lead Ruppert by 300 votes going into the night-shift voting. If Ruppert, however, won 80 percent of the night shift, he would have a 720 vote margin on nights and beat Beltran by 420 votes. If Ruppert carried the second shift by 70 to 30 percent, he would have a 560 vote margin on nights and win the election by 260 votes. If Ruppert's margin on nights was reduced to 65 to 35 percent, he would still have a 420 vote margin and win the election by 120 votes. It was only at the 60 to 40 percent mark that Ruppert's second-shift lead could be reduced to 280 votes, falling just short of Beltran's 300 vote first-shift margin. If those figures held, Beltran would win by 20 votes. With those rough estimates as the cornerstone of their plan, the second-shift Beltran supporters had two weeks to convince 280 voters who were leaning toward Ruppert to vote for Beltran, while preventing any erosion among the voters leaning toward Beltran.

The War of the Leaflets

Contrary to many antiworker stereotypes, autoworkers as a group are highly intelligent, with the vast majority quite literate as well. They read election leaflets carefully and are influenced by the battle of ideas--especially in an election in which the stakes are so high. While, in other elections, walking the line and shaking hands were major factors in rounding up votes, in this election written leaflets were the decisive factor. When the second shift returned to work on May 20, 1987, Mark Masaoka put out his own leaflet, "The View of a Returning Worker":

> All of us who have been on lay-off these past 10 months feel a tremendous sense of relief about the return of the second shift....But my enthusiasm is tempered by the

> following concerns: 1) GM has no long term future planned for the Van Nuys plant; 2) the plant manager's lies about "team concept saving the plant and bringing the second shift back" will divert people from continuing to fight for a new car model and a long-term commitment, and 3) unless we renegotiate objectionable portions of the team concept agreement we will work in a divisive and undemocratic system with excessive and unsafe amounts of work....These are the kinds of objections to the present team concept that President Beltran feels must be changed to produce a team-concept agreement we can live with, even if it means delaying implementation of the team concept....
>
> Although local management tries to depict our local President Beltran as insensitive to the future of the plant, it was under Beltran's leadership that the Campaign to Keep GM Van Nuys Open began. We have a broad Labor/Community Coalition who pledged in a meeting with President Jim McDonald that GM would face a Los Angeles area boycott if they closed Van Nuys. The impact of this organizing work is sometimes better understood by GM and the nation's business magazines than by some of our own members.[11]

Masaoka's leaflet, in an effort to make Beltran's position less threatening to the second-shift workers, in fact softened it too much, implying that Beltran wanted to modify the team concept's worst excesses when, actually, he wanted to dismantle it. Still, it was the first effort to move the debate from "are you for or against the team concept?" to a more thoughtful discussion of its specific provisions. It offered the Campaign as an alternative to the team concept's claims of job security.

Beltran then put out his first leaflet explaining his position:

> Contrary to the rumor mill, I am not seeking the closure of our plant in Van Nuys,

let alone the permanent layoff of the second shift. Even our court action demands the recall and retention of the second shift. Surely then, my critics jest when they think I want to be the Shop Committee Chairman of nothing.

Four years ago, when General Motors first started threatening the closure of our plant, I joined with our community leaders in putting together one of the broadest-based coalitions in Southern California, the Coalition to Keep GM Van Nuys Open. That Coalition has not disappeared--but rather will marshall its resources to prove to GM that if the Company reactivates its threat to close our plant, Southern California will FIGHT BACK! by spearheading a door-to-door and dealer-to-dealer boycott of GM.

Unfortunately, up till now, the Company has not threatened your livelihood, but rather certain of your so-called union leaders have. These people are telling you that it is either *Team Concept or Nothing*. In turn, they tell you about plants that closed or are closing because the Union refused Team Concept. Nothing could be further from the truth. One year ago today these very same union reps proclaimed the motto: *No New Product, No Team Concept*. Boy, how quickly we forget.

I am sure you can recall the announcement in the early 1980s that St. Louis Truck and Bus was going to close; not long thereafter we were told that the plant had been spared. Why? Team Concept? No! Truck and bus sales went up. Now, some six years later, GM can no longer secure air pollution waivers and so it must close the St. Louis facility. (I am sure that the recent gutting of Cal/OSHA has assured GM, and particularly Uncle Ernie, of amnesty from future criminal sanctions at Van Nuys.)

> Remember that in 1947 our first UAW Local 645 members were assured that our plant had a guaranteed lifespan of fifty years. That meant 1997. However, the State of California has only given you a 90-day assurance of continuing employment after team training, while General Motors states only that it will keep the plant open for the "foreseeable future." I ask you what type of guarantee is that?...
>
> The $20 million [State of California training grant to GM and the UAW] hasn't bought you any security, only awareness training on such critical topics as first-aid, earthquake preparedness, listening skills, and how to get along with your neighbors....
>
> *No, I'm not trying to close our plant. I'm simply trying to restore integrity into the collective bargaining process*, rather than to permit certain alleged union officials to continue making a mockery of your rights as union members.
>
> Remember, We Must Stand For Something
> Or We'll Be Forced to Stoop to Anything.[12]

A few days later, Beltran put out another leaflet clarifying his position:

> The company and my opponents are trying hard to distort what I stand for....In the mass meetings held in the plant last year I made 3 main points. First, I do not philosophically like the team concept and its emphasis on peer pressure. Secondly, I told the membership that if you are willing to work under those conditions, that is your decision to make, but *make sure you get a long-term commitment.* Thirdly, I said that if you accept the team concept be prepared to fight the company's exploitation of it, particularly in the areas of job over-loading, seniority and treatment of injured workers....Ray Ruiz and Richard Ruppert

are delinquent in their responsibilities in not joining with me in seeking enforcement of the provision requiring a GM commitment of a new car model....

I get the impression that any day a plant manager and shop chairman agree on something, the contract can be changed. If that continues, we might as well just show up for work every day and look on the bulletin board for the latest marching orders. That is not why I joined the UAW and I believe that is not what you want either. I see other abuses beginning to take place that alarm me:

Overloaded jobs and line speed: Right now is the honeymoon period, when GM is telling us a lot about cooperation. But an increase in line speed can make an average job unbearable. At NUMMI [the GM-Toyota joint venture in Fremont, California] they sped up the line, added work to the jobs, and sped up the line again, to the point it reminds people of the sweatshop conditions that existed before the UAW.

On-the-job injuries: Work at GM is hard and over the years, many workers become seriously injured. I will not allow workers to be forced to accept dangerous levels of work. GM is starting to kick out many workers with medical restrictions who were injured in the plant. Workers coming back with restrictions are being told to get them removed or stay out on disability. I do not support abuses of the system, but I will make sure GM has a responsibility to find suitable work within one's restrictions, and certain union officials are not fighting for that.

Seniority: The people who fought to build the UAW recognized that seniority rights insure equality. Regardless of who you were, with sufficient seniority you could progress to a better job, or would not be laid

> off. Seniority rights are being replaced with favoritism and politics.
>
> Finally, what worries GM the most about me is I will give my aggressive support to an LA area labor and community boycott of GM products if they eventually close the Van Nuys plant. Without the support of local union leadership like myself, the community will not make that move. And GM knows that I will not be bought off by positions in retraining programs or as an International rep. The accompanying article, from the book *Inside the Circle*, describes how closing down one of Ford's model Employee Involvement (team concept) plants was as easy as taking candy from a small child. I ask for your vote and support to ensure that a similar story will never happen here.[13]

Beltran argued that rather than protect the worker's job security, the team concept was an effort to dismantle the Campaign, dismantle the union as an instrument of power in the political arena, and pave the way for a future plant closing with little resistance on the part of the workers. The article which Beltran included in his leaflet is reprinted below.

> In November 1982, Ford Motor Co. gave six months notice that it would permanently close its Milpitas, California assembly plant. Up to 2,400 hourly and salary employees with seniority up to 37 years would lose their jobs...The workers had voted heavily for contract concessions and had an extensive Employee Involvement (EI) program. One might have predicted resistance, or at least that there would be some difficulties in maintaining production during those last six months. But not at Milpitas, according to Stan Jones, Chairman of the Bargaining Committee of UAW Local 560 and Hal Axtel, Labor Relations Manager.

> Jones admits that when the closing decision was announced, a few union committeemen wanted to find a way to fight the closing. But thanks to EI, he and other union leaders had "developed some kind of trust" and understood that the best course would be to work with the company....
>
> The EI program at Milpitas had been extensive. The entire plant shut down for a half hour every week for circle meetings....Management also credited EI with reducing costs. Absenteeism declined by 50 percent, says Axtel, "as a result of peer pressure."
>
> The cooperative atmosphere also saved the company money on the costs of closing down. A job retraining program cost only $650,000 and, according to Axtel, helped avoid the bitterness that was a part of other plant closings. "If we had a closure [like other auto plants in the area] with mass Workers' Comp cases filed, we would have lost four to five million dollars."[14]

With less than ten days left in the election campaign it was hard to assess opinion in the plant, but Beltran's leaflets were beginning to have some impact, and the efforts to stereotype him as a hard-headed obstructionist were finding less fertile ground. Mark Masaoka observed: "I don't know if we're going to win their votes, but a lot of people are starting to say, 'Beltran's raising some good points.' If we had a few more weeks I think we could change a lot of minds, but this is a race against the clock."

In the last week of the Campaign, Richard Ruppert put out a leaflet that was the clearest explanation of his strategy:

> All the mudslinging and name-calling is probably as frustrating to the membership as it is to me as a candidate. What is really important is what the candidates stand for. What is their plan for the future?...I propose

a strategy that is proactive, not reactive. We can no longer simply react to the decisions of management but must be actively involved in the decision-making itself.

The principle of hourly participation in the workplace does not begin and end on the assembly line. We must extend our involvement into other areas of the business which affect our job security. The best example is in the area of quality. Hourly workers should be contacting the customers who buy our cars to make sure they are satisfied. We should help them with the dealers and zone representatives if they are not getting proper treatment. *If all else fails, let's go to their homes and fix the car to their satisfaction.* In the future we must be able to approach those who drive the cars we build, thank them for buying our product and be in a position to guarantee its quality....

A whole new exterior is proposed [for the Camaros and Firebirds] in 1992. We have already proposed that the designers be located in the Van Nuys plant so we can be involved. ...None of us are happy with the marketing strategy used for the Camaro and Firebird. The car should be advertised on the West Coast as built in California. The people who built the car should be featured in the ads.

Pricing is another area of concern. The UAW members at the Linden, New Jersey plant raised a ruckus when the East Coast dealers were raising the price of their car when it first came out. They were successful in ending this practice. We should certainly insist that if we become more efficient and productive the customer must benefit in the form of lower prices....The flex plant concept [whereby the plant would produce a wider variety of models] is still the best way to cut our costs by decreasing back shipping through

> increased sales closer to the plant. Building one model makes us more dependent on the marketplace. We must continue to propose multiple model production.
>
> These are certainly changes in the role of the union, but they are necessary changes which will benefit the membership. The Responsible Representation candidates are committed to an aggressive involvement in the decisions that affect our future. It is a new world, which demands new approaches and strategies to secure our future.[15]

Ruppert's strategy raised many concerns that workers shared, such as a greater worker voice in actual design and manufacturing decisions. Still, workers on the shop floor raised several criticisms:

– He was accepting the company perspective that the future of the plant was not a management decision but, rather, was "in the workers' hands," even to the point of workers going to customers' homes to fix defective cars to save their own jobs. Since Ruppert himself criticized GM for poor design, marketing, and sales strategies, it put the workers in a situation where they would suffer the consequences for management decisions over which they had no control.

– Many of Ruppert's suggestions were good ones; but, for example, making "proposals" to GM about multiple car production (which had long been a demand of the Campaign) without the threat of a boycott, strike, or some other form of leverage, meant relying solely on persuasion. Ruppert could propose, but GM would dispose.

– Ruppert's strategic perspective openly advocated reduced class conflict with the corporation; in another leaflet he argued that "blaming others, such as GM or the International union, for our situation is no help." While Beltran's growing attacks on the undemocratic and heavy-handed practices accompanying the team concept were gaining acceptance, Ruppert, to the surprise of many of his own supporters, chose to cede to Beltran the issues of speedup, overloaded jobs, violations of contractual rights, and interference with union representation.

While Ruppert had won great respect from many of the members through his past confrontations with the company, it was perceived by some that he was becoming too close with the company, and with plant manager Schaefer in particular. As one second-shift worker expressed it: "Sometimes I worry that Beltran will fight the company too much. But now I'm also starting to worry that Ruppert won't fight the company at all."

Ruppert's leaflet was followed by a joint statement by several candidates from the Fighting Back slate ("The Team Concept or Pete Beltran--Is This Really The Choice") which had considerable impact on the debate:

> We are being lied to. The company wants us to believe that we have only two choices: either go with the team concept and their hand-picked candidate Richard Ruppert, and keep our jobs; or vote for Pete Beltran, who opposes the team concept, and lose our jobs. But we have a mind of our own and those are not the true options.
>
> We have a better choice--accept some of the changes that go under the umbrella of the team concept, reject the parts we think are harmful, vote for Beltran and Goldener, and keep our jobs and our self-respect.
>
> General Motors wants us to believe that the team concept has saved our jobs. But when General Motors says that it decided to keep another plant in the California new-car market they acknowledge the impact of four years of community pressure, demonstrations and rallies that have raised the threat of a GM boycott if GM runs away. But now that they have decided to stay here, understandably they want to make as much profit as they can....
>
> Remember what we heard from Schaefer's own Pontiac Fiero plant. At first workers were promised no layoffs, then layoffs did occur. That is why they are spending so much money

sending us to class, so we will be paralyzed as job after job gets eliminated and our work is shifted to the remaining workers....

Richard Ruppert has tried to take credit for the return of the second shift, and the company has paid for several letters to be sent to laid-off workers' homes to present Ruppert as our hero. For when the company said, "Let's forget about this commitment of a new car line," Ruppert and Ray Ruiz cooperated in erasing this protection from the local agreement.

What they should have done is told GM, "We don't have the power to erase a portion of the local agreement--that has to be approved by the membership. And if you want the membership to approve it you are going to have to provide some things, such as some basic seniority rights and a legally binding commitment to keep the plant open for ten years." But that is Pete Beltran's approach, not Ruppert's. *And it is Beltran's insistence that cooperation be a two-way street that makes him the best representative of our interests under the team concept.*

In the meantime, local unions with strong, independent leaderships are fighting back against the worst excesses of the team concept....

At Wentzville the company has team concept. But the workers struck for 11 days to reduce the mandatory job training and to make participation in teams optional.

At Orion the company has team concept. Favoritism was running wild in job placements, so the workers approved a strike vote to reinstate over 20 basic job classifications. The company resisted, but on the eve of the walkout, GM settled and brought back the desired protections.

At Pontiac Truck the company has team concept. Just several weeks ago the workers

> went out on strike to bring back basic job classifications and to stop subcontracting and outsourcing. Again, the strike was successful in winning the workers' demands.
>
> *So what is the lesson for Van Nuys?* That despite all the talk about cooperation and common interests, we the workers have different interests from the company. *The company wants a company union; we want a strong, independent union.* The company wants a weak local agreement that they can change at any time, a so-called "living agreement." We want a clear, written agreement that applies equally to all, that can be changed only by both the membership and the company.
>
> Of course there are issues we agree with the company on, such as improving quality by allowing workers to stop the line when a vital repair is needed, or increased technical (not psychological) education of the workforce. But we need a union leadership that, when it sees abuses, arouses the workers around the injustice. And if polite requests fail, and there is widespread sentiment for action, we need a union leadership that is willing to take the company on and win the best solution it can....We want a president and chairman willing to lead us in standing up to the company and not simply being an echo for the company. That's why we urge you to vote Beltran for Chairman, Goldener for President.[16]

The leaflet was signed by Mark Masaoka, Jose Silva, Nate Brodsky, Manuel Hurtado, Kelley Jenco, Chris Dorval, and Mike Gomez.

The leaflet war escalated daily. Almost one hundred leaflets were distributed to the membership from dozens of candidates, since every shop floor and executive office was up for election. While many of the leaflets on both sides involved personal attacks, charges, and counter-charges, Ruppert's assessment was right: nobody was very interested. This was a time for strategic debate.

While there were many secondary issues and many strong candidates in the field, as one long-time union activist, Buddy Maxwell, said: "This is the most important election in the history of the local. It all comes down to one question and one vote: Are you for or against the team concept? Are you for Beltran or Ruppert for shop chairman?"

On the Saturday before the election, the Fighting Back caucus held their last preelection strategy meeting at the Acapulco restaurant in San Fernando. Beltran chaired the meeting and began with his own assessment of the situation.

> I think we're going to win big. Paul Goldener and I walked around the second shift Thursday and Friday night, and the response we got was incredible. Many of the younger workers told me that their parents were on the first shift and they didn't want us to give up what their parents had fought so hard for. But we have some problems as well. Even on the first shift there are people with hard feelings toward Paul. We have to explain to them that many old battles are not important. We are in a new battle, and Paul Goldener, Pete Lopez, Cal Gutierrez, Mike Velasquez, and I are all on the same side in a war.

Several second-shift activists were not as sanguine. "It's about time Pete and Paul came on the second shift; where have they been the last two weeks? They are making up ground but this is a hell of a time to start." Others questioned the Goldener candidacy. "If these first-shift guys are still angry at Paul for disagreements ten years ago, they're not going to change their mind in two days."

While most of the attention focused on the Beltran and Goldener candidacies, there were over thirty people in the room running for office, excited about their own prospects, and providing a grass roots structure to the Fighting Back movement.

Privately, most of the caucus members assessed that both Ruppert and Shrieves were running ahead, while both Beltran and Goldener were narrowing the gap. But with only two days remaining, was there enough time? Caucus members pledged to spend the last two days working one shift and campaigning the other, talking to people one at a time. As the election day drew near, behind the optimistic rhetoric there was a growing sense that both Beltran and Goldener might lose. Many caucus members made a "no sleep until the polls close" pledge, motivated by the frightening scenario of being driven from power in the local.

While the battle had been mainly an internal one for weeks, as was usual with events at the Van Nuys plant, it seemed that an entire city was watching, or at least the city's labor movement and those concerned about its developments. On the Monday before the election, the *Los Angeles Times* ran a feature story on the Beltran-Ruppert race:

> The election Tuesday for the chairmanship of the union bargaining committee at the General Motors factory in Van Nuys is far more than a contest over who will hold the most powerful position in the United Auto Workers local at Southern California's last auto assembly plant.
>
> It is a contest that raises fundamental issues about just what a union should be in the late 1980s, and the results may be interpreted as a plebiscite on how workers feel about Japanese-style production methods.
>
> Beltran unabashedly paints himself as a traditional unionist and argues to fellow members that the new system will erode union protections, damage the national UAW and eventually cost jobs at the Van Nuys plant. Ruppert is viewed as a new style "cooperative" union leader and favors the Japanese-style system--dubbed "team concept"--that already is being phased in at Van Nuys. He tells

> colleagues that the team concept will give workers more responsibility and power on the job. He also contends it is essential to prolong the life of the factory, which until late last year was in danger of closing....
>
> Ruppert, 34, an auto worker since 1976, calls Beltran out of touch with changing realities. "Walter Reuther always argued that workers were fighting for their piece of the pie, their fair share," said Ruppert. "Now the existence of that pie is at stake. A lot of adversarial things we did are extremely destructive."
>
> Beltran, 47, who first went to work on the assembly line at Van Nuys in 1958, asserted that the changes could have long-term detrimental effects on the entire UAW. He said that allowing the introduction of Japanese-style production systems with individual plant variations on a piecemeal basis is giving local unions so much autonomy that local agreements will, in effect, supersede the national agreements. "It sets up the potential for the breakdown of a national structure of a national union."[17]

The lines were clearly drawn. Now, after several major articles, scores of leaflets, and thousands of individual conversations, the workers were ready to vote. On election day, June 2, 1987, the polls opened at 5 a.m. At 10:54, the lunch break for the day shift, hundreds of workers came rushing across the street to vote. The Responsible Representation slate staked out the turf in front of the liquor store on the corner of Blythe Street and Van Nuys Boulevard to get first shot at the workers as they crossed the street from the plant. "Vote Brown slate all the way. Save your jobs. Hey, Jose, don't forget me, man. Remember those names, Shrieves and Ruppert." The Responsible slate pushed a slate card in the hand of every passing voter.

The Fighting Back slate members staked out Mi Casita restaurant, only twenty yards past the liquor store--the last legal campaigning place before the workers entered the union hall--so as to get the last word in.

"Vote the Green slate, Beltran and Goldener. Don't forget Joe B. Remember, we want a union, not a company union." They pressed their own slate cards into the voters' hands, hands that were already filled with election materials.

Hundreds of workers squeezed through the swarm of candidates like people walking the gauntlet. When they approached the Responsible slate crowd, many voters gave their candidates the thumbs up sign. Twenty yards later, as they had to pass through the Fighting Back crowd, many of the same voters gave the candidates a knowing wink, mumbling under their breath, "You got my vote, brother." Joe B. Garcia observed: "Hey, they call us politicians; but the biggest politician of them all is an autoworker at election time. Even if you end up with ten votes, a hundred people swear they voted for you."

Before one vote had been counted, the entire process reflected well on labor unions in general and the UAW in particular. In the election for shop chairman, 3,094 workers voted out of an eligible group of 4,400, a voting percentage of 70 percent--far more than the 57 percent of eligible California voters who had voted in the 1984 Reagan-Mondale election.[18] Compared with voters in the usual exit polls, who appear shockingly uninformed as to the issues, the autoworkers polled that day were a model of an informed and thoughtful electorate. They understood the issues and had made their choices. The only thing left was to count the votes.

Finally, at two in the morning, after all that talking, there was silence. The election committee, having been awake since 4 a.m. the previous day, locked up the ballots, took them to a local police station, and went home to get some sleep. They would begin to count them the following day.

The Election Results: The Moment of Truth Arrives

At 6 p.m. on Wednesday, June 3, the first election results were in. Jerry Shrieves, the Responsible Representation candidate for the office of president, had defeated Paul Goldener, the Fighting Back candidate, by 220 votes (1,834 to 1,614).[19] Joe B. Garcia, the incumbent financial secretary-treasurer from the Fighting Back slate had defeated Manny Granillo from the Responsible Representation slate by 695 votes (1,987 to 1,292). Thus, the two top executive offices had been split.

As the evening wore on, it became clear that the Responsible slate was winning the majority of the executive board seats, but that virtually every election was being decided by less than 200 votes and many by margins of less than 20. By three in the morning, all eyes were on the ballots for shop chairman, at least all eyes that were still open. Throughout the late night and early morning, the phone at the union hall rang every five minutes as supporters from both sides replied: "No word yet; they're still counting."

At 6 a.m., after the final tally had been counted and recounted, the election committee announced:

> Pete Beltran is the new shop chairman of UAW Local 645, defeating Richard Ruppert by 116 votes (1,605 to 1,489).

Loraine McDaniel Rodriguez, one of the Fighting Back caucus' best campaigners, gave Beltran an early morning champagne toast, all over his carefully coiffed hair. "You know how Pete never has a hair out of place. Well, I wish the press had been there to take his picture at that minute."

The Fighting Back caucus held its postelection caucus meeting the following Saturday, back at the Acapulco restaurant. The mood was jubilant. The magnitude of the victory, combined with the close brush with defeat, produced a triumph that was not marred by arrogance. George Encinas, a retiree and long-time friend of Beltran said:

> You know, I grew up on the farm. And the dogs, they would guard the chickens all night, bark enough to wake up everyone in the whole village, and then they would congratulate themselves and go to sleep. Then

> the coyotes would come in the morning and eat the chickens. That's why the coyotes wanted to have Pete's ballots counted at five in the morning. But we were smarter than the dogs. We didn't bark so loud; we just stayed awake to make sure that Pete got a fair count.

Beltran spoke next, in tones that combined a religious revival and an election sum-up:

> I lost faith around 5 a.m.; I thought I had lost. I was 135 votes ahead and then 80 votes ahead and then 60 votes ahead and I couldn't take it anymore. So I went out to breakfast with two of my oldest friends, Sam Mancaruso and Gil Luna. I told Sam, "For the first time in an election, I feel I have lost." Sam said, "How does it feel?" I checked out my own emotions and said, "I feel free, free at last." And then Sam said, "That's a sign that you'll win." We went to Denny's for breakfast and I said a prayer. And when I got back to the union hall people were yelling and screaming, "We did it, we won." My prayer had been answered.

Candidate after candidate, those who had won and those who hadn't, gave moving testimonials. Whereas traditionally caucuses had been alliances of convenience in which one's perception of victory or defeat was solely measured in individual terms, for virtually all of the seventy people in that room, Beltran's victory meant that "we" had won.

A closer look at the election statistics showed that the strategy and projections outlined by many of Beltran's second-shift supporters had proven uncannily accurate. On the first shift, Beltran had received 968 votes, while Ruppert received 656. That gave Beltran a 312 vote lead going into the second and third shift vote. On the second shift, Ruppert had received 756 votes to Beltran's 523, a margin of 233 votes that cut Beltran's lead to 79 votes. On the third shift, where there is no auto production, the maintenance workers voted 114 for Beltran to 77 for Ruppert, a margin of 37 votes which gave Beltran a final margin of 116 and the victory.

In a count that not only approximated the projections but virtually duplicated them, Beltran's margin on the first shift was 60 percent, while Ruppert's was 40 percent. On the second shift, the percentages were almost exactly the reverse, with Ruppert winning 59 percent to 41 percent for Beltran. The ballpark estimate that Beltran would win the first shift 60 to 40 and would have to win at least 40 percent of the second shift had proven accurate. The assessment that the third shift would provide a small margin of victory for Beltran had underestimated his support there--since he carried the third shift by a 60 to 40 margin.

The prediction that the traditionally higher vote totals on the day shift (as many as 300 more votes than nights) would be narrowed to perhaps as little as a 100 vote margin did not prove true. On the second shift, 1,279 workers voted, an impressive 58 percent of those eligible and yet, on the first shift, 1,624 workers voted for shop chairman, better than 73 percent of those eligible. This led to 345 more votes cast on the day shift than the night shift.

Thus, the substantially larger day-shift vote, Beltran's last-minute increase in his night-shift support, and his strong showing on the third shift combined to provide the margin of victory.

In the shop committee elections, two candidates supportive of the team concept, Michael Wilson and Jess Pacheco, had been elected on the night shift, while two candidates opposed to the team concept, Pete Lopez and Cal Gutierrez, had won the same positions on days. Thus, the Fighting Back slate had a three-to-two numerical majority on the shop committee, although politically the margin was even greater, for traditionally--and even more so with Beltran in the office--the shop chairman's word was decisive.

After analyzing and savoring the Beltran-Ruppert results in minute detail, congratulating Joe B. Garcia for the only landslide victory in any of the races, and giving heartfelt thanks to virtually everyone in the room, there was still more work to be done. The following Tuesday there would be a runoff election for many positions in which no candidate had received a majority of the votes.

The stakes were quite high. In the executive board elections (the traditional base of support for the Campaign and progressive political causes), Shrieves had been elected president and six of the eight at-large seats had been won by Responsible Representation candidates. Also, several key Campaign activists suffered defeat. Incumbent unit chairman Nate Brodsky lost his reelection bid by several hundred votes; Kelley Jenco lost reelection to the executive board by five votes (1,204 to 1,209) and Mark Masaoka lost a bid for unit recording secretary and a seat on the board by fourteen votes (1,437 to 1,451). The progressive board majority was in jeopardy. However, there were still six additional seats on the board up for grabs in the runoff, making that election critical from the perspective of the Campaign.

The Runoff Results

In theory, since both the Fighting Back and Responsible Representation caucuses had split the two most powerful offices in the local, it could be argued that the June 2 election was a draw. But since the company, the media, and the Responsible slate itself had made defeating Beltran the central issue, his victory shaped the perception of who had won the election. The view that Beltran and his allies had won the election shaped the results in the runoff. Fighting Back candidates swept five of the six remaining executive offices:

– Mike Velasquez, already elected committeeman on the first shift, was elected vice-president.

– Mike Gomez, the political action chair, who had trailed in the first election, was elected recording secretary. (Thus, along with Joe B. Garcia, three of the four top executive offices were won by Fighting Back candidates.)

– Fighting Back candidates Ray Knudson and Fernando Fuentes were elected trustees and Art Rodriguez was elected guide.

– Responsible Representation candidate Michael Browning was elected trustee.

Another election that offered encouragement about the future of the Campaign and the local itself was the race for committeeman and alternate committeeman in the second-shift trim department. Campaign leaders Kelley Jenco and Manuel Hurtado ran together as a slate for those positions. Jenco had been active in organizing classes for workers wanting to get a high school degree, had helped revive a then-dormant women's committee, and had been one of the Campaign's main spokespeople since its inception. Hurtado had been the leading spokesperson for the Latino immigrant workers, had fought for greater equality for Spanish-speaking workers in union activities, and had devoted almost five years to the Campaign. While both of them had outstanding records of service to the membership, both of them had obvious electoral handicaps--Jenco was a woman and Hurtado was less than fluent in English.

Hurtado had run a strong campaign for committeeman two years previously, losing to the incumbent by a vote of approximately 95 to 70. Many workers felt he was the best person for the job, but at the last minute were dissuaded by the argument that his English, characterized by a strong accent and frequent grammatical lapses, was insufficient for the job. In reality, however, Hurtado's English was quite expressive and functional; he was a brilliant if unorthodox communicator; and his Spanish (which his opponent did not speak at all) was excellent. Most importantly, he loved the union, had a compelling vision of the job, and had not the slightest fear of the company. When he lost, he was inconsolable for several weeks:

> I would understand if the Anglos didn't vote for me; but many of my own people didn't vote for me, even the ones they don't speak as good as me. Even the ones who need my Spanish, they want a committeeman who speaks perfect English. I say to them, "So I don't speak English as good as him, and sometimes I can't find the words. So you

> want someone to sell you out in perfect English?" They laughed, but they don't vote for me.

After a few weeks, however, Hurtado returned to being one of the most visible union activists in his district and the second shift, and an outspoken critic of the team concept.

In union elections, sometimes perseverance is the most important quality. In the June 1987 elections, Jenco and Hurtado ran for two offices. They both ran for the executive board on the Fighting Back slate, and both lost. But they also ran as a team for committeeman (Jenco) and alternate committeeman (Hurtado) in their district. Hurtado was elected outright in his election, by a margin of 80 to 60. Jenco, his running mate, ran against an incumbent committeeman. The vote was 75 for Jenco, 72 for incumbent Louie Barron, and 10 for a third candidate, which necessitated a runoff. As the runoff election approached, Jenco was worried: "Maybe I took him by surprise the first time, but now he has a week to campaign while I am stuck on the line. And besides, for a lot of the workers it's hard for them to picture a woman representing them."

But, apparently, they could picture it. With Manuel Hurtado, who had already been elected, campaigning for her, and with Campaign activist Nancy Thomas and other workers on the line offering support as well, Jenco won the runoff 78 to 52.

The Jenco-Hurtado election is of considerable significance for the future of both the Campaign and the union local. First, two of the Campaign's most visible activists were elected to positions which involve the day-to-day enforcement of the contract. Along with Beltran's election, this breaks down the stereotype that the Campaign is mainly for those concerned with "outside" issues; whereas the opposition to the Campaign comes from those who care more about "shop floor" issues. While Beltran has been and will continue to be the center of both the movement to oppose the team concept and the movement to keep the plant open, the development of new leadership in the local is essential. Hurtado and

Jenco represent a new generation of leadership that has developed through the ranks.

Neither Hurtado nor Jenco represent the traditional charismatic electoral prototype. They won in spite of those expectations, based on hard work and years of developing their ties to the people with whom they work. Through their upset election victories, both Jenco and Hurtado helped expand the conception of who was "electable" in the local.

In Jenco's case, her election is a milestone--the first time in the forty-year history of the local that a woman has been elected committeeman. For the first time, "committeeperson" will find its way into the union's terminology.

THE ELECTION SUM-UP: HOW DID BELTRAN WIN?

In retrospect, even the most committed members of the Fighting Back slate will admit they had strong doubts about Beltran's chances of victory. He had three major institutions lobbying against his election and supporting his opponent--the company, the International union, and the press. To compound his problems, there was the very real threat of a plant closing hanging over the workers' heads, with strong suggestions from the company that a vote for Beltran would jeopardize their jobs. Beltran's election was, at the least, a major upset, given that Ruppert had had a six-month appointed incumbency; that Ruppert and Schaefer had conducted a systematic direct-mail campaign to the laid-off workers; and, perhaps coincidentally, that the second shift had been called back right before the elections. Under those conditions, Beltran's victory was, perhaps, the electoral miracle that his supporters claim. But since miracles in the political arena are more often the product of strategy and tactics than of divine intervention, an analysis of the Beltran victory is in order.

It is difficult, methodologically, to determine why people vote for a particular candidate, and even more difficult to characterize why 1,605 people vote for that candidate. Obviously, there are many factors involved. Fortunately, though, in this case the issues were far more sharply drawn than in most elections, and the electorate was exposed to, if not saturated by, the competing political perspectives. In an election in which 3,094 workers voted and the winning margin was 116 votes, it needs to be emphasized that Richard Ruppert and the advocates of the team concept also made a very strong showing. The main question, however, is that since Ruppert was both the incumbent and the favorite, how did Beltran turn the situation around? Through an extensive interview process with many workers who were willing to candidly express their views, the basic contours of the Beltran victory can be understood.

To begin with, Beltran had to reverse the stereotypes. The Responsible Representation slate tried to characterize Beltran as an irresponsible candidate who would rather fight the company to the death than keep the plant open, and who would rather hold onto archaic union protections than confront the hard realities of a competitive world auto market. In response, the Fighting Back slate characterized Ruppert as an adjunct of the company who would sacrifice both the union's integrity and the workers' job security for an illusory promise of future employment.

As Mark Masaoka observed: "The election was really Ruppert's to lose. He began with a big lead, and the stereotype of Pete was far more accepted than some of our caucus members wanted to acknowledge. Pete's job was to make *his* charges stick and to successfully rebut the charges against him."

Two workers who were long-time admirers of Beltran and supporters of the Campaign, but who ended up voting for Ruppert, were reflective of some of the obstacles that Beltran had to overcome. The first worker said:

> Beltran causes too much tension. Don't get me wrong; I love and respect Pete. But sometimes I get the sense that he just wants to fight for its own sake. I'm a team leader;

> I want to give the new system a try. I feel that he's not really being open-minded and wants to fight just because he hates the company. As they explained in the classes, it's time for more cooperation on both sides. Beltran's view is out of date.

The second worker added:

> Look, I know we may end up slaves here, but at least this slave will be able to support his family. I joined the Campaign to keep this plant open; but I think Ruppert will do a better job of saving the plant. I left El Salvador because the government was killing the guerrillas and the guerrillas were killing the soldiers. I don't want any more warfare up here. On the other hand, I respect all that Pete has done for us, and now I worry that with my bad back they will kick me out if the work gets too hard.

The conflict within the mind of that one voter is indicative of a larger trend. There is an effort to simplistically describe the first shift as 60-40 Beltran and the second shift as 60-40 Ruppert; but, in fact, except for several hundred committed supporters on each side, many workers were themselves 60-40 in their own minds, wavering back and forth between two candidates, both of whom raised legitimate concerns. It was the deep ambivalence that many workers felt that allowed substantial voting shifts over a period of a few short weeks. The question was: how did Beltran translate ambivalence into political support?

In discussions with many workers who were not partisans of either caucus, several major reasons stand out:

Beltran's long history of service to the membership. Beltran was considered by friend and enemy alike to be an excellent president. While he had a broad vision about the union, he also had a long history as committeeman, shop chairman, financial secretary, and president.

He always emphasized that the individual member's grievance and the union's day-to-day servicing of the membership were the building blocks of larger strategies.

While he was not the best administrator, he was scrupulous almost to the point of religious principle about taking up individual workers' cases. He defended workers when their unemployment claims were denied, handled many arbitrations, and helped grieving families with funeral arrangements. Once, when a well-known television personality came to do a prearranged interview, Beltran kept him waiting for almost an hour as he handled a worker's immigration case. When the reporter pressured one of the other officers to prod him, Beltran snapped, "They can wait. They get paid good money at CBS, but I get paid to represent these people. The members come first." During the second-shift layoff, more than one thousand workers received surplus butter and cheese as well as defense against evictions and foreclosures because of a program that Beltran sponsored through the Community Services Committee. More than fifteen years of good works created the foundation of his support.

The weakness of the company's training program and the team concept itself. At the Fighting Back caucus meeting in which the workers summed up the June 2 elections, Chris Dorval said, "Thank God for those team concept classes; we couldn't have won the election without them." At first people were incredulous, but Dorval explained, "When we first got there it seemed like most of the people were for the team concept and for Ruppert. But because the company paid us to talk all week, we had a chance to talk about the election, much more than we could have on the line. I know a lot of people who changed their mind at the end of the week and decided to vote for Pete." Mark Masaoka amplified Dorval's observations:

> While the classes certainly helped Ruppert to consolidate his support among some team leaders and gave him considerable visibility, they also produced a great deal of cynicism among other workers. The opening session at which Ernie Schaefer and Richard Ruppert

welcomed the first-shift workers was met with a very cool and restrained mood. People would ask, "Where is the contract?" And "Could you explain exactly what type of commitment GM has made to the plant?" And most of the trainers couldn't answer effectively. That led to some erosion of support. The company told people that they were on the honor system, but then took roll several times a day and placed guards at the door to record peoples' badge numbers in case they left early.

It wasn't mainly the classes, though, it was the team concept itself. Even in its first few weeks people saw things that raised a lot of doubts. There were expectations that things would be quite different; but when people got back, the foreman had a new name--"group leader" or "advisor"--but he was still barking orders. Some of the team leaders assumed their new positions with a great deal of arrogance, threatening to take people they had worked with for years to labor relations for discipline, which is a management function.

The company told the workers that there would be mandatory job rotation but had to back down after considerable resistance. They arbitrarily instituted a much harsher absentee policy, but kept postponing its implementation as people yelled. Cumulatively, all these things undermined the credibility of the whole effort. Some enterprising entrepreneurs printed up hats saying "Team Conflict." They were hot sellers.[20]

The Role of the Campaign To Keep GM Van Nuys Open

Beltran's past years of service made him a formidable candidate, and the growing skepticism about the team concept created the possibility of picking up enough votes to win. However, the decisive factor that transformed Beltran's candidacy from a valiant effort to a victory was the Campaign. The Campaign made three major contributions to Beltran's election:

First, it provided an answer to the company's threats to close the plant, and offered an alternative to the team concept on the issue of job security. The central issue in the election contest was GM's threat to close the plant if the workers did not enthusiastically carry out the team concept. As Ernie Schaefer had warned: "If we're successful, then this plant has nothing to worry about. On the other hand, if we don't do a good job, then we, like all the other plants in the General Motors system, will appear on the endangered species list." The efforts to portray Beltran as a "dinosaur" and the plant as "an endangered species" could not be answered simply by arguing "Fight Back" or "No Concessions." The Campaign provided Beltran with far more than a critique. It was an alternate strategy. In virtually every leaflet Beltran put out, the Campaign was counterposed to the team concept:

> What worries GM the most about me is I will give my aggressive support to a LA area labor/community boycott of GM products if they eventually close the Van Nuys Plant. Without the support of local union leaders like myself, the community will not make that move.
>
> Four years ago, when General Motors first started threatening the closure of our plant, I joined with our community leaders in putting together one of the broadest coalitions in Southern California, the Coalition to Keep GM Van Nuys Open. That Coalition has not disappeared--but rather will marshall its resources to prove to General Motors that if the Company reactivates its threat to close our plant, Southern California will Fight Back! by spearheading a door-to-door and dealer-to-dealer boycott of GM.

While some had cautioned Beltran about taking too adversarial a stance, he felt that without a clear alternative to the team concept the workers could not conceptualize an effective resistance. Without the strategy of the Campaign, how could Beltran have answered the company's threats--threats that, unfortunately, they had shown the capacity to back up.

At the Fighting Back caucus meeting after the election, Ernie Moreno, who had just been elected alternate committeeman among first-shift skilled-trades workers, gave a first-hand account of how the Campaign had influenced his thinking:

> I used to be with the other caucus. I was from Southgate and I didn't know Pete personally, but I had heard a lot of criticisms of him from the other side. When I went to the other caucus, their meetings were very undemocratic, and they made me uneasy. Then my son, who works in the plant, brought home this film, *Tiger By the Tail.* It really turned me on and opened up my mind. I realized that they had been lying to me. They said the team concept had saved the plant, but after seeing that movie I realized that the Coalition saved the plant. I called Pete and asked, "Can I run with you guys?" and I'm happy to be here and happy to be elected.[21]

Moreno's experience, while more dramatic than most, was not unique. Several workers expressed the idea: "I am not sure that the Campaign can save my job and I'm not sure the team concept can, but, since I'm against the team concept anyway, at least the Campaign gives me a fighting chance. This way, I can vote my conscience." Many voters said the Campaign was a factor in reinforcing their conviction to vote for Beltran.

Second, the Campaign provided Beltran with considerable visibility among second-shift workers. Ruppert, as night-shift committeeman-at-large, had walked the line every night for the year before the layoff. Unlike a district committeeman, his "district" was the entire shift;

which obviously helped his visibility and electoral chances. Beltran, by contrast, had not utilized the two years before the election to campaign on the second shift; and his normal presidential duties did not bring him into day-to-day contact with the people on the line. But over the years, the Campaign's mass meetings, rallies, and marches had brought the second-shift workers to the union hall, where Beltran--even in the company of Ed Asner, Jackson Browne and Jesse Jackson--was clearly the main spokesperson and unquestioned leader of the movement. The four hundred to five hundred workers from the second shift who frequently attended those Campaign events were the initial core of Beltran's second-shift voting strength.

Third, the Campaign helped provide a core of new leaders, especially on the second shift, who contributed to Beltran's vote totals. Kelley Jenco, Manuel Hurtado, and Mark Masaoka were highly visible leaders who had strong, independent bases of their own. Jenco received 1,204 votes and Hurtado 985 votes for executive board members at large, and Masaoka received 1,437 votes for the position of unit recording secretary. While none of them was elected, their strong campaigns brought many additional votes to Beltran and other Fighting Back candidates, especially because they spent a good deal of their own campaign time trying to convince undecided voters to support Beltran.

Fourth, the Campaign helped consolidate and solidify Beltran's support on the first shift. While it had been agreed upon that the second shift would be the main battleground of the election, there was nothing guaranteed about Beltran's strong showing on the first shift. Richard Ruppert had been functioning as shop chairman since November 1986 and, with the second shift laid off, had eight hours a day for six months to represent the members--and to campaign--on the first shift.

While the first shift was Beltran's strongest base of support, Ruppert's first-shift vote was impressive. Ruppert received 656 votes on the first shift, and in many individual districts the vote was far closer than 60-40. In a race with such a small margin of victory, a slight increase in Ruppert's first-shift vote would have changed the outcome. For example, in the actual vote, Beltran carried the first shift by a margin of 312 votes. Had the first-shift voting shifted only four percentage points (to 56 percent for Beltran and 44 percent for Ruppert), Beltran's first-shift margin would have been reduced to 194 and he would have lost the election by two votes.

While the Campaign was *not* the main factor in the first-shift vote, it was a significant factor in solidifying and protecting Beltran's strongest base. Joe Vasquez, who was elected to the executive board, was a long-time supporter of the Campaign's activities; Willie Guadiana, a high-seniority maintenance man who had become re-involved in the local through the Campaign, ran on the Fighting Back ticket and, although he lost, received 995 votes.

The Campaign's electoral influence on the first shift went beyond the involvement of individual activists. Over four years, the Campaign organizers had distributed more than fifty individual leaflets to the membership. The response on the first shift was always less enthusiastic than on the second, with early morning insults and a generally apathetic attitude greeting the leafleters--who often wondered what they were doing putting up with abuse and indifference at 5 o'clock in the morning. But then there were the good moments, with Willie Gastelo, Robert Garrett, Michelle Reyes, Ernest Pringle, Dorothy Travis, as well as committeemen Mike Velasquez and Pete Lopez saying: "Give me some of those leaflets; I'll distribute them on my line." And, while at times it seemed like the search for the proverbial needle in the haystack, out of the blue an old-time worker would say: "We appreciate what all of you are doing; Walter would be proud of you." Thus, support for the Campaign grew, one worker at a time.

On the first shift, while opposition to the team concept was perceived as the main issue, the Campaign reinforced those who wanted to resist. No more than fifty first-shift workers could have been called *active* Campaign supporters. Over the first four years of the Campaign, no more than two hundred first-shift workers attended any of its rallies, marches, or press conferences. But that, in itself, provided fifty activists and two hundred supporters on a shift of twenty-two hundred workers, a strong infrastructure. Those people magnified their influence by bringing back their own first-hand experience to the people on their line and generating discussion and debate.

Thus, the first-shift opposition to the team concept, reflected in the vote to remove Ray Ruiz from office and the 60-40 margin of support for Beltran, was partially a reflection of the earlier traditions of trade union militancy symbolized by the Reuther years; but also, more than some might recognize, it was a reflection of four years of the Campaign's organizing work.

By the June 1987 elections, the movements to keep the plant open and to resist the team concept had reached their greatest synthesis. In part because of the Campaign's impact, the first shift began and ended the election as a stronghold for Beltran.

Thus, the Campaign provided Beltran with an answer to the question: "What is our alternative to the company's threats?" and gave him his own "job security" platform. His constant references to the Campaign, and the workers' belief that the Campaign was viable, successfully rebutted the charges that he had no strategy and made his own charges of company unionism against the opposition more effective. The Campaign provided Beltran with four years of high visibility on an issue that the vast majority of workers in the plant supported. It provided him with a new group of allies, many of whom were effective campaigners, on the second shift. It reinforced his allies on the first shift and brought him a few new ones; and it built upon the excellent record of service and leadership he had established over twenty-eight years. In short, the Campaign provided Beltran with his margin of victory.

THE VOTERS SPEAK FOR THEMSELVES

In an effort to develop a deeper understanding of how the workers perceived the two candidates and the issues separating them, this author conducted interviews with second-shift workers on Wednesday, June 24, 1987, three weeks after the election results were announced. The methodology used was to approach workers on several lines in the plant where the workers knew the author well, thus allowing a more frank expression of their views. Groups of eight or ten workers in a row were interviewed, with no one excluded, to make sure that the sample was not arbitrarily selected. Surprisingly, of the forty workers questioned, only two chose not to participate. They expressed their views freely with the understanding that their statements would be quoted but their names would not be used. What follows are nine statements by second-shift workers that reflect the most commonly expressed views:

> I voted for Pete. When I got here ten years ago, Pete was here. You can't beat experience. Pete is sincere; or if he's strokin' me, he's so good at it I don't even notice. I think the politicians and ministers that we organized would not let this plant close. I've been at the rallies. GM is not going anywhere.

> I voted for Ruppert. It was a hard choice. I agreed with many of Pete's ideas, like the company is trying to pit local against local; but I heard many criticisms of Pete and I didn't know who to believe. I finally voted for Ruppert because I want to believe in the team concept. It sounds like such a good idea. But just in the last three weeks they've added more clips onto my job, and you know my job is one of the hardest on the line already. If the election was held today, I might reconsider my vote.

I voted for Pete. I'm a team leader and I believe in the team concept, but it's a question of checks and balances. This way, if the company goes too far one way, we have Beltran to push the other way.

I voted for Ruppert. I felt that Pete was too radical. I'm worried about the plant closing, and sometimes I get the impression that Beltran is unwilling to try new ideas. I thought Ruppert was more open to new ideas, although I know he made deals behind our back. Overall, I am neither radical nor passive, but I'm more afraid of radicalism. So I voted for Ruppert.

I voted for Pete. When Ruppert was my committeeman he was very good, but as he got up there I watched him change. I get the feeling that Ruppert will be taken care of even though he lost. Pete gave up the presidency to run for shop chairman. That impressed me.

I voted for Ruppert. He was the only one who cared about the second shift coming back. Pete said he did, but I didn't believe him. Ruppert really cares about the people. If you have a problem, he's the one you want to defend you.

I voted for Ruppert because I believe in the team concept. But I'm already having second thoughts, not about the team concept, but about how the company is applying it. I'm a team leader. I have already learned seven jobs, and now they tell me they want me to learn seven more. I've told them, "Enough." I am strongly against this idea of the "living contract." They are trying to make it seem that if you support the team concept, then they can change the contract any time they want to. I want Pete to tell the company that the team concept doesn't mean that they can violate our rights. You know, its funny. During the election I voted for Ruppert, but now I'm glad Beltran is in there. Before the election a lot of us were worried that he would be too militant, but now we're worried that he'll be just like the rest of them and we'll never see him on the line--until the next election.

I voted for Ruppert. I didn't know either candidate too well, so I depended upon my friend's opinions. I'm not a follower, but I trust my friends more than the politicians. Ruppert had always been visible, and I do want to give the team concept a try. I don't see what is gained by provoking the company before you even try it.

I voted for Pete. I don't trust these guys to negotiate local contracts. They're not smart enough or honest enough. Contracts should be negotiated at the national level and be the same for everyone. That way, they can't play plant against plant--that's what Pete has been trying to explain to these people. I go up to people on the line and they say they're for the team concept. So I say, "Describe the team concept," and they really can't; it's just a name that sounds good. I've been to all the rallies. If there is one word that is poison to GM, it's "boycott." They know about Gallo and Coors, and I don't think they'll risk it. Whether these people know it or not, they owe their jobs to the Campaign.

NOTES

1. "GM Workers at Van Nuys Express Relief," *Los Angeles Times,* Business section, November 7, 1986, p. 1.
2. *Los Angeles Herald-Examiner*, February 4, 1987, p. 10.
3. Interview with the author, July 9, 1987.
4. Conversation with the author, May 5, 1987
5. Richard Ruppert, letter to the membership, December 15, 1986.
6. "Van Nuys Plant Status," letter to all laid-off employees, November 6, 1986.
7. "Return of Two-Shift Operations," letter to laid-off workers, April 7, 1987.
8. "Militant UAW Officials Sue GM in Bid to Halt Team Concept's Implementation," *Los Angeles Times*, Valley Edition, Business section, April 14, 1987, pp. 9A, 9B.
9. *Methods of Resolving Conflict*, GM-UAW Joint Training Activities Manual, p. 9.
10. Interview with the author, May 22, 1987
11. Mark Masaoka, "The View of a Returning Worker," leaflet distributed at GM Van Nuys, May 21, 1987.
12. Peter Z. Beltran, "An Open Letter to the Membership," May 13, 1987.
13. Pete Beltran, "A Message to the Membership," distributed to GM workers May 22, 1987.
14. Mike Parker, *Inside the Circle: A Union Guide to Quality of Worklife* (Boston: South End Press, 1985), p. 27.
15. Richard Ruppert, "Elect Richard Ruppert Shop Chairman," leaflet distributed May 20-June 1, 1987.
16. "The Team Concept or Pete Beltran--Is This Really the Choice?", leaflet distributed to GM workers.
17. Henry Weinstein, "UAW Van Nuys Vote: Where Does Union Go in the 1980s?", *Los Angeles Times*, Metro section, June 1, 1987, p. 1.
18. November 6, 1984, statistics compiled by California secretary of state.
19. All figures in this discussion are from the official election committee report, UAW Local 645.
20. Interview with the author, June 22, 1987.

21. Remarks to Fighting Back caucus meeting, June 6, 1987.

Chapter Thirteen

THE FUTURE OF GM VAN NUYS, THE FUTURE OF THE CAMPAIGN

There have been times in the history of the Van Nuys plant when you could take a two-year vacation only to return and find things relatively unchanged. "How's everything been since I've gone?" "Well, you know, same old, same old." And after an hour back on the line, it would be as if you had never left--as car after car rolled by, co-workers told the same tired jokes and the cafeteria food looked and tasted its same old, same old.

In 1986 and 1987, however, the sweep of events moved so quickly and forcefully that two days away from the plant required a lengthy update, and two weeks away required a full-length narrative. GM Van Nuys had become more than a case study or even a workshop in organizing; it had become a highly symbolic confrontation between an individual UAW local and mighty General Motors in the era of America's fall from world economic domination. The battle of classes and events prevented a stable synthesis, as new contradictions and new possibilities for both progress and reaction exploded almost daily.

In the summer of 1987, when this narrative ends, General Motors was still committed to implementing the team concept. The Fighting Back caucus was committed to reasserting a collective bargaining relationship with the corporation and defanging, if not dismantling, the team concept. The new local president, Jerry Shrieves, was committed to rolling back many of the policies and approaches of Beltran's administration, while Beltran was equally committed to rolling back what he perceived to be the regressions of the previous Ruiz-Ruppert regime. GM was committed to closing down more plants in its system, while the Campaign was committed to keeping Van Nuys open and building a broader movement against plant closings within the UAW.

In this context, it is difficult to predict future events. There are too many powerful forces with mutually contradictory interests to reach any stable political agreements--at least in the short run. The demands of the Campaign and the newly elected shop committee are directly contradictory to corporate objectives. Until the corporation comes to terms with those concerns, future confrontations are not just probable, but inevitable. Within this dynamic situation, however, we can take a closer look at the main forces in order to understand the conflicts that will shape the plant's future.

GENERAL MOTORS' EVOLVING VIEW OF THE VAN NUYS PLANT: THE REASONS CHANGE, BUT THE THREAT CONTINUES

When the Campaign began in 1982, the corporation was pursuing a regional disinvestment strategy. It had closed two of its three West Coast plants and was obsessed with "consolidation"--concentrating parts manufacture and assembly in the Midwest to emulate the "Japanese-style," "just-in-time" inventory system.

The counterstrategy of the Campaign was to oppose such a dramatic, regional restructuring of GM's operations. Its main tactic was to use the threat of a boycott in the Southern California auto market to impose some social responsibility on GM's manufacturing decisions.

By 1987, however, that period of history was over. If it were simply a question of stopping GM's efforts to consolidate all production in the Midwest (a business decision which many auto analysts took issue with anyway, since *some* decentralized assembly is necessary), it could be argued with some confidence that the Campaign had accomplished its objectives. Through the Coalition's efforts GM, it appeared, became convinced that it was "good business" to keep at least one plant open in Los Angeles. The Coalition's work could have been scaled down to an annual jogging of GM's memory about the boycott with dramatic, if somewhat ritualized, Keep GM Van Nuys Open rallies.

But the GM of 1982, no matter how embattled it seemed at the time, was far more stable and vital than the GM of the late 1980s. Once again, the future not only of the GM Van Nuys plant, but many other GM plants as well, is in jeopardy. As was developed in an earlier chapter, GM's problems are structural and serious and, some believe, are approaching crisis proportions:

– In June 1987, GM's sales, continuing a decline that industry analysts called a "free fall," were only 34.9 percent of the U.S. auto market, while Ford's increased more than two full percentage points to 20.6 percent of the U.S. market. (At the time the Campaign began, in 1982, GM's total market share was more than 42 percent.)

– GM's sales, in the second quarter of 1987, declined 16.9 percent, while Ford's increased five percent.

– GM reported a 28 percent *decline* in pretax earnings from operations, while Ford's operating profit jumped 36.4 percent.[1]

Thus, at the conclusion of the June 1987 elections, the Van Nuys workers were dealing with an employer in trouble. And, with the growing challenge from imports, captive imports, and a revitalized Ford and Chrysler, there was no foreseeable end to GM's difficulties.

As demand for GM cars continued to drop, the danger of more plant closings, including one at Van Nuys, became more pronounced. Regardless of the team concept or the Campaign, or whether Ruppert or Beltran won, or whether Van Nuys or another plant was closed, once again many workers would pay for the mistakes of GM management and the structural crisis of overproduction, in which too many companies produced too many cars competing for too few customers. Thus, in 1987, on the economic front, the Van Nuys workers were facing a GM that had just announced the closing of eleven plants, and that was facing the prospect of more plant closings due to declining sales.

Politically, GM's assessment of the situation was changing as well, based on the unexpected and, from its perspective, unpleasant election results in the Van Nuys local. In the year prior to the 1987 local elections, GM had had things all its way. While the corporation was still well aware of the Coalition and its boycott potential, the press was minimizing the Campaign's accomplishments and lauding those of the team concept. The corporation set a new economic objective: to stay in Van Nuys and to maximize its profits at that location. To that it added political objectives: to accede to the pressure from the Coalition without acknowledging that it was doing so, and to promote the "Van Nuys model" and utilize it as a lever against other GM plants.

Beltran's election, however, upset that political equation. His election was the subject of widespread media attention. The media's long-standing preparation of the public for a "plebiscite at Van Nuys" was encouraged by the corporation, with the assumption that Beltran would be defeated. When the workers at Van Nuys did not vote according to expectations, the GM public relations department had unwittingly magnified the political impact of Beltran's victory.

The day after the election, early editions of the *Los Angeles Times* ran the story on page three (and later editions ran it on page one), with the headline, "Team Concept Foe Wins UAW Van Nuys Vote":

> Pete Beltran, a union traditionalist who opposes the Japanese-style "team concept" production system being put in place at General Motors' Van Nuys factory, was narrowly elected chairman of the union's in-plant bargaining committee, union officials announced Thursday.

> Beltran, 47, won a two-year term by defeating Richard Ruppert, 34, a more conciliatory union leader and a strong advocate of the team concept approach....
>
> The Beltran-Ruppert election campaign was viewed by many as a plebiscite on the Japanese-style production methods at the factory. But interviews with workers at the plant Thursday revealed that not all of the winner's supporters opposed the team concept. ..."He'll help everyone," said Calvin Liggins, a 21-year veteran of the plant...."We need him more in the plant than across the street at the union hall (as president)," Gilbert Pacheco said, "He'll protect our rights...."
>
> For months, Beltran has asserted that the team concept would erode traditional union protections, damage the national UAW and eventually cost jobs at the Van Nuys plant. He also asserted that the system which eliminates job classifications and calls on workers to perform a variety of tasks, would create friction within the union by pitting employees against one another.
>
> "My victory is a victory for the workers and a victory for people who believe the union should represent the workers not the company," Beltran said....Ernie Schaefer, GM's Van Nuys plant manager, declined to speculate on the effects of Beltran's election. "Implementation of the team concept is well under way," he said, but added, "I'm sure there will be some changes. We'll find a path through the forest."[2]

Schaefer's melancholy mood was shared by his superiors in Detroit, accompanied by, word in the plant had it, some hard questions as to how a seemingly surefire election victory had slipped away. If GM officials had argued that the plant had been kept open because it was a "model" for other plants, no such rationale was possible after the Beltran victory. Now the plant had become a model of resistance, with Beltran once again a figure in national UAW politics and the "Van Nuys model" something that many other UAW locals would want to reverse-engineer.

Beltran's victory was seen as a news story of national import. *Labor Notes*, a nationwide newsletter read by union insurgents, carried the story "Foe of 'Team Concept' Wins Narrow Election in California Auto Local" and concluded: "At least half the workers in the Van Nuys plant feel that they do not have to give in to General Motors' pressure, despite the plant's vulnerable position as the company's only remaining assembly plant on the West Coast."[3]

A *Chicago Tribune* article, along with several others in major newspapers throughout the country, reflected the national attention given to the election results:

> Pete Beltran knows that the troubles of American manufacturing have given birth to the belief that Japanese methods are needed substitutes for outmoded industrial practices and labor conflict.
>
> He begs to disagree--and his doubts may mushroom into a high-stakes confrontation over cooperation in the U.S. auto industry....
>
> Fear of shutdown at Van Nuys prompted formation of a vibrant, wide-ranging coalition of labor, church and other groups. Actor Ed Asner and Rev. Jesse Jackson, who called the workers "freedom fighters" became involved. The coalition threatened a boycott of GM products statewide if it closed Van Nuys....
>
> Beltran, who joined the plant's trim department in 1958, has "no problem with becoming more efficient." But he argues that the team concept will undermine the local and national union and, in effect, destroy the seniority system, as "team leaders" possibly evolve into union-exempt managers.
>
> "Team concept represents the most devious scheme they've ever conjured up to

> screw workers," said Beltran. "It places the burden on them to eliminate the jobs of others and to eliminate union rights."[4]

From the perspective of the Campaign and the Fighting Back movement, the change in media attitude was a major victory. After a year of being misrepresented, discounted, and ignored, Beltran and the Campaign activists found a newfound respect reflected in the postelection media coverage.

But this also placed even greater pressure on the Van Nuys workers and the Campaign. While the election victory certainly heartened like-minded UAW activists in other locals, it erased one factor that was contributing to the plant's short-term safety--GM's political investment in portraying Van Nuys as a "once-militant" plant that had succumbed. As top GM officials mulled over the implications of the election results, workers at Van Nuys could expect a stormy future.

The Fighting Back campaign had warned the workers that the storm was coming anyway. With another virtually inevitable round of plant closings scheduled for the late 1980s or early 1990s, had the Responsible Representation slate swept the elections, two or three years of their unchallenged union leadership would have set the political and ideological conditions for a weak, or nonexistent, response to a future plant closing. They predicted that if Beltran was replaced by more "cooperative" officers, after several years of the team concept, a closing at Van Nuys would have ended with local union officers lamenting the closing, blaming the Japanese, and beginning the ritual of setting up "job training programs" for the permanently displaced workers.

But with Beltran in leadership, there *were* additional dangers as well as possibilities. If GM decided to close the Van Nuys plant, even several years in the future, its script could have been written the day after the election: "We regret to announce the closing of the Van Nuys plant. We knew that Van Nuys was more expensive to operate, being on the West Coast, but we valued the Los Angeles community and did everything we could to salvage the plant. We brought in exciting new plans for a cooperative effort with our employees and new production methods to make the plant more efficient and more competitive. But a self-destructive union leadership challenged us at every point. We opted for cooperation; but they chose confrontation. We urge the public to disregard any talk of a boycott. We kept Van Nuys open as long as we could but, ultimately, we are a business and the union destroyed the viability of the plant they claimed they wanted to save."

Anticipating such a response from GM, the Campaign once again became of great strategic significance. Since the Beltran candidacy had offered the Campaign as an alternative to the team concept, it was essential that the Coalition escalate its preparation for the boycott--one it hoped it would never have to carry out.

Once again, the political battle for the plant's future was back in the workers' hands. What they would do with that opportunity, however, would be a major factor in determining the ultimate outcome of the story.

THE FUTURE OF THE TEAM CONCEPT

While the election created the possibility of increased political influence for both the Campaign and the Fighting Back movement, any new strategies would have to begin with the reality of a deeply divided and highly ambivalent workforce. The turmoil in the auto industry, the UAW, and American society itself was reflected in the minds of the Van Nuys workers. The team-concept/new-car-model contract of May 1986 was ratified 53 to 47 percent. Jerry Shrieves defeated Paul Goldener for president by 53 to 47 percent. Beltran defeated Ruppert for shop chairman by 52 to 48 percent.

In addition to the sharp divisions in the workforce, postelection interviews with many workers indicated that most felt deeply conflicted. They had questions and doubts about both of their newly elected leaders and their respective strategies, as well as doubts about the plant manager and the corporation itself. Except for several hundred workers on each side whose loyalties and political convictions were clear, the vast majority of workers perceived themselves to be in the middle--caught between forces within their own union and caught between their union and the corporation they worked for. In the next few years, the strategies and organizational capabilities of both caucuses would be put to a test as both sides attempted to move the plant toward a clearer consensus.

Upon assuming office, Beltran explained the first steps of his strategy:

> The first thing I am trying to do is just to find the contract. Pretty radical, huh? It's outrageous what Ruiz allowed to happen over the past few years. First, I asked for the contract the day after I won the election. For weeks, people have been scrambling around telling me they will get it for me, but I'm not sure they even know where it is.
>
> They created a system in which the contract is now a series of signed letters or "side agreements." Some are in Detroit; some are in the plant manager's office; some are signed by our local people and not theirs; some have cover sheets signed by International officers, while the actual agreement is not signed. I think the whole process is illegal. My first job is to round up all these letters and compile them so I know what has been agreed to and who has agreed to it. Then I can figure out how to fight back.
>
> My second goal is to try to unify the shop committee and reestablish even the most elementary sense of negotiations. When I first sat down with the people from labor relations and we tried to clear up the dozens of outstanding grievances the meetings took five days. For years, the company had been able to drop in, say what they want, and get it.

> Now they had to bargain again, and they didn't like it at all.[5]

Upon assuming office, Beltran had to answer several tactical questions: How much of the team concept to take on at once? What type of mandate existed to do so? How could he successfully mobilize the workers to support his initiatives? But while the answers to those questions were far from clear, it *was* clear that the early stages of the team concept's implementation had produced certain widespread concerns among the workers.

Health and safety. The strong electoral support for Beltran among the skilled-trades workers was partially because they felt the company would exploit classifications they had earned after years of apprenticeship, but also because of their genuine concerns about health and safety. Local management, in its efforts to reduce manpower, for example, was pressing millwrights to help electricians, even when they were working on high voltage electrical equipment.

The problem, however, extended to the production workers as well. For years the union had fought for and finally won "thirty and out," a retirement plan based on thirty years of employment regardless of age. But workers at Van Nuys worry that efforts to speed up the line will make thirty years in an auto plant a physical impossibility.

Since the assembly line moves at an average of sixty cars per hour, leaving each assembler sixty seconds to do each job, the addition of even three or four seconds of work per car can make the difference between a comfortable pace and back fatigue. Another two seconds of work per minute and back fatigue is transformed into back spasms, or a sore hand is transformed into carpal tunnel syndrome. While the public may not understand those distinctions, the autoworkers do, and company efforts to add additional work once the line reaches full speed will provoke considerable resistance.

Giving management functions to "team leaders" who are members of the bargaining unit. Beltran and many other committeemen--with strong support from many line workers--oppose the use of team leaders to discipline co-workers. Many of the team leaders, in just a few short weeks on the job, came to oppose that part of their job description, and several voted for Beltran partially for those reasons.

There was growing sentiment that one union member should not threaten another with discipline--discipline that under the contract can only be meted out by the corporation. There was also sentiment among some of the team leaders that their role should be as a skilled and responsible worker, not as a management agent.

Demanding a written contract. It was a distressing sign of the times that Beltran's first "militant" act was to demand a copy of the contract. Kelley Jenco was elected in her district partially because of that demand, and many workers had become increasingly angry about the idea of "the living contract." As one worker joked, "That damn contract is so alive that when you try to pick it up, it runs away."

In the first weeks after Beltran's election the workers expressed more of a sense of having options. They discussed which parts of the team concept they agreed with and which parts they didn't with a newfound sense of choice, a far cry from the "adopt the team concept or we will close down the plant" mood that was sweeping the plant just a few weeks before the election. After the election, many workers who were sympathetic to the team concept told Beltran they would support his efforts to eliminate its abuses, but they worried when he said he wanted to "dismantle" the whole system.

Beltran's view, however, was that many of the so-called "abuses" of the team concept were integral to its functioning. The elements of the team concept that the workers liked the most were the promise of worker input into the production process, the opportunity to rotate jobs, and the possibility of greater respect from management.

But from GM's perspective, giving workers greater input, job satisfaction, and respect were means to an end--greater productivity and lower labor costs. Thus, the elements of the plan many workers disliked--efforts to involve co-workers in time-and-motion studies to "eliminate wasteful effort"; cross-training on jobs in order to absorb additional work as many of those who retire or leave on disability are not replaced; reduced emphasis on health and safety; using "team leaders" to encourage workers to accept additional work on their jobs--were, from the corporation's perspective, not the abuses of the team concept, but its essence.

As a result, any efforts by Beltran and the shop committee majority to challenge those provisions would meet stiff resistance from management. Before Beltran would be able to modify, let alone dismantle, any of the team concept's provisions, he would have to communicate his concerns to the membership and mobilize them effectively.

Beltran Attempts to Dismantle the Team Concept, While GM Attempts to Dismantle His Shop Chairmanship

As Beltran, Pete Lopez, Cal Gutierrez, Mike Velasquez, and other committeemen attempted to respond to the contract they had inherited, the company made efforts to circumvent Beltran's election victory by refusing to recognize his authority. In virtually every UAW local, the shop chairmanship is the most powerful position. The shop chairman functions as the leader of, in the case of Van Nuys, more than fifteen full-time committeemen. He is the last word in handling grievances, interprets the contract, negotiates with management's labor relations staff, and is the chief bargainer during local contract negotiations. In Beltran's case, during his presidency, his political leadership and personal charisma gave that office greater visibility and power than in other UAW locals. As a result, it was assumed that he would exert even more influence in his newly won position.

At least in the first two months of Beltran's tenure, however, that did not prove to be the case. In essence, General Motors attempted to carry out a policy of nonrecognition of his office.

In July, Beltran spoke to the press and explained that he planned to reopen negotiations and challenge many of the aspects of the team concept. A *Los Angeles Times* article carried the headline "Team Concept Must Go, GM Workers Warn"[6] The next day the article was reprinted, accompanied by handwritten headlines, "Pete Must Go." That would have been par for the course had they been left at workers' stations, but they were posted on locked, glass enclosed company bulletin boards throughout the plant. Once again, union officials friendly to the company had been given access to company property to attack Beltran--even calling for his removal from office.

While there were many incidents of this nature, the most important one was the company's assertion that the local union did not have the right to reopen local negotiations on the team concept agreement.

Based on the UAW's past practice, all local agreements expire simultaneously with the national agreement. The common expiration date gave locals greater bargaining clout. National strikes, even when concluded, would not deliver the workers back to the plant unless the local agreement was ratified as well. Thus, if management wanted labor peace, it had to pay attention to local demands.

With Beltran elected in June 1987 and the UAW national contract due to expire in September 1987, he had the perfect opportunity to bring the team concept back to the bargaining table in a contractual way that was consistent with UAW past practice and the workers' own experiences. It would not be "Pete Beltran demanding to reopen negotiations," as much as "Pete Beltran conducting local negotiations at the expiration of the contract."

Unfortunately, local GM management refused to recognize Beltran's efforts to serve the legally mandated sixty days' notice of intent to reopen negotiations. They argued that the team concept agreement did not expire with virtually all of the other UAW local contracts in the GM system but, rather, extended until 1990--at which time local negotiations would be allowed.

From Beltran's perspective, the immediate consequences, if not reversed, would be devastating. In essence, the local would have relinquished its right to reopen the contract--without having voted to do so. Certainly something as basic as the expiration of the contract should have been a matter of public record; and virtually everyone on the shop floor, for or against the team concept, assumed that the contract expired in September 1987.

The May 1986 official report to the membership by the shop committee chaired by Ray Ruiz, which urged ratification of the just negotiated team concept agreement, contained a boxed section titled, "Duration, ratification, text." This section stated, *in full:*

> None of the provisions of the proposed Local Union contract between the union and GM-Van Nuys plant will take effect until the agreement is ratified by a majority vote of the membership of UAW local 645, and then only on the effective date specified. If ratified, this agreement will become effective only when a new product is announced for the Van Nuys plant.[7]

Thus, the original agreement had no clear *beginning date*. In fact, the recall movement against Ray Ruiz charged that he violated the membership's right to ratify by attempting to implement an agreement that was not supposed to go into effect until GM made a commitment for a new car model. As Pete Beltran explained:

> When I ran for office, I charged that the company had unilaterally implemented a contract before it had complied with its provisions. But now they are telling us that they and Ray Ruiz reached agreement, behind the members' backs, not just on when it would start, but on when it would end--and no one ratified a 1990 expiration date.[8]

Obviously, the battle on these points as well as many others like them will continue and, in the tradition of GM Van Nuys, will go through endless and unexpected twists and turns. These postelection incidents, however, indicate that, for Beltran and his allies, winning the election is only one in a series of battles with the company. While future events cannot be predicted, Beltran's strategy must contain at least three essential elements if he is to consolidate his election victory.

First, stabilizing the collective bargaining situation. There is some possibility that GM may choose to deal with Beltran. The corporation, as has been shown through its history, is extremely flexible and adaptive to political realities. So is Beltran. There is an outside chance that the company will back down from its efforts to remold the consciousness of its workforce, and focus its efforts on quality and productivity. (This may occur, since the press reported that, after seven weeks of the team concept, "productivity is 15 percent behind schedule."[9])

If that is the case, an accommodation is possible. Beltran's statement that he is willing to increase efficiency and encourage technical--as opposed to psychological--training of the workforce should be carefully considered by the corporation. A possible compromise between the newly elected shop committee and local management would have to contain some of the following elements:

– Full recognition of the newly elected shop committee. Local management must understand that efforts to circumvent the local's elected leadership will not achieve increased productivity, but will provoke greater shop-floor rebellion.

– Training line workers on several jobs, organizing groups of workers into production teams, and soliciting greater worker input into the production process are potentially positive developments, and can serve the objectives of both the company and the union.

– Efforts to impose contracts without full union participation, efforts to create "joint-committees" in which nonelected union officials engage in bargaining functions, and efforts to supplement written contracts with an endless stream of "side letters" outside of the ratification process are thoroughly unacceptable.

– Management efforts to place job elimination at the heart of any new work organization are in contradiction to the union's responsibility to protect the jobs of its members and the company's stated goal of increased product quality. The *long-term* ability of workers to keep up with the pace of the line and carry out their jobs consistent with their health and safety must be central to any new production processes.

– Efforts by management to characterize union opposition to specific proposals as "endangering the future of the plant" must be stopped immediately. Management's acceptance of the Campaign's demand for a ten-year commitment is the key to improved worker cooperation, morale, and productivity.

Within those parameters, there is considerable room for negotiation. Given GM's declining national sales and credibility, and the critical role of the Los Angeles and California new-car markets in any GM strategies for a rebound, a commitment to the plant's long-term future and the reestablishment of collective bargaining with the Beltran administration is in some ways in the corporation's interest.

Second, communicating his concerns to the rank-and-file workers on the line. Some of Beltran's closest supporters have raised concerns about his visibility and availability since assuming office. While Beltran's commitment and skills are unquestioned, his visible presence on the shop floor is essential to any plans for reestablishing a strong union presence. While certain weaknesses could be compensated for in an election campaign, over the next two years of his term the workers will be watching carefully.

If he relies on dramatic court cases and occasional leaflets to the membership, a backlash of resentment will begin to develop, and the opposition will exploit the "Where's Pete?" issue. On the other hand, if he systematically walks the line each week and has discussions with the opinion leaders in each department, he will be able to expand both his own base and that of the movement to rebuild the union.

Third, explaining his case to the public. The battle for "public opinion" has been, and will continue to be, a critical element in this ongoing drama. The pendulum of public opinion has swung in favor of the Campaign, and then against it. From the perspective of both the shop-floor movement and the Campaign itself, there is a new opportunity to recapture significant public support.

In the first phase, from 1982 until 1986 the Campaign was on the offensive. Church leaders, liberal and moderate politicians, and the media asked General Motors: "Why can't you keep open at least one profitable plant in Los Angeles; how can you sell all these cars in Los Angeles and want to leave?" "The Chicano and black communities say that a closing at Van Nuys is a civil rights issue. Do you have any concern about civil rights?" "Why do you have to close down a profitable plant just to make some more profits somewhere else?" "We recognize your need for a profit, but don't these people have any rights in the situation?" "Would you really close down this plant and risk a boycott of your products in Los Angeles?"

In the second phase, from January 1986 until June 1987, the Campaign was placed on the defensive. "Don't you people want to produce a quality product?" "GM wants to involve you in the production process, but it seems that you prefer a position of permanent opposition. Don't you want any voice in the plant's future?" "GM is trying to compete with the Japanese, but you don't seem to care. Isn't competitiveness a legitimate corporate objective?" "If you keep saying you want to keep the plant open, why are you opposing a bold new plan by the corporation to save the plant?" "You say you speak for the workers, but you keep losing elections. Isn't it true that your ideas have been rejected by the workers themselves?"

In the third phase, beginning in June 1987, Beltran and his allies have new opportunities for recapturing public support; but those opportunities are by no means assured. If Beltran is able to project himself as an embattled labor leader attempting to protect his members, and a practical union official attempting to meet GM halfway, then the burden of proof can once again be shifted back to the company. Several examples of issues that Beltran can turn to the workers' advantage are:

Quality. If Beltran argues that the workers want to build a quality product but GM management practices interfere with that objective, the public will be interested. If he says that GM claims to want quality but eliminates jobs and pressures inspectors to overlook product defects in the interest of profits and quantity, he can shape the debate and once again place the company on the defensive.

Collective bargaining. If Beltran portrays himself as a duly elected union official whom the company is trying to circumvent, there will be considerable sympathy for his position. Support for free elections is an integral element of America's democratic values as well as its mythology. Beltran's challenge to the public--"With all the articles written against me, with all the company support for my opponent, and with management's threat of a plant closing if I was elected, doesn't it indicate that something must be drastically wrong in this plant for the workers to have elected me?"--can strike a responsive chord. An appeal to the public for their help in getting GM to sit down and talk seriously with the new union leadership would gain considerable support.

The ten-year commitment. There is a certain weariness and resentment in the public mind in Los Angeles about the never-ending company threat to close down the plant. If Beltran went on a speaking tour of community groups, he could explain: "I am willing to meet GM halfway, but I need your help. The company must end, once and for all, its use of the plant closing as an instrument of labor relations. A ten-year commitment is the fundamental building block to a constructive labor and community relations policy." An articulate and persuasive speaker, Beltran could win substantial community support for his point of view--support which would be transferred into pressure on General Motors.

Obviously, all those "positions" would have to be implemented as part of an overall organizing strategy, not just floated into the air. But the ability--or inability--to interpret the shop-floor events to a broader public may become the key to the success--or failure--of both Beltran's shop chairmanship and the Campaign itself.

THE FUTURE OF THE FIGHTING BACK CAUCUS

There is a tendency to abbreviate the shop-floor movement as "Beltran and allies." But, in fact, the grass roots movement that produced the impressive electoral victory was comprised of more than fifty union activists and another fifty supporters. In order to preserve that grass roots movement, however, they will have to transform the Fighting Back caucus--or at least the grouping of union activists who organized it--from a short-term electoral caucus into a long-term workers' organization.

In most UAW locals, "caucuses" are almost exclusively electoral alliances of convenience, coming into being as the election approaches and dissolving--often in acrimony between winners and losers--the day after the election. The victorious candidates from each caucus begin to work together, reach compromises in order to function, and make deals when possible. Over time, new personality conflicts and divisions take place, often leading to dramatically realigned caucuses as the next election approaches.

The idea of a union caucus based on a common commitment to issues is in itself unusual in today's UAW. The idea that elected officials, once elected, would be subject to influence by rank and file members is even more unusual. In recent years, there has been a marked decline in the membership's involvement in the day-to-day life of the UAW. Ritual has replaced participation and power. Every three years there is a contract, preceded by "rallying the troops" from above to create a "bargaining mandate." Then, if necessary, there is a strike, followed by a "quieting of the troops" in order to achieve the necessary ratification. Then there is silence, as the workers are sent back to the line and the committeemen are empowered to represent them and enforce the contract.

The local elections follow a similar pattern. As the workers complain:

> Every two years these guys come out here and run around saying that we are being sold out and should vote someone else in. The guys who are in power come around and remind us of all that they've done for us, and

> tell us that the guys running against them are drunks and troublemakers and just trying to get off the line. Then we go to vote and we don't see any of them for two more years.

In this context, the Campaign was the first *sustained and nonelectoral* movement in the local's history. It maintained a core of more than twenty workers over a five-year period, expanded that core to as many as seventy-five workers during periods of intensified activity, involved another one hundred workers in some form of activity--phone banks, leafleting, rally monitoring--and hundreds more who attended marches, rallies, and showings of *Tiger By The Tail.*

Unlike the elections, which by necessity hinge on the politics and personalities of a few top candidates, the Campaign developed a conscious strategy of building and promoting new leadership. But can the Fighting Back caucus develop a similar organizing strategy?

The possibility is there. From June 1987 until the elections of June 1989, the Fighting Back caucus will have a voting majority on the shop committee and, until the elections of 1990, a narrow majority on the executive board as well. Given the narrow voting margins on both bodies and the substantial differences on the issues, there is a need and a basis for a genuine two-party system in the local.

Some members of the Fighting Back caucus want to involve new people, prepare for executive board meetings, continue to write leaflets to the membership, and plan strategy. This kind of activity, however, may meet with resistance from a few elected officials, who will not oppose it directly, but will prefer to function free of collective and issue-oriented constraints.

Like the Campaign itself, transforming the caucus will be an organizing challenge. If successful, it will continue and even expand the grass roots involvement of the workers on the shop floor. If not, the Fighting Back victory may be a brief one, overwhelmed by company forces far more powerful and organized than itself.

THE FUTURE OF THE CAMPAIGN: THE UAW LOCAL 645 COMPONENT

For almost five years, The Campaign to Keep GM Van Nuys Open has enjoyed the full and enthusiastic support of the local president. To some degree, the form the Campaign takes in the future will depend upon the stance of the incoming president, Jerry Shrieves.

Based on Shrieves' early practice, there is little room for encouragement. His first major policy change was to move from an open committee system to a closed one. This is not a technical change, but a political one. During the eight years of his presidency, Pete Beltran operated with an open committee system. For example, while Beltran appointee, Mike Gomez, was chair of the Community Action Committee, all CAP meetings were posted on union bulletin boards and open to any member of the union.

The test of Beltran's commitment to this principle came in May 1983 at a meeting at which the CAP committee was voting to send a delegation of five Campaign leaders to the UAW convention in Dallas. Because Shrieves and others had opposed using union funds for this project, the CAP members had raised the money privately--including having a fund-raising party on the Friday before the Saturday vote. But while they had spent the week raising money, the opponents of the Campaign had spent the week organizing. They showed up at the meeting with a bloc of thirty votes, and put themselves up as candidates to go to Dallas. This caught the Campaign organizers completely off guard. For, although seventy-five workers had been at the party the night before, only about thirty Campaign supporters attended the actual vote.

Campaign organizers appealed to Beltran to disallow the anti-Campaign members from voting. They had never attended meetings of the Campaign, had done nothing to raise money for the trip, and were clearly there to smash the meeting. But Beltran replied: "It's dirty politics; but the reality is that we got out-organized. I am not going to bar a union member from voting at a committee meeting."

As it turned out, Campaign leaders Dorothy Travis, Jose Silva, and Eric Mann won narrow victories, while two union members opposed to their leadership also were elected. The lesson from that experience, as Beltran explained, was not to attempt to exclude union members on a technicality, but to out-organize your opponents at future meetings. For the next three years, the meetings of the CAP committee continued to be publicly posted and open to *all* union members.

Immediately upon assuming office, however, Shrieves reversed that policy. In July 1987, he posted notices that people interested in serving on union committees should "apply" to him. Then, he personally selected the members of all committees, virtually excluding any workers allied with the Fighting Back Caucus from participating. Thus, after five years of work, more than one hundred workers who had attended CAP committee meetings over the past five years, and the twenty most active organizers of the Campaign, were barred from the Political Action Committee by presidential decree. The previous CAP chairman, Mike Gomez, was the only Campaign member appointed, with the clear understanding that he would be voted out of his chairmanship at the first meeting by the newly appointed committee members.

Those who disagree with this policy have many options available to them. They can write leaflets to the membership protesting these actions, bring their case to both the executive board and general membership meetings, and bring excluded members to the meetings and demand to be seated. The problem isn't coming up with ideas; the problem is developing a strong enough movement to convince President Shrieves to reverse his policy and open up the committees to the membership.

What has become clear is that, like Beltran, Shrieves has a clear political agenda--and moving against the Campaign and its architects appears to be an integral part of it. There is the very real possibility that with the power of the presidency behind them, the Campaign's opponents will feel emboldened, and will move from their previous behind-the-scenes attacks to a more frontal assault. If some of the Campaign's supporters underestimate the danger, or fight back in a disoriented and half-hearted way, the Campaign could suffer significant defeats. If the shop committee leadership--which is a critical element of the Campaign's in-plant coalition--becomes preoccupied with the collective bargaining fight and gives only lukewarm support to the battle to maintain the Campaign, a terrible setback could result.

Again, this is the complexity and beauty of a democratic labor union. Just as the June 1987 election campaign provided the workers with some clear political choices, so would a similar battle over the Campaign. If the Shrieves administration attempts to attack or disband the Campaign, it could be expected that at least one hundred active workers, including many committeemen and the shop chairman, would launch a worker-by-worker, line-by-line movement in support of the Campaign. Judging by its past organizing successes, the Campaign would be in a strong position to win any battles at the general membership meetings.

Moreover, the Campaign's leaders would not be defensive. They would openly question the objectives of union officials who would leave the Van Nuys workers isolated and unprotected in the face of company threats to close the plant. Community leaders would become involved as well. For, although they have scrupulously avoided the internal union conflict over the team concept, they would aggressively oppose any move to sever the relationship between the union and the community.

The local presidency is a powerful position. Considerable power and initiative are in Shrieves' hands, and he is obviously free to exercise the power that comes with electoral victory. But if Shrieves chooses to move against the Campaign--one of the most popular issues in the local--it is possible that, like Ray Ruiz before him, his "mandate" would be rapidly eroded.

Whatever the specific developments, there will have to be some major readjustments in the Campaign's strategy. Unless the battle over the Campaign's future prompts a change of heart by the new president, the Campaign's organizers can expect a difficult and uphill fight during the three long years of his term.

THE FUTURE OF THE CAMPAIGN: THE ROLE OF THE COMMUNITY

From May 1986 to June 1987, the Labor/Community Coalition had been in a state of suspended animation. Beltran's defeat in the April 1986 delegate elections, followed by the membership's vote (no matter how narrow) for the team concept in May of that year, had dramatically weakened the Coalition's mandate. This was exacerbated by a systematic, if uncoordinated, media campaign that hailed the team concept, projected Beltran's political demise, and made the Campaign and its Coalition a nonevent.

April 27, 1986, *Los Angeles Times*:

> Ruiz's stance is gaining favor in the plant, according to him and a number of others in the union. They said the growing sentiment for accommodation with the company was manifested last week when a slate of delegates headed by Ruiz defeated Beltran's slate to be the local's representatives at the UAW convention in Anaheim in June.[10]

May 27, 1986, *Los Angeles Times:*

> UAW's Van Nuys Chief Stung by Challenge From Within Ranks
>
> When thousands of United Auto Workers delegates gather in Anaheim on Sunday for the union's national convention, Pete Beltran will be just an observer....Beltran, president of UAW Local 645 in Van Nuys, says he's marched, picketed and fought for the working class all his life, bucking General Motors and, at times, the national union....
>
> Then, on April 22, the rank and file snubbed Beltran. Union members, worried that the layoffs could be a prelude to the eventual shutdown of their plant, selected a slate of

seven convention delegates who support the "team concept," a GM-backed production method styled after Japanese techniques.

Beltran, who adamantly opposes the idea, finished ninth, making it the first time the local hasn't named its president a delegate to the national convention. Worse yet, as far as Beltran is concerned, negotiators for the local last week reached a tentative agreement with GM that could bring the team concept to the Van Nuys plant.[11]

May 31, 1986, *Los Angeles Times:*

GM Van Nuys Workers Approve Team Concept in Effort to Save Plant

"I'm pleased," said Ray Ruiz, bargaining committee chairman for UAW Local 645. "We wouldn't have had a future without this new contract." Ernie Schaefer, manager of the Van Nuys plant echoed these sentiments. "I think this vote is the thing we've needed to move this plant from the bottom of the list in Detroit to near the top of the list to get a future product," Schaefer said.[12]

April 7, 1987, *Los Angeles Times*:

GM to Resume Second Shift at Van Nuys Plant: Team Concept Techniques Help Save Jobs

Van Nuys plant manager Ernest D. Schaefer said resumption of the night shift was a direct result of the workers' approval of "team concept" techniques. "A lot of union folks took a big risk, and it's paid off for everybody," Schaefer said. "Team concept has saved this plant."

These articles, and more than a dozen others like them, created a public relations bonanza for both the corporation and its advocates in the local union. In liberal circles throughout Los Angeles there was a media-cultivated party line: "Oh, you work at GM Van Nuys. Isn't that where there used to be a lot of trouble, but the workers have voted to cooperate with the company and now they are making a better car and the plant has been saved?"

In November 1986, shortly after GM announced the closing of eleven plants and the decision to keep the Van Nuys plant open, Eloy Salazar, one of the Campaign's most active community members, observed:

> The whole thing gets me sick. Here we work for four years; we have that meeting with McDonald; we march and picket and hold press conferences. You know, I must have sent Roger Smith a couple of hundred letters just from the Machinists alone. And then it's like we're invisible. Even guys in my own union tell me, "Hey, I read in the paper where those guys at Van Nuys are trying to save their plant by cooperating with the company."
>
> After GM announced that Van Nuys was going to be kept open, I was so glad we could have a press conference to explain how the Campaign helped to save the plant. At the press conference, I go up to this reporter from the *L.A. Times* and say, "I'm glad you're finally going to tell our side of the story." And he says, "What story? I said I would attend the press conference, but I don't see any story here." The next day, I kept re-reading the paper figuring I must have missed the article; but there was no story at all.
>
> There was excellent coverage on the TV stations, and some of them even said it was the community boycott more than the team concept that kept the plant open. But those messages were just a half-minute and then they were gone. There was nothing in any of the papers. If we can't turn this situation

> around, I'm worried that support for the Coalition will dry up.[13]

Coalition members such as Reverend Dick Gillett, Rudy Acuña, and Nadine Kerner, who had extensive community contacts, attempted to explain that Beltran was still the president; that virtually half the workers had voted *against* the team concept; and that community pressure on GM was still essential to protect the long-term future of the plant.

But few were listening. Politics is a complex formula of moral authority, initiative, popular support, and power. A movement eventually must possess all four of those attributes to achieve its objectives, but it needs at least one of them to continue to exist. From June 1, 1986, the opening of the UAW Convention, to June 2, 1987, the day of the UAW Local 645 elections, the Coalition had only one of those qualities--moral authority--but was lacking initiative, public support, and power.

The team-concept advocates were taking the initiative, claiming they were being "proactive, not reactive." They *claimed* the moral authority as well, arguing that they were working together with management to stop destructive confrontations, produce a quality product, and save their jobs. Thanks to the press, they had popular support. They were portrayed as the modern, state-of-the-art union leaders, whereas the Campaign's advocates were portrayed as dogmatic and archaic. Most importantly, they had power--the power of an elected delegate slate, the power of the shop chairmanship, the power of the company, and the power of the press.

The elections of June 1987, however, gave the Labor-Community Coalition a new lease on life. The Coalition could once again take the initiative, redoubling its boycott preparations in order to protect a beleaguered shop chairman and the workers who voted for him. Coalition activists went back into the community with some questions of their own: "Can workers in the UAW ever have a free election if, after electing a candidate the company opposes, the company is allowed to shut down a plant?" "Regardless of the merits of the team concept itself, how can it claim to be based on 'cooperation,' if GM tells the workers to accept it or they will close the plant?"

After the election of Beltran, the Coalition received many invitations from community groups wanting speakers to address their meetings. Once again, there were requests for showing *Tiger By the Tail*. Friends of the Coalition proposed new meetings with GM officials; press conferences; ecumenical meetings of the clergy; and a new petition campaign. There was no shortage of energy or new ideas.

Once again the Coalition had a clear mandate from the workers. As Pete Beltran explained the day after the election: "We are like the South Africans. They cannot get rid of apartheid alone; we cannot save our plant alone. They need world public opinion to keep the pressure on the apartheid regime; we need the community to keep the pressure on General Motors."

Public opinion began to swing back in the direction of the Coalition, if not actively, at least in terms of its openness to the Campaign's point of view. Many liberals, who were favorably predisposed toward the team concept, wondered why the workers elected a shop chairman adamantly opposed to it.

In discussions with dozens of professionals, liberal businesspeople, academics, and Democratic party regulars (constituencies that are important to the Campaign's strategy), a marked change in attitude was apparent following the election. As one attorney, reflective of this change, observed:

> I read a lot of the articles about the turmoil over at Van Nuys, but I never quite know what is going on over there. I had read a lot of articles saying how good the team concept was, and it sounded like both GM and the union were on the right track. I certainly know that the workers want to hold on to their jobs. So, when I heard that the workers had elected Beltran, even after the company told them it might close the plant, I figured that GM must be doing something

> wrong. Maybe the team concept is not as good as it's cracked up to be.

The day the election results were announced, every television station in Los Angeles ran a major story about the workers electing an opponent of the team concept at Van Nuys. And while most reporters had difficulty explaining the workers' vote, especially after dozens of stories over the past year had lauded the team concept, they did convey the simple message that there was a "yes" vote for Beltran, which in some way reflected a "no" vote for the team concept. The news coverage created a rebirth of interest in the Campaign and the Coalition. As Eloy Salazar observed: "Now all of a sudden people are interested in my opinion again."

THE FUTURE OF THE VAN NUYS PLANT: CAN THE CAMPAIGN KEEP GM VAN NUYS OPEN?

This analysis of the complex set of political forces and their interrelationship is a prelude to the most difficult practical question--what will eventually happen to the Van Nuys plant? Ultimately, taking on General Motors is a question of power. As a team-concept committeeman and long-time opponent of the Campaign explained:

> You know, a lot of people in my district hate me. I know it. And they always find someone to run against me. And sometimes I only win by two or three votes. But I always win. The guy who loses tells all his friends how good he did and how close he came to beating me. But, for two years, he is stuck back on the line and I am the committeeman. That's all that matters--who wins and who loses.

In many ways, he is right. GM Van Nuys will, ultimately, either be kept open or will close. The movement will, ultimately, either succeed in its objectives or fail. Given the balance of forces--a single UAW local and a labor-community coalition against the number one corporation in the Fortune 500--it is certainly possible that a defeat will occur and the plant will close despite the workers' best efforts. Even if that is the ultimate eventuality, the labor movement has already won many victories at Van Nuys. This is not a case in which organized labor has underachieved. The perpetuation of the Van Nuys movement for five years, and its uncanny ability to land on its feet, have provided an important symbol and a rich organizing experience for a labor movement desperate for victories. Nonetheless, the Campaign organizers are not preparing for noble defeat. They have every intention of winning the ten-year commitment they have been demanding.

The Campaign organizers have developed a two-pronged approach to continue their movement. *First, the Coalition intends to reestablish, if not escalate, its public presence.* As Congressman Howard Berman explained: "A man like Roger Smith has so many things on his mind. When we are not directly in front of his face we become invisible." The Coalition's strategy is to reappear in front of Roger Smith and General Motors, and to once again become a major factor in the corporation's decision-making process. Jim Wisely, a demographics expert who has followed the Campaign since its inception, observed:

> In many ways, the potential for the Campaign and its boycott is greater than ever. When it began, the whole American auto industry was in trouble; but now it's mainly General Motors. I can't think of anything Iacocca would want more than a boycott of GM products in Los Angeles.
>
> Ford and Chrysler couldn't admit it publicly, but in the world of business, one company's hard luck is another's opportunity. GM is getting famous for making bad business

> decisions, but underestimating the boycott might prove to be one of its all-time worst.[14]

Coalition members are discussing several new tactical options--a series of meetings with car dealers in Los Angeles county to impress upon them the reality of the boycott and to ask their help in averting it through mutual efforts to get a long-term commitment from GM; a community leadership meeting with local plant manager Ernest Schaefer; a greater focus on college campuses and the formation of Keep GM Van Nuys Open first-time buyer committees; and the formation of an ecumenical committee to organize church-by-church, boycott petition drives to GM Chairman Roger Smith.

Second, pressuring GM to come to terms with the new shop committee. The shop-floor movement has to convince General Motors management in Detroit that if they are sincere about wanting quality and reasonably orderly industrial production, they have to back away from their efforts to break the union. There are many plants throughout the GM system that are producing cars without the team concept--and doing so quite profitably. There are also many so-called "team concept" systems that have been modified dramatically by the union to restrict their worst aspects. There is no reason why GM cannot back down from its efforts to make GM Van Nuys into a "showcase" and just allow it to be an auto plant producing high-quality Camaros, Firebirds, and future models that GM agrees to produce there.

Just as the Flint strikers finally convinced GM that its efforts to push for the last dollar of profit and the last ounce of capitulation would generate nothing but resistance, Beltran, as a "traditionalist," is trying to convince GM that his election signals the end of a brief period of company unionism, and that dramatic adjustments on the part of the corporation will be necessary.

If GM comes to accept that it is in Los Angeles to stay, and that it must abandon some of its more overt efforts to bend the workers to its latest schemes, the Van Nuys plant can continue to provide cars for the public, profits for General Motors, and jobs for the workers and their families.

While such a "happy ending" may not be in the cards, at least the workers are now back in the game with a strong hand of their own. With a rebuilt and revitalized community coalition, a majority on both the shop committee and the executive board, and growing public support for their movement, the workers and their Campaign are once again in a strong position to take on General Motors should that become necessary. While future events are hard to predict, it appears that, at least for several more years, GM Van Nuys will remain open; the workers will continue to have their jobs; the union will continue to function as a vital institution--and the battle will continue.

NOTES

1. James Risen, "Ford's Earnings Up; GM's Drop," *Los Angeles Times*, Business section, July 24, 1987, p. 1.
2. Henry Weinstein, "Team Concept Foe Wins UAW Van Nuys Vote," *Los Angeles Times*, June 5, 1987, p. 3.
3. *Labor Notes*, July 1987, p. 16. This newsletter provides the best coverage, much of it written by union activists, of insurgent and left strategies being attempted in today's labor movement. For subscription and other information: P.O. Box 20001, Detroit, Michigan, 48220.
4. James Warren, "GM Team Faces Tough UAW Opponent," *Chicago Tribune*, Section 7, July 5, 1987, p. 3. This article was one of the best efforts to present Beltran's views, as well as the role of the Campaign, fairly and systematically.
5. Interview with the author, June 25, 1987.
6. *Los Angeles Times*, Business section, July 7, 1987, p. 3.
7. "Summary of Proposed Agreement," Special Report to the Membership, UAW-GM Local 645, May 1986.
8. Interview with the author, July 20, 1987.
9. "Team Concept Must Go, Workers Warn," *Los Angeles Times*, July 7, Business section, 1987, p. 3.
10. "Coalition Supports Bid to Keep GM Plant Open," *Los Angeles Times*, Metro section, April 27, 1986, p. 5.
11. Alan Goldstein, "UAW's Van Nuys Chief Stung By Challenge From Within the Ranks," *Los Angeles Times*, Business section, May 27, 1986, p. 1.
12. "GM Van Nuys Workers Approve Team Concept in Effort To Save Plant," *Los Angeles Times*, Business section, May 31, 1986, p. 1.
13. Conversation with the author, November 12, 1986.
14. Conversation with the author, June 30, 1987.

Part Four

DRAWING LESSONS FROM THE VAN NUYS CAMPAIGN

Chapter Fourteen

GM VAN NUYS IN THE BROADER PICTURE

In the first stages of the Campaign, when some of its early achievements had captured the imagination of a few labor activists, the organizers were encouraged to sum up the lessons of the Van Nuys movement. At that point, however, the pressures of building the movement were so overwhelming that disseminating information and ideas to a broader audience had to be postponed. After five years of organizing work, however, it is time to discuss the broader applications and the larger issues raised by the Van Nuys Campaign.

Taking a Campaign to Keep Auto Plants Open to the UAW as a Whole

Almost from its inception, the Campaign organizers talked about, even dreamed about, the possibility of a *coordinated*, *nationwide* UAW response to capital flight; corporate intimidation of communities; and the whipsawing of UAW locals. In the absence of that historical possibility, the Campaign did the next best thing--it demonstrated a local model of a "job and community protection" campaign that could serve as the prototype for a national UAW campaign against the Big Three.

A national strategy could begin by subjecting company plant closing plans to union and community scrutiny. The goal would *not* be to prevent auto companies from ever closing down a plant. Every auto company must have a relative balance between plant capacity and the demand for its products. In order to compete, it must introduce new technology, modernize its plants, and eventually phase out antiquated ones. That is not the problem. It is the unwillingness of corporations such as GM to develop socially responsible methods of carrying out those closings and, worse, their use of plant closings as a management weapon to browbeat workers and communities that the UAW should be challenging.

While some plant closings may be inevitable, many others can be stopped. If GM, Ford, or Chrysler claim that the problem is overcapacity, the UAW must examine which corporate policies led to that surplus plant capacity. How much of that "excess" was the product of "captive imports"--foreign-made imports brought into the United States under their own nameplates?

> General Motors, which already sells two small cars built in Japan [Isuzu and Suzuki] ...will introduce the LeMans, a Pontiac subcompact built in South Korea by GM's joint venture with Daewoo Motor Co.
>
> Ford will introduce the Ford Festiva, a Japanese-designed subcompact produced in South Korea by Kia Motors, Ford's new Korean partner...and the Mercury Tracer, built in Ford's new plant in Hermosillo, Mexico....
>
> Chrysler has held discussions recently with Proton Industries of Malaysia. For now, though, Chrysler is planning to make do with Japanese subcompacts built by Mitsubishi Motor Company.[1]

The UAW research department estimates that by 1990 11 percent of GM's sales, 26 percent of Ford's, and 26 percent of Chrysler's will come from captive imports.[2] Obviously, that will lead to further closings of domestic plants. While the UAW has done a good job of researching the problem, it has, in practice, placed too little emphasis on opposing U.S. captive imports and too much on opposing Japanese imports.

Politically, it is the *domestic* companies that are most culpable and vulnerable. It makes complete sense that Toyota would build cars in Japan and import them to the United States. But why are General Motors, Ford, and Chrysler taking capital produced by the labor of American workers, building cars overseas, and then importing those cars back into the United States--leading to the layoff of many of those same workers and the closing of their plants?

If the UAW International leadership asked that question forcefully and persistently, there would be widespread support for policies to restrict those practices. A national campaign restricting the export of domestic capital for investment abroad would place the UAW on the high ground, focus the workers' anger against their own employers (instead of the Japanese) and, if successful, could cut down on the threat of plant closings.

The UAW need not appear to be "antiprogress" or "antitechnology." The union should encourage the retooling of existing plants and the building of new plants as a constructive use of corporate capital. However, the UAW should replace GM's policy of "plant closures as a management weapon" with a "job and communities preservation" policy.

Under that plan, corporations such as GM would be forced to recognize "*plant and community seniority*"; whereby communities with the longest time in the GM system would be given first preference for the construction of new auto plants. In instances in which it was necessary to close down older, outmoded plants, corporations would be required to replace them with new, state-ofthe-art ones within twenty miles of the original site.

This strategy would place the UAW on a collision course with GM executives who believe that the corporation should be allowed to pursue the highest rate of profit possible--regardless of the social consequences. This narrow perspective allows GM to view communities and workers who have contributed to its profits for decades as the unfortunate, if inevitable, victims of a plant closing. Past loyalty and years of service to the corporation become a liability; while new, virgin communities become the most attractive.

A job and community preservation policy would offer an alternative to the present situation in which corporations use the stick of plant closings to shake down communities with existing plants and the carrot of plant openings to demand tax and labor-law concessions from communities desperate to attract "new" jobs. This affirmative, nationwide strategy to protect workers and communities from "job blackmail" could involve the UAW in alliances with other labor unions, minority communities, consumer, and environmental groups and grass roots leaders throughout the country--a coalition that could become a building block for a revitalized labor and progressive movement.

At this point in the UAW's history, however, neither a job and community preservation campaign nor a program to empower local unions and communities is on the agenda. The international leadership is strategically opposed to such a confrontational strategy, and the locals are too divided and isolated to carry it out themselves. Thus, before there can be a leap from coalitions rooted in a single UAW local, such as the Van Nuys Campaign, to an eventual change in strategy at the international level of the UAW, there will have to be a proliferation of regional movements based on new politics and new directions. Through initiative and pressure from below, it may be possible, over a period of years, to produce new leaders and new policies at the top levels of the UAW.

Building Regional Movements in the UAW: The New Directions Movement

The New Directions Movement is one example of an encouraging regional model of UAW insurgency. In 1986, a group of local leaders in Region 5 (the UAW region representing 75,000 UAW members in eight South Central states, including Missouri, Oklahoma, Louisiana, Texas, and Kansas) organized the New Directions movement.

They disagreed with what they believed was the union's concessionary strategy and the lack of democracy in the region--initiating their movement out of a directly felt need more than a coherent philosophy or strategy.

They decided to challenge the incumbent regional director, Kenneth Worley. Their view that they were mounting that challenge "within channels" was reflected in their choice of incumbent assistant director, Jerry Tucker, a fourteen-year veteran of the International staff, as their candidate to run against Worley. Their slogan, "Justice, Not Just Us," reflected their concern with greater solidarity between white and black workers in a region in which racism was still quite overt, and with greater solidarity among individual locals in order to reverse the company practice of whipsawing local against local.

Their movement was based on more than a critique; it had an impressive track record. Under Tucker's leadership, many of the locals had waged resourceful struggles to resist concessions, such as the 1984 UAW campaign at LTV-Vought, the aerospace firm in Dallas-Fort Worth. In that situation, the company demanded concessions in an attempt to provoke the union into a lengthy strike, with the hope that the financially drained workers would return in a more pliable mood.

Tucker and the local union leadership countered with a tactical plan they called "running the plant backwards." They used work slowdowns, mass grievance filings, passive resistance, and other forms of "in-plant strategies" to involve hundreds of new workers in the process and wear the company down--choosing to use the strike weapon on their timetable not the company's. Finally, a one-day strike in June 1985, as the culmination of more than a year of organizing, forced the company to back down. None of management's concessionary demands was imposed.[3]

With their movement rooted in successful rank-and-file resistance, the New Directions delegates went to the June 1986 UAW convention in Anaheim, California, with hopes of electing Jerry Tucker. At a convention that celebrated the fiftieth anniversary of the union's founding, many delegates from other regions saw the feisty New Directions people as a harbinger of hope. Its top-to-bottom racial integration, the prominent role of women workers in the movement, and its call to once again confront the corporations made New Directions the talk of the convention. If Tucker could win, perhaps Region 5 could become a workshop for new strategies that could eventually impact the entire UAW.

When the election was held for Region 5, hundreds of delegates from other regions packed into the ballroom to watch the roll call vote--as if their own future was at stake as well. When the votes were finally counted, Ken Worley was declared the winner over Jerry Tucker by an announced margin of 325 for Worley and 324.8 for Tucker--a difference of two-tenths of a vote.

The Tucker delegates contested the election results based on charges of irregularities. Tucker retained the services of attorney Joseph A. "Chip" Yablonski (whose father, "Jock" Yablonski, a reformer in the United Mine Workers, was murdered for his efforts to democratize his union). After an investigation of Tucker's charges, the U.S. Department of Labor, according to Yablonski, found the following election violations in the Tucker-Worley race for regional director: several delegates who had voted for Worley had never been properly elected in their locals; two delegates who had voted for Worley received payments of approximately $5,000 in UAW funds; and Jerry Tucker, after fourteen years on the staff of the International union, had been fired from his position as assistant regional director four days after he announced his candidacy.[4]

The New Directions activists demanded a completely new election for regional director, including new elections for all convention delegates in the region. In many union reform movements, drawn out legal proceedings, even if eventually successful, often discourage the activists and lead to dramatic declines in organizing momentum. In the case of New Directions, however, a year after the UAW convention, as they awaited the decision of the courts, their movement was, if anything, growing stronger. They were publishing an attractive newsletter with articles debating the union's future; organizing local officers to raise job security demands for the 1987 auto contract negotiations; and running slates of officers in virtually every local election in the region.

To its credit, their movement does not place undue emphasis on Tucker. It trains and encourages dozens of grass roots leaders, through programs such as all-day strategy workshops addressing union responses to whipsawing, concessions and plant closings. The New Directions organizers are developing an advanced model involving building a coalition of UAW locals in an eight-state region.

If the courts order a new election and Tucker is elected regional director, the character of the insurgent movement will have been transformed, in at least one region, from protest to program. The New Directions leaders will have the opportunity (and the responsibility) to try out new strategic approaches with which to confront the auto and aerospace companies. If new elections are not ordered, or if they are and Tucker is not elected, the New Directions people will focus their energies on the shop floor--and prepare for the 1989 UAW convention where the next regularly scheduled regional director's election will be held.

One possible program for a regionwide movement such as New Directions would be a campaign to make UAW Region 5 a "plant-closing-free zone." UAW locals in an eight state area could warn GM that any actions to close down a plant in their region would lead to local strikes and regionwide boycotts.

The prospect of UAW locals and community leaders in an eight state area engaging in *regional economic planning* and taking on corporations such as General Motors to achieve their objectives is certainly a long shot at this point in history. But, based on the successes and lessons of the Van Nuys model, it offers exciting possibilities. If New Directions adopted a "plant-closing-free zone" strategy and the idea took off, it could exponentially expand the impact of the Van Nuys movement--creating a true domino effect that could influence the policies both of the International UAW and General Motors management.

In this context, the movement for greater internal democracy in the UAW assumes even greater importance. There is a crying need for an open and widespread strategic debate within the UAW as to its future direction. For many in the UAW, the most distressing development is not the union's orientation toward concessions, workplace cooperation, and protectionism, but its unwillingness to subject those strategies to widespread membership debate.

There is a great deal of enthusiasm, militancy, and programatic initiative at the local level. The vast majority of dissident local leaders, while highly critical of the *strategies* of the international leadership, are offering their views constructively. Those views should be considered and debated, rather than suppressed, if a declining union with a proud history and a potentially proud future is to rebuild itself.

APPLYING THE VAN NUYS EXPERIENCE

How applicable are the lessons of the Van Nuys Campaign to the problems of labor unions and community groups across the country? Some have argued that the unique set of conditions in Los Angeles provided highly favorable circumstances for such a Campaign--circumstances that other workers and communities do not enjoy. Activists who have watched the Van Nuys Campaign for years feared that workers in areas where there was not a large regional market to make a boycott feasible, workers who produce products that are not sold in mass consumer markets, or workers in service industries or in smaller-scale production might find the Van Nuys story more inspiring than applicable.

Those fears are only valid if activists attempt a literal application of the Van Nuys model. This dogmatic approach could never succeed, even if the objective situations were virtually identical, since organizing is a highly creative process involving the utmost attention to the specifics of each situation. Every political situation is unique. Organizing involves accurately understanding the inner dynamics of situations and translating those understandings into strategy.

The view that the Van Nuys Campaign achieved a certain level of success because of uniquely *favorable* conditions has only been raised by a few observers in retrospect. At its inception, however, virtually everyone advised the Campaign's initiators that the strategy could not succeed because of *unfavorable* conditions: the plant was so isolated from other UAW locals in the Midwest that there was no possibility of other locals joining the movement; the closure of five of the six California auto plants had created a public opinion already accepting the eventuality of Van Nuys' demise; the focus on the the Chicano and black commnities was romantic since "the civil rights movement is dead"; the expectation that large numbers of consumers would boycott something as personally important as a car was utopian because this is the "yuppie era" and Californians are even more selfish and "laid-back"; the plan to build a movement *before* a plant closed wouldn't work because no one would take the threat seriously and GM could always deny it; the past practice at other closed industrial plants in the Los Angeles area (Goodyear, Firestone, Southgate, Bethlehem) had not generated much organized resistance, and so on.

So, while it is true that the conditions in which the Campaign developed were unique, they were by no means uniquely favorable. It is the *methodology and political approach* of the Campaign, not its specifics, that are most applicable to other situations. A few of the elements of that approach are:

Developing A Strategic Plan

In every successful struggle there must be an objective balance sheet of the union's strengths and weaknesses, as well as those of the corporation. Too often, union leaders are predisposed toward defeat and are narrow and mechanical in their analysis. This frequently leads them to miss the historical possibilities of a situation. Local union activists can develop the skills of strategy-building and can get help from specialized organizations such as the Midwest Center for Labor Research in Chicago and the Labor Institute in New York.

In the Van Nuys experience, the organizers began with a hard-nosed analysis of whether a boycott was feasible. The strategy began with a predominantly minority workforce (50 percent Latino and 15 percent black) located in a major urban center (Los Angeles, whose population was 35 percent Latino and 14 percent black). The viability of the strategy was reinforced by the enormity of the Los Angeles new-car market--with more than 155,000 cars and trucks sold per year.

In other struggles, management may be vulnerable for a variety of reasons: because its abuse of the environment impacts a far larger community than the workers themselves; or because its policies are in conflict with state and local political forces; or because it depends upon government contracts; or because a religious denomination sympathetic to social concerns owns substantial blocks of its stock; or because it has a highly seasonal business that makes it especially vulnerable to strikes. In some instances the company's product itself is vulnerable to consumer pressure and in others major stockholders are heads of firms or banks that are vulnerable. In some cases individual corporations are targetable; and in others it may be better to target several corporations at once whose overall policies impact a wide constituency that can be organized. There are few corporations that do not have some window of vulnerability; the job of the union and or community group faced with a possible plant closing (or other antisocial corporate behavior) is to analyze both the company's vulnerability and the possibilities of broader coalitions--and then attack.

The Adversarial and Confrontational Model

It is paradoxical that at a time of labor's greatest weakness in fifty years and the systematic attacks by large corporations on union rights, so many labor leaders are caught up in the rhetoric of cooperation. By contrast, the Van Nuys Campaign was built on the following premises:

– Workers and communities have a *right* to keep the plant open.

– Closing down a profitable plant to pursue greater profits elsewhere is an unacceptable use of corporate power.

– Since the interests of the corporation and those of the workers are in strategic contradiction, class confrontation is the only way to resolve that conflict in the interests of the workers.

– The workers need economic and political weapons in order to override GM's short-term, profit-oriented decisions; otherwise the corporation will have no motivation to change its behavior.

From those basic premises, countless hours went into researching the specifics of the situation, and countless more were spent in debate in order to combine strategic firmness with tactical flexibility. To the degree that the Campaign succeeded, a rejection of class cooperation and an affirmation of class struggle was, as the corporate executives say, the "bottom line."

The Alliance Between the Labor Movement and Minority Communities

There is virtually no objective that labor can win alone. In the 1930s, as the UAW and the CIO were developing, capitalism was at a stage in which the scale of production and the degree of competition still gave labor some leverage. In the 1980s, however, new strategies for labor must address the development of gigantic conglomerates and multinational corporations.

Organized capital has reached dimensions of frightening scale and has created new political conditions in which even the most militant and united international union (let alone a single local) is no match for the company. It is only in conjunction with the broad community--with black, Chicano, Asian-American, and other minority groups; with small-business owners, consumers, environmentalists, peace activists, and organized religious organizations--that labor can win any structural changes in governmental and corporate policy.

While the Van Nuys coalition encompassed all those constituencies, the core of the movement was the alliance between the GM workers and the black and Chicano communities. *It was the successful integration of the issues of class and race that gave the coalition its vitality and power.*

The gains of the civil rights movement in the turbulent sixties that were over a century in the making lasted less than a decade before a "white backlash" was orchestrated to roll them back. From the Bakke decision with its cry of "reverse discrimination" to a Reagan administration that brazenly opposed affirmative action, the fragile efforts to unite workers of all races against discrimination were replaced by racist appeals to white workers to perceive their own interests as threatened by the progress of minorities.

This reappearance of racist ideology was used to justify draconian cuts in urgently needed social programs (even though many of the victims were poor whites). Millions of black and Latino families, after a brief period of hope, saw the reemergence of overcrowded schools, deteriorating housing, and dramatically reduced medical services.

While a small stratum of minorities had been able to make well-deserved and long overdue gains in the 1960s and early 1970s, by the late 1970s and continuing into the 1980s the window of opportunity had been slammed on the hands of millions of others. Many minority workers trying to climb out of poverty and racially imposed deadend jobs found themselves locked into structural unemployment, underemployment, and lower-paid categories--an intolerable situation made even worse by the deterioration of the nation's industrial base.

The Van Nuys Campaign was able to tap deep reservoirs of class anger as well as racial and national sentiments in Los Angeles' Chicano and black communities. It engaged community leaders in a battle that had tangible objectives, while also serving the broader goals of political and economic empowerment. For many in those communities, a confrontation with General Motors took on a symbolic meaning--a showdown with the number one corporation in the Fortune 500; a chance for minority leaders to tell corporate America: "Enough!" As was argued previously, GM apparently concluded that the Chicano and black communities in Los Angeles, with long histories of struggle against big business and an orientation towards direct action, should not be challenged on the Van Nuys issue. Of the many critical elements of the overall community strategy, the active and visible role of the Chicano and black community leadership was the decisive factor in the Campaign's initial success.

In every city, regardless of the specific objectives and demands, the ability of workers, many of whom are themselves black, Latino, or Asian, to ally with minority communities and organizations is critical. Even in situations in which the majority of the workers are white, if there is a genuine element of the problem that concerns minority communities, it is critical to seek out their help. In most cases, their participation will be pivotal to the success of any labor-community coalition.

IMPACTING NATIONAL POLICY FROM THE BOTTOM UP

There has been no shortage of proposals for a restructured economic system in America that would involve labor unions and local communities in some type of democratic economic planning. The problem has been how to build sufficient political pressure from below to get those in power to consider, let alone implement, those proposals.

In the early stages of the civil rights movement, the debates about social policy objectives and movement-building proceeded simultaneously; but in the absence of a powerful social movement, developing strategies and tactics for *organizing* was given the highest priority. Out of the freedom rides and sit-ins, voter registration drives, and boycotts, the broader demands of the Civil Rights Act of 1964 were developed. And, although the initial drafting of the legislation was handled by specialists and more moderate political forces, the most militant civil rights groups discussed the draft provisions of the bill in great detail. The same organizers whose risks, sacrifices, and ingenuity had created the conditions for the Civil Rights Act understood that those very same attributes would be necessary for its effective implementation.

The leaders of the civil rights movement, from the Student Nonviolent Coordinating Committee (SNCC) to Martin Luther King, taught a generation of organizers that the main objective of the political establishment is social order--not social justice. Thus, without social activism and at least the threat of economic or social disruption at the bottom, there is little incentive for those at the top to consider reforms.

The Van Nuys organizers shared a similar perspective--that grass roots movements with the power to disrupt corporate objectives were the key to changes in corporate policy. But while the Campaign placed almost all of its emphasis on a direct challenge to GM's decision making, many interesting possibilities for regional economic planning and social policy opened up.

For example, in the initial discussions with officials of the Van Nuys and United Chambers of Commerce of San Fernando Valley, the UAW organizers limited the discussions to their mutual interest in keeping the plant open. But as GM began to repeat its claims that the costs of importing parts from the Midwest were too great, several local businessmen countered that if the community pressure to keep the plant open succeeded GM might offer contracts to local manufacturers who could produce those parts in Los Angeles County. At one meeting of the United Chambers, local businesspeople speculated about the availability of vacant land and the possibility of local companies building an industrial park for West Coast auto parts production.

Similarly, when GM argued that it was too costly to ship completed cars from Van Nuys to dealers in the East, Christopher Cedergren, a senior analyst at J.D. Powers and Associates, an auto market research firm, proposed the following solution:

> If I was General Motors, I would convert the Van Nuys plant to Cadillac production. California is one of the great markets for Cadillacs [with 13 percent of all U.S. sales]. GM is saying that it wants to upgrade the Cadillac and make it directly competitive with the Mercedes and other top-of-the-line companies. For that to happen, GM will have to move towards an exclusive assembly plant that only builds Cadillacs, which is sorely needed to regain its luster. If GM focused on quality by slowing down the assembly line and focused on high-profit Devilles and El Dorados, Van Nuys would be the perfect place to build them after the Camaro and Firebird are phased out. For GM to build its finest cars in its strongest market would help the image of the car.[5]

The reason it warrants even mentioning the ideas of local businesspeople or industry analysts as to the best uses of the Van Nuys facility is that there is a social movement forcing GM to stay in Los Angeles. In the Van Nuys situation, GM has a greater interest than usual in proposals about the future of the plant because, at least in the short run, the corporation believes it is stuck in Van Nuys.

In reality, the Campaign will not be strong enough to venture further into this aspect of GM's management prerogatives. But, in terms of longer-term possibilities reflected in the Van Nuys case study, it is interesting that while the workers began with the more immediate goal of saving the plant, as they reached out for allies, new possibilities of social and economic planning from the bottom up became evident. The irony of the Van Nuys experience is that a movement initially organized to confront corporate management and restrict the mobility of its capital ended up providing opportunities for the creative and constructive use of that capital.

The model of workers, businesspeople, community residents, and professionals working together to develop community-based and regional economic models is an exciting one. But it can never be generated by liberal economists and social architects working in isolation or attempting to convince those in power to carry out a top-down reform strategy. Rather, it will require intellectuals, academics, and professionals with skills in community economic development working closely with union and community movements that are directly confronting capital.

In Harlem in the 1960s, local architects and professional educators worked in concert with neighborhood movements of black community residents. It was the black movement that created the political mandate to persuade federal and local officials to fund neighborhood community centers and community-run public schools. In that context, professionals, technicians, and planners were able to play a progressive social role.

While there is no need to mechanically separate the important contributions of social theorists and economic planners from those of labor and community organizers, in this historical moment, when there is so little organized, farsighted mass activity at either the union or community level, one pressing priority for social theory is to address the ways that academics and intellectuals can best contribute to the rebuilding of those movements.

RESTRICTING CAPITAL FLIGHT: PLANT CLOSING LEGISLATION, LABOR LAW REFORM, AND A CONTRACTUAL BILL OF RIGHTS FOR UNIONS

For forty years, from the passage of the National Labor Relations Act in 1935 to the beginning of America's industrial decline of the mid-1970s, the basic contours of the social compact between management and labor worked reasonably well for the workers in unionized, oligopolized industry. Labor relations were characterized by the codification of labor-management relations in collectively bargained contracts; the agreement by the union not to strike during the life of the contract; the limitation of most of the workers' options during the life of the contract to individual grievances solved one at a time; the development of the mediation and arbitration industry to reconcile class conflict; and the mutual agreement that the government's National Labor Relations Board would be the arbiter of most labor disputes.

While there was still class conflict, in the unionized industries it was attenuated and, for the most part, orderly. The corporation received dependable labor and uninterrupted production, while the workers received dependable wages and, for the most part, uninterrupted work.

Of course, a few union activists dissented from this approach. During the postwar years, it was common for left-wing trade unionists in the auto industry to complain about the "management rights" clause in the UAW contract. But they could gain little support from their co-workers. As long as the union was able to restrict the speed of the assembly line to a bearable rate, provide a constantly improving package of wages and benefits, and use the grievance procedure to curb management's worst abuses, most workers saw little reason to challenge management's authority. Ater all, this was capitalism, wasn't it? Why was it so shocking, they argued, that management wanted to run its own company?

But that thinking began to change during the 1970s as the wave of plant closings reached epidemic proportions. Bluestone and Harrison estimate that "all together, over 38 million jobs were lost through private disinvestment during the 1970s. That would seem to be deindustrialization with a vengeance."[6] As plant after plant closed, many autoworkers wanted to reevaluate the management rights clause in the contract that stated:

> ...the products to be manufactured, the location of plants, the schedule of production, the methods, processes, and means of manufacturing are solely and exclusively the responsibility of the corporation.[7]

In the era of plant closings, "the location of plants" can no longer be the sole prerogative of the corporation; and, if it is not, there are implications for corporate policy, federal law, and union contracts.

Throughout the advanced capitalist world, there has been a growing demand for some form of greater social control over corporations whose sole reason for existence, by their own admission, is to invest capital in order to maximize its return.

The position paper of the National Conference of Catholic Bishops, *Economic Justice for All*, sharply expressed the church's concerns:

> When companies are considering plant closures or the movement of capital, it is patently unjust to deny workers any role in shaping the outcome of these difficult choices.. ..While such decisions may sometimes be necessary, a collaborative and mutually accountable model of industrial organization would mean that workers not be expected to carry all the burdens of an economy in transition. Management and investors must also accept their share of sacrifices, especially when management is thinking of transferring capital to a seemingly more lucrative or competitive activity. *The capital at the disposal of management is in part the product of the labor of those who have toiled in the company over the years, including currently employed workers.*[8]

Decisions such as plant closings, with their enormous social impact and ripple effect throughout the community, can no longer be allowed to be the sole "property" of the corporation. In a capitalist society with any pretension of industrial democracy, in which the working class is not just an adjunct to production but a powerful political force, the pursuit of corporate profit must take place within strictly defined social constraints. In the "era of plant closings," the labor movement has to win major reforms in both the legislative and contractual arenas to reestablish even a modicum of working class influence over critical corporate decisions.

Plant Closing Legislation

The most far-reaching plant closing legislation must be at the federal level in order to establish uniform regulations on corporate behavior and to prevent corporations from punishing more progressive states by running away to more backward ones. However, those who argue that plant closing legislation at the state level is not feasible in the absence of federal laws are simply passing the buck. In practice, virtually every piece of progressive federal legislation has been preceded by far more advanced laws at the state level. States like California and New York, with enormous markets, access to seaports, national media centers, and other unique reasons for companies to locate there are in the strongest position to initiate strong plant-closing laws that could call the bluff of corporations threatening to run away.

Whether at the state or national level, two critical provisions of effective legislation are *an advance notice clause of at least six months* and *requirements for community impact hearings* to ascertain the social costs of a plant closing before it can be finalized. Such provisions, applicable to plants of, say, more than two hundred workers, would allow community groups and unions the advance notice to *organize.* As the size of the plant increased, thereby increasing the community impact of its closing, the burden of proof would shift more to the employer and make it increasingly difficult to close.

Many corporations, after predictions of doom, would learn to place greater attention on product differentiation, design, and quality, instead of compensating for their own deficiencies by browbeating workers and communities. In the era in which "competitiveness" has become a cliche, corporations would be forced to compete for profits without being able use the threat of a runaway to compensate for their poor perforance.

Just as during the 1930s, when mass movements were able to impose union contracts, minimum wages, and social security laws on the corporations; and during the 1960s, when a civil rights movement forced corporations to implement affirmative action programs, in the 1980s it is way past time to impose similar restraints upon corporations to prevent them from closing down productive plants as they see fit. The new ground rules would acknowledge a large productive plant as "community property," and the pursuit of profit as a privilege, not a right.

In 1982, when the Van Nuys organizers openly challenged GM's right to take the capital and run, some within the union itself felt that the theory was too radical--essentially arguing that the plant (and to some degree the workers themselves) were GM's property, to dispose of as it wished. The Campaign organizers responded that at least part of that capital had been produced through the workers' labor. Thus, they had *rights* in the situation and could demand, not just request, that GM stay in Los Angeles. As the 1986 Catholic Bishops' position paper reinforcing that perspective stated:

> The size of a firm or bank is in many cases an indicator of relative economic power. With this power goes responsibility and the need for those who manage it to be held to moral and institutional responsibility....
>
> Owners and managers have not created this capital on their own. They have benefited from the work of many others and from the local communities that support their endeavors. They are accountable to these workers and communities when making decisions.[9]

Plant Closings Protection in Union Contracts

Collective bargaining agreements do not, in themselves, guarantee power to workers or their union. But a strong contract can be a valuable weapon in the hands of an activist union. Just as in the past, when union contracts were developed to protect workers' wages, hours, and working conditions, new contractual breakthroughs are needed to protect workers' job security.

There is a need for contractual provisions to require that any corporate plans to close a plant be submitted to the union *at least a year in advance.* Instead of omnipresent and constantly shifting "danger lists," management should be strictly limited to the number of plants under discussion for a possible closure. These discussions must begin at the international union level and then involve local unions as well. When particular plants are considered in danger, the UAW should involve community organizations in those discussions at the earliest possible moment.

For example, had there been greater contractual restraints upon management behavior, and had a UAW-initiated "regional protection program" been in place, GM, once having closed Southgate in Southern California would have been prevented from closing its Northern California Fremont plant and its last remaining Southern California plant in Van Nuys. That would have allowed workers from Southgate to continue to draw benefits until openings developed at Fremont or at Van Nuys, rather than being forced to accept work in Shreveport, Louisiana, or Wentzville, Missouri. Similarly, once Ford had closed its Pico Rivera plant in Los Angeles, it should have been compelled to keep open its Milpitas plant in Northern California.

Virtually every idea proposed for federal legislation is also possible in union contracts. The UAW could call for a mandatory community impact study before any plant was closed and could win advance notice provisions of at least one year. Even more advanced, it would be possible to negotiate a moratorium on plant closings, company by company, over the life of each contract.

At this time in history, however, there is strong opposition to these contractual provisions on the part of management, and little commitment to them on the part of the UAW leadership. Thus, until grass roots movements at the bottom are strong enough to impact new strategic thinking at the top, many of these ideas will remain on a wish list.

Changes in Federal Labor Laws in the Era of Plant Closings

It is not just the indiscriminate closing of plants, but the use of the plant closing (or its threat) as a weapon with which to impose management control that must be prohibited. The policies of General Motors in this respect have become a prototype of socially intolerable behavior.

In the United States since World War II, traditional models of labor-management relations have been based on the premise of a fixed and relatively permanent plant. Although class conflict still took place, both sides assumed the existence of the plant over which they were struggling.

In recent years, however, the collective bargaining process (already structured in favor of management) has been further redesigned to restrict labor's already declining influence. This can be seen in the Van Nuys case history:

– In 1982, management at GM Van Nuys explicitly warned the workers that plants would be "rated" in terms of many factors, including "labor climate." "Excessive grievances," management asserted, could be a factor in a possible plant closing.

– Beginning in 1985, management at the plant told the workers both at public meetings and in publicly distributed flyers that if they did not accept the team concept the plant would not receive a new product to be built and would be closed down.[10]

– At the meeting with the Labor/Community Coalition in January 1984, GM President McDonald produced a slide show in which five GM plants (including Van Nuys) were on the "danger list." By 1986, however, at the time that GM announced the closing of eleven plants, plant manager Ernest Schaefer argued that if Van Nuys did not perform according to expectations "we, like all the other plants in the General Motors system, will appear on the danger list."[11] In two short years, the "danger list" had expanded to cover every plant in the GM system.

The strategy of placing its entire workforce on the danger list is not just rhetorical: GM is attempting to carry it out. In the early stages of the Campaign, Van

Nuys activists looked longingly at newer, state-of-the-art plants such as the one in Wentzville, Missouri. The Van Nuys workers reasoned that organizing worker militancy at a plant such as Wentzville would be a lot easier, since the workers would feel the security of a Midwest location and a brand-new plant.

Apparently, GM felt that the prospect of workers in newer plants feeling a greater sense of security was contradictory to its overall strategy for worker control. Thus, by 1987, the Wentzville workers were told that they too were vulnerable to a possible plant closing.

In an open letter to Wentzville workers, entitled "Cooperation is a two-way street but GM wants it all one way," Peter Downs, a New Directions activist, and several co-workers wrote:

> Wentzville plant manager Nick Bozich is talking about "team development" lately. He made clear in the pages of the *St. Louis Post Dispatch* exactly what he means. He wants to increase "the efficiency" of workers in order to decrease labor costs. The same article also repeated a theme that "advisors" recite in team meetings: "*If workers don't get more efficient the plant will close.*"
>
> Such misleading threats to close the plant are exactly what we would expect from traditional management, but they have no place in cooperative labor relations.[12]

Reading the Wentzville newsletter one has a sense of deja vu. Substitute the name Ernie Schaefer for Nick Bozich and one could reprint the newsletter in its entirety and the Van Nuys workers would think it was written about their plant. Change the name again and it could be distributed at Leeds, Missouri; Framingham, Massachusetts; or Oklahoma City, Oklahoma.

One must ask what is wrong with a corporation that has placed all of its 350,000 hourly employees on the "danger list"; and what is wrong with a society that tolerates that type of corporate behavior? The practice of corporations like General Motors in applying threats of plant closings to all their workers belies any claims that plant closings are an "inevitable" response to declining market demand or outmoded factories.

Plant closings have become an essential instrument of GM management policy and corporate policy in general. Under those conditions, collective bargaining as it has been traditionally understood no longer exists in the GM system.

What should be the penalty for a corporation that tells its workers that if they file too many grievances or if they do not accept certain contract demands their plant will be shut down? The specific changes in labor law should be the subject of brainstorming discussions between union activists, legislators, and attorneys. But there is a clear need for amendments to the National Labor Relations Act that would include:

– Workers and unions who can demonstrate that a corporation is using the threat of a plant closing to extract wage concessions and/or a weakening of workplace protections should be able to collect substantial cash damages from the corporation.

– Corporations threatening to close a plant as an instrument of bargaining strategy should be subject to court injunctions and restraining orders *preventing* such a closure for periods of at least two years--thereby defeating the very intention of the threat.

– Any damages payable by the employer or restraints upon the employer should be immediately enforceable, while the employer is free to file appeals. In that way, the corporations cannot use their immense legal resources to evade social constraints while they tie the workers' movement up in the courts for years.

It is sadly ironic that at this point in history those modest demands seem utopian--but no more so than collective bargaining appeared in the reactionary climate of the 1920s or the prospects of a civil rights movement seemed in the "apathetic" 1950s. Yet, many forget that impressive labor organizing took place during the 1920s which laid the foundation for the mass upsurge of the 1930s; and the battles for school integration at Little Rock, Arkansas, and many other locations set the stage for the more full-fledged mass movements of the 1960s.

Similarly, while neither the Van Nuys movement nor the victorious strike of the Watsonville, California, cannery workers nor the New Directions insurgency nor the Hormel strike in themselves can turn labor around, the embryonic experiments with new strategies and approaches are creating the conditions for a time when labor can once again play a major role in the political life of the country.

USING THEORY AS A GUIDE TO PRACTICE: THE BATTLE FOR AN OPEN MARKETPLACE OF IDEAS IN THE LABOR MOVEMENT

When one stands on a stage and looks out at a thousand community and labor supporters at a rally to Keep GM Van Nuys Open, one is shocked to see the enormous potential for labor's increased political influence at a time in history when the media keep repeating that "the public" is "anti-labor." One key that unlocked that support was a break with a traditional "representational" model of unionism and a move towards bold, creative, and confrontational politics.

In recent decades, "militant unionism" has meant fighting hard at the bargaining table once every few years, and electing a few full-time fighters on the shop floor to enforce the contract that was negotiated. The Van Nuys model, however, out of both conviction and necessity, attempted to *empower* large numbers of workers, to train them in political as well as technical leadership skills, and to involve more and more workers in the movement--at a time in history when there was little reinforcement for a participatory model of working class activity.

But it would be a vast oversimplification to assume that the Campaign's movement-building successes were the product of a gut-level militancy or a simplistic view of "worker involvement." From its inception, the Campaign was driven by political ideas that gave the movement a distinctive character. Because it was a coalition, there were many political views that both clashed and impacted each other, creating an evolving political perspective that became more refined as the movement progressed. The strategic thinking of the Campaign had several distinct historical roots that gave the movement its dynamism and direction:

– The imagery and mythology of the Flint sit-down strikers provided a model of autoworkers occupying factories and fighting police to win their demands against the same General Motors that was threatening to close down the plant.

– The Reuther period of the UAW's history provided a sense of class solidarity and militant collective bargaining that many of the older workers still embraced.

– The Marxist view of class struggle offered a philosophy in which the broader political interests of the working class were asserted. The view that the capitalists had, in fact, accumulated their capital through the exploitation of the workers gave legitimacy to union demands to restrict capital--such as demands to keep plants open.

– The civil rights philosophy, exemplified by SNCC and Martin Luther King, argued that direct action, moral and physical confrontation, and broad-based coalition building against more powerful opponents was essential to any organizing victories.

– The Chicano movement emphasized the alliance between the Chicano working class and the Chicano community--exemplified by the successful grape boycotts of the United Farm Workers--and the need to preserve the last auto plant in the Southwest, the area of greatest concentration of Chicanos.

– The progressive economic teachings of the Catholic Church--represented by the views of Father Luis Olivares who called the Van Nuys movement part of a social revolution empowering the poor and working people--gave a moral authority and legitimacy to far-reaching ideas of social reform.

– The anti-concessions movement in the UAW offered a sense of strategic disagreement with the overall direction of the union and provided a national network of resistance to management's demands.

– The example of the Canadian Auto Workers, who broke away to form their own union based on both national self-determination and a more class conscious approach to the employers brought home to some of the Campaign organizers that for those in the American UAW they had a responsibility to fight for their own view of the union's future.

At the theoretical and strategic level, the Van Nuys movement was able to create an atmosphere in which the battle of ideas and the ability to draw from many seemingly contradictory strategies could produce an exciting atmosphere of experimentation and synthesis.

And yet, that atmosphere did not develop without quite a struggle. The battle against red-baiting, important in itself, was even more important for the type of intellectual attitude necessary for a vibrant social movement. If new strategies are to be attempted, no ideas can be rejected out of hand. In fact, some of the ideas offered by Marxists and communists were quite helpful, while others were dogmatic, sectarian, and unhelpful to movement-building. But it was the ability to draw upon and synthesize ideas--from Marx and the *Wall Street Journal*; from the Catholic Church and the Chamber of Commerce; from the UAW's pioneers (including socialists and communists); and from Martin Luther King and Cesar Chavez--that gave the Van Nuys movement the intellectual power to take on General Motors. Today's labor movement is urgently in need of new strategic thinking. Union members need not fear new ideas; rather, they need to fear those who prefer censorship to open debate.

THE CRITICAL ROLE OF LABOR UNIONS IN ANY DEMOCRATIC VISION OF A NEW SOCIETY

Finding new directions for the labor movement cannot be separated from the direction of American society itself. As this book is being written in the late 1980s there is a prevailing sense of despair on the part of many activists in the labor movement and on the left. By contrast, in the 1960s the growth of civil rights, antiwar, and progressive electoral coalitions encouraged broader discussions about institutional changes in American society. Was socialism possible in the United States and, if so, would it be an improvement? What types of socialism were people even talking about--Yugoslavian, Chinese, Soviet, Swedish? Was Sweden really socialist or simply capitalism brought to a more civilized level; and could strictly regulated capitalism provide a better integration of economic and political democracy? What were Social Democratic parties doing in Western Europe, and what political experiments were taking place in the Third World? Could America be reformed through the Democratic party; should some form of "third party" or "labor party" be built; or would it take a revolution to bring economic and racial justice to the society?

What types of social welfare and community empowerment laws could be passed to make America more democratic--laws that could be both ends in themselves and stepping stones to greater power for minorities, workers, and communities? Those were exciting and hopeful times, when human imagination and intellect were pushed to their limits--until, eventually, reform was beaten back by the left's weaknesses and the far greater strength and political sophistication of the corporate establishment.

Today, however, it is not merely the ebbing of reform but the advent of reaction that sets the tone of debate. Discussion among social reformers and activists focuses on being "practical" to win "achievable" victories, and to recognize society's "limits."

As today's liberals and leftists discuss new strategies, it is important to remember the still critical role of labor unions in any future coalitions. While American labor's decline from representing 32 percent of the workforce in 1955 to 18 percent in 1987 is often mentioned, few outside of the labor movement seem to understand the direct threat to their own future reflected in that trend.

Labor unions are not simply economic vehicles for wages and benefits. They are one of the few remaining democratic institutions that offer the possibilty of resistance to the growing and frightening concentration of power in the hands of a tiny number of corporations. General Motors' annual report provides a vivid illustration of the problem:

- 8.6 million cars and trucks sold worldwide.
- $4.5 billion in net income.
- 731,000 employees world-wide.
- $22 billion annual payroll.[13]

In this context, the existence of democratic institutions such as the almost one-million-member United Auto Workers is a critical counterweight, not just to General Motors' economic power, but to its political power as well.

America's claims to democracy, always exaggerated at best, are becoming structurally threatened by the growth of mega-merged corporations. The scale of both corporations and the state apparatus has become so enormous that the concept of an enlightened or outraged citizenry organizing to impact their activities is rapidly approaching folklore. No matter what the progressive social objective--stopping the frightening growth of chemical pollutants; organizing another wave of civil rights activity; stopping the nuclear arms race before it is too late--there is little historical possibility of effecting those objectives without the active participation of the labor unions.

Unfortunately, unless a new generation of labor leaders can democratize and reorient today's labor unions, develop a broader political program, and reverse the trend of their decline, both the workers and the larger society will suffer immensely; and a lurking totalitarianism will become an even more imminent threat.

The late twentieth-century experience of both capitalist and socialist societies offers some common dangers: the growing concentration of power in the hands of political elites who dominate the supposedly popular political parties; frightening concentrations of economic power; awesome technological and military power concentrated in the hands of the state. In both capitalist and socialist societies there is a dominant view of labor unions as enforcers of labor discipline and productivity; as adjuncts of the productive process rather than independent economic and political institutions of the working class.

Any vision of a democratic society must involve not just "pressure" from the bottom up but *power* residing in smaller units of production and governance--local community organizations, coalitions of small businesses, regional development councils, and revitalized labor unions. The Van Nuys movement involved Latino, black, white, and Asian autoworkers, women, men, local business-people, Catholic priests, Baptist ministers, and Chicano college students--all joined in a coalition against General Motors, the number one corporation in the Fortune 500. The coalition slogan--"The future of GM Van Nuys is not just for GM to decide; workers and communities demand a voice"--offers, in microcosm, a vision of a civilized and democratized industrial society.

This study has tried to present the problems and achievements of the Van Nuys Campaign quite soberly. In the five-year period that this case study analyzes, the Van Nuys movement has been able to push the theory and practice of the labor movement a small step forward. It is hoped that by reverse-engineering this study and the Campaign it describes, others can take the movement to a higher level.

NOTES

1. James Risen, "A Gridlock in Autos," *Los Angeles Times*, Business section, September 28, 1986, p. 1.
2. "Moving the Auto Industry Back in Gear," *Solidarity*, December 1, 1986, p. 13. (This is the official magazine of the UAW and an excellent source of information on the auto industry.)
3. Jack Metzgar, "Running the Plant Backwards in UAW Region 5," *Labor Research Review*, Midwest Center for Labor Research, Fall 1985, pp. 36-43.
4. Comments of Joseph A. "Chip" Yablonski: "Election violations which the United States Secretary of Labor found as a result of his investigation of the [Tucker-Worley] election," *Voice of New Directions*, February, 1987, p. 2.
5. Interview with the author, February 20, 1987.
6. Barry Bluestone and Bennett Harrison, *The Deindustrialization of America* (New York: Basic Books, 1982), p. 35.
7. *Agreement Between General Motors Corporation and the United Auto Workers*, September 21, 1984, paragraph 8, "Rights of Corporation," p. 13.
8. *Economic Justice for All: Catholic Social Teaching and the U.S. Economy*, National Conference of Catholic Bishops, June 4, 1986, p. 82.
9. *Economic Justice for All*, p. 31.
10. "Statement from Plant Manager Ernie Schaefer," *Positive Press*, Special Edition, December 16, 1985.
11. "Reprieve for GM Plant Has No Guarantee," *Los Angeles Times*, Business section, November 7, 1986, p. 1.
12. "An Open Letter to GM-Wentzville Employees" from Mike Bullock, Peter Downs, Mark Haefner, Lisa Lehnbeuter, and Butch Spencer, undated.
13. *General Motors Annual Report*, 1986, p. 1.

BIBLIOGRAPHY

Selected Books and Pamphlets

Acuña, Rodolfo. *Occupied America: A History of Chicanos.* New York: Harper and Row, 1981.

Barnard, John. *Walter Reuther and the Rise of the Auto Workers.* Boston: Little Brown, 1983.

Bluestone, Barry, and Bennett Harrison. *The Deindustrialization of America.* New York: Basic Books, 1982.

Boyer, Richard O., and Herbert M. Morais. *Labor's Untold Story.* New York: United Electrical Workers Union (UE), 1982.

Braverman, Harry. *Labor and Monopoly Capital: The Degradation of Work in the Twentieth Century.* New York: Monthly Review Press, 1974.

Chandler, Alfred D., and Stephen Salsbury. *Pierre S. DuPont and the Making of the Modern Corporation.* New York: Harper and Row, 1971.

Cray, Ed. *Chrome Colossus: General Motors and Its Times.* New York: McGraw Hill, 1980.

Davis, Mike. *Prisoners of the American Dream.* London: Verso, 1986.

Foster, William Z. *History of the Communist Party of the United States.* New York: International Publishers, 1952.

Gartman, David. *Auto Slavery.* New Brunswick, New Jersey: Rutgers University Press, 1986.

Georgakas, Dan, and Marvin Surkin. *Detroit: I Do Mind Dying*. New York: St. Martins Press, 1975.

Geschwender, James A. *Class, Race, and Worker Insurgency*. Cambridge: Cambridge University Press, 1977.

Gustin, Lawrence R. *Billy Durant, Creator of GM*. Grand Rapids, Michigan: William B. Eerdmans, 1973.

Haas, Gilda. *Plant Closures: Myths, Realities and Responses*. Boston: South End Press, 1985.

Halberstam, David. *The Reckoning*. New York: William Morrow, 1986.

Iacocca, Lee. *Iacocca: An Autobiography*. New York: Bantam, 1984.

Keeran, Roger. *The Communist Party and the Auto Workers' Unions*. New York: International Publishers, 1980.

Lacey, Robert. *Ford: The Men and the Machine*. Boston: Little Brown, 1986.

Lang, Lucy Robins. *Tomorrow is Beautiful*. New York: MacMillan, 1948.

Lichtenstein, Nelson. *Labor's War at Home: The CIO in World War II*. Cambridge: Cambridge University Press, 1982.

Meier, August, and Elliott Rudwick. *Black Detroit and the Rise of the UAW*. New York: Oxford University Press, 1979.

Morris, Charles J., ed. *The Developing Labor Law*. Washington, D.C.: Bureau of National Affairs, 1971.

Mortimer, Wyndham. *Organize! My Life as a Union Man*. Boston: Beacon Press, 1972.

National Conference of Catholic Bishops. *Economic Justice For All: Catholic Social Teaching and the U.S. Economy*. Washington, D.C.: United States Catholic Conference, 1986.

Olney, Peter et al. "A Feasibility Study of a Boycott of General Motors Products in Southern California." Masters thesis. University of California, Los Angeles, Graduate School of Management, 1986.

Prickett, James Robert. "Communists and the Communist Issue in the American Labor Movement," 1920-1950." Ph.D. dissertation, University of California, Los Angeles, Department of History, 1975.

Reuther, Victor G. *The Brothers Reuther*. Boston: Houghton Mifflin, 1976.

Richmond, Al. *A Long View from the Left: Memoirs of an American Revolutionary*. New York: Dell, 1972.

Serrin, William. *The Company and the Union*. New York: Alfred A. Knopf, 1973.

Sloan, Alfred P., Jr. *My Years With General Motors*. Garden City, New York: Anchor Books, 1972.

Wright, J. Patrick. *On A Clear Day You Can See General Motors*. New York: Avon Books, 1979.

Selected Articles

Alperovitz, Gar. "The Coming Break In Liberal Consciousness." *Christianity and Crisis*, March 3, 1986.

Benson, Herman. "Circling the Wagons Inside the UAW." *Union Democracy Review*, January 1987.

Brody, Michael. "Can GM Manage It All?" *Fortune*, July 8, 1985.

Hampton, William J., and James R. Norman. "What Went Wrong at GM." *Business Week*, March 16, 1987.

Ingrassia, Paul, and Doron P. Levin. "A Gathering Glut: Auto Industry Faces Era of Plant Closings." *Wall Street Journal*, February 14, 1986.

Keil, Roger. "Keep GM Van Nuys Open: Perspektiven eines sudkalifornischen Arbeitskampfes." *Kommune*, June 1987.

Mann, Eric. "Workers and Community Take on GM." *The Nation*, February 11, 1984.

Mann, Eric. "Strike Diary." *The Nation*, November 10, 1984.

Mann, Eric. "UAW Backs the Wrong Team." *The Nation*, February 14, 1987.

Mann, Eric. "Labor's Silent Partner Role Harmful to Workers and Public." *Los Angeles Times*, Opinion section, September 1, 1985.

Mann, Eric. "Unions Absent on Sunday Are Dead on Monday." *New York Times*, September 1, 1986.

Mann, Eric. "Keeping GM Van Nuys Open." *Midwest Center for Labor Research Review*, Fall 1986.

Metzgar, Jack. "Running the Plant Backwards." *Midwest Center for Labor Research Review*, Fall 1985.

Morales, Rebecca. "Made in L.A.: Automobile Manufacturing in Southern California." Graduate School of Architecture and Urban Planning, University of California, Los Angeles, Summer 1986.

Russo, John. "Saturn's Rings: What GM's Saturn Project is Really About." *Midwest Center for Labor Research Review*, Fall 1986.

Risen, James. "GM Shedding Smokestack Image." *Los Angeles Times*, Business section, October 28, 1984.

Risen, James. "GM Chairman Smith's Image Changes from Bumbler To Guru." *Los Angeles Times*, Business section, October 28, 1984.

Risen, James. "A Gridlock in Autos." *Los Angeles Times*, Business section, September 28, 1986.

Risen, James. "GM Opts for the Quick Fix." *Los Angeles Times*, Business section, August 29, 1986.

Sandercock, Leonie, and John Friedmann. "Economic Restructuring and Community Dislocation: The Challenge to Planners." Graduate School of Architecture and Urban Planning, University of California, Los Angeles, December 1985.

Shapira, Phillip. "The Crumbling of Smokestack California." Institute of Urban and Regional Development, University of California, Berkeley, November 1984.

Sorge, Marjorie et al. "GM: A New Kind of Global Conglomerate." *Automotive News*, January 21, 1985.

Tasini, Jonathan. "Jobs on the Line." *LA Reader*, March 23, 1984.

Tucker, Jonathan B. "GM: Shifting to Automatic." *High Technology*, May 1985.

Warren, James. "GM Team Faces Tough UAW Opponent." *Chicago Tribune*, July 5, 1987, Section 7.

Weinstein, Henry. "Factory Becomes Focus of a Cause." *Los Angeles Times*, Metro section, December 5, 1983.

Weinstein, Henry. "UAW Van Nuys Vote: Where Does Union Go in the '80s?" *Los Angeles Times*, Metro section, June 1, 1987.

INDEX